ROMMEL

as Military Commander

PEN & SWORD MILITARY CLASSICS

We hope you enjoy your Pen and Sword Military Classic. The series is designed to give readers quality military history at affordable prices. Pen and Sword Classics are available from all good bookshops. If you would like to keep in touch with further developments in the series, including information on the **Classics Club**, then please contact Pen and Sword at the address below.

Published Classics Titles

Series No.

1	The Bowmen of England	Donald Featherstone
2	The Life & Death of the Afrika Korps	Ronald Lewin
3	The Old Front Line	John Masefield
4	Wellington & Napoleon	Robin Neillands
5	Beggars in Red	John Strawson
6	The Luftwaffe: A History	John Killen
7	Siege: Malta 1940–1943	Ernle Bradford
8	Hitler as Military Commander	John Strawson
9	Nelson's Battles	Oliver Warner
10	The Western Front 1914–1918	John Terraine
11	The Killing Ground	Tim Travers
12	Vimy	Pierre Berton
13	Dictionary of the First World War	Stephen Pope & Elizabeth-Anne Wheal
14	1918: The Last Act	Barrie Pitt
15	Hitler's Last Offensive	Peter Elstob
16	Naval Battles of World War Two	Geoffrey Bennett
17	Omdurman	Philip Ziegler
18	Strike Hard, Strike Sure	Ralph Barker
19	The Black Angels	Rupert Butler
20	The Black Ship	Dudley Pope
21	The Argentine Fight for the Falklands	Martin Middlebrook
22	The Narrow Margin	Derek Wood & Derek Dempster
23	Warfare in the Age of Bonaparte	Michael Glover
24	With the German Guns	Herbert Sulzbach
25	Dictionary of the Second World War	Stephen Pope & Elizabeth-Anne Wheal
26	Not Ordinary Men	John Colvin

Forthcoming Titles

27	Plumer: The Soldier's General	Geoffrey Powell
28	Rommel as Military Commander	Ronald Lewin
29	Legions of Death	Rupert Butler
30	The Sword and the Scimitar	Ernie Bradford
31	By Sea and By Land	Robin Neillands
32	Cavalry: The History of Mounted Warfare	John Ellis
33	The March of the Twenty-Six	R. F. Delderfield
34	The Floating Republic	G.E. Manwaring & Bonamy Dobree
35	Tug of War: The Battle for Italy 1943–45	Dominick Graham & Shelford Bidwell
36	Churchill & The Generals	Barrie Pitt
37	The Secret War	Brian Johnson
38	Command on the Western Front	Robin Prior & Trevor Wilson
39	The Operators	James Rennie
40	Churchill and The Admirals	Stephen Roskill
41	The Battle for North Africa	John Strawson
42	One of Our Submarines	Edward Young
43	The Battle of Trafalgar	Geoffrey Bennett

PEN AND SWORD BOOKS LTD

47 Church Street • Barnsley • South Yorkshire • S70 2AS

Tel: 01226 734555 • 734222

E-mail: enquiries@pen-and-sword.co.uk • **Website:** www.pen-and-sword.co.uk

ROMMEL

as Military Commander

Ronald Lewin

"'Rommel, Rommel, Rommel, Rommel!" he cried. "What else matters but beating him?"'

Winston Churchill at the Cairo Conference, 8 August 1942
(from the diary of Lieut.-Gen. Sir Ian Jacob)

PEN & SWORD MILITARY CLASSICS

First published in 1968 by B. T. BATSFORD LTD
Published in 2004, in this format, by
PEN & SWORD MILITARY CLASSICS
an imprint of
Pen & Sword Books Limited,
47, Church Street,
Barnsley,
S. Yorkshire,
S70 2AS

ISBN 1 84415 040 2

A CIP record for this book is
available from the British Library

Printed in England by
CPI UK

Contents

Acknowledgements

The student of ancient warfare would be happy to have had an opportunity of consulting Brasidas or Belisarius: anyone who writes about contemporary war must recognise the opportunity he has enjoyed of referring to those who were actually involved in the conflicts with which he is concerned. I am most grateful for the insight, information, advice, criticism and encouragement which have come my way from Field-Marshal Sir Claude Auchinleck, Brigadier John Bagnall, General Sir Richard Gale, Major-General Gambier-Parry, Professor Norman Gibbs, Major-General Holden, Captain Sir Basil Liddell Hart, Stuart Hood, Major-General W. G. F. Jackson, Vice-Admiral I. L. M. McGeoch, Major Kenneth Macksey, Brigadier C. J. C. Molony, The Earl of Ranfurly, Brigadier John Stevenson, General Siegfried Westphal and Brigadier E. T. Williams. My debt to John Connell and Chester Wilmot is for other reasons inexpressible and is recognised in my dedication. I alone, of course, am responsible for every statement of fact or opinion in this book.

I am indebted to the following for permission to quote from copyright material: Captain Sir Basil Liddell Hart on behalf of Frau Rommel, for quotations from *The Rommel Papers*, and Messrs. Collins; to Messrs. Collins also for quotations from *Rommel* by Desmond Young and *The Struggle for Europe* by Chester Wilmot; to Messrs. Macmillan for quotations from *The Nemesis of Power* by Sir John Wheeler-Bennett; and to the Controller, H.M. Stationary Office, for sundry quotations from the *Official History of the Second World War*. I am also grateful to *The Sunday Times* for permission to quote from an article by Dr. Hans-Adolf Jocobsen and to the Hamlyn Group (incorporating Odhams) for a quotation from Blumentritt's *Von Rundstedt*.

The Author and Publishers wish to thank the following for permission to reproduce the illustrations included in this book.

The Ullstein Bilderdienst, for figs. 1, 7, 10, 19, 23, 28 and 32; Associated Press Ltd., for figs. 9, 25 and 31; the R.A.C. Tank Museum, for fig. 15-18; the Imperial War Museum, for figs. 26, 27 and 29; the Süd-deutscher Verlag, for figs. 2 and 30; Dr. Eugen Dollman, for fig. 22; Frau Rommel, for figs. 3-6, 11-14, 20, 21 and 35. Figs. 33 and 34, by Erwin Rommel, are reproduced in *The History of 79 Armoured Division* (privately printed).

vi

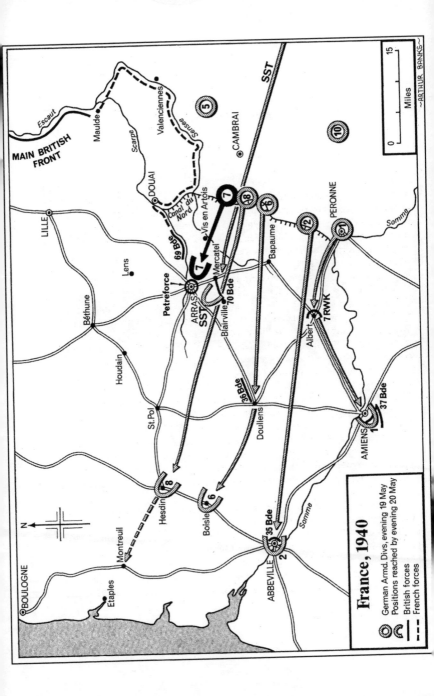

France, 1940

German Armd. Divs, evening 19 May
Positions reached by evening 20 May
British forces
French forces

MAIN BRITISH FRONT

BOULOGNE
Etaples
Montreuil
Hesdin
Boisle
ABBEVILLE
35 Bde
Somme
AMIENS
37 Bde
PERONNE
Somme
Albert
7 RWK
Doullens
36 Bde
St. Pol
Houdain
Béthune
Lens
LILLE
Petreforce
ARRAS
SST
Blairville
70 Bde
Mercatel
Vis en Artois
Canal du Nord
DOUAI
Scarpe
Maulde
Escaut
Valenciennes
Sensée
CAMBRAI
Bapaume
69 Bde

Miles
0   15

~ARTHUR BANKS

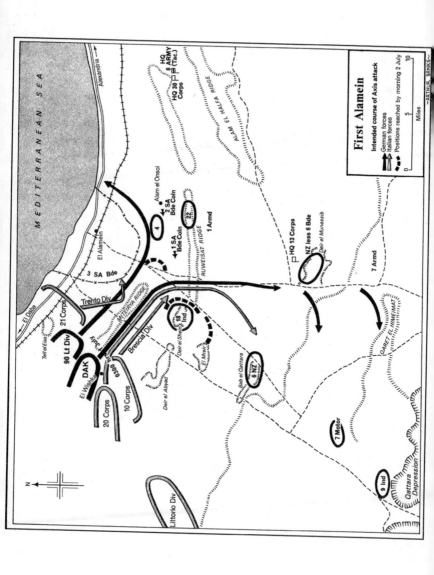

First Alamein

Intended course of Axis attack

➤ German forces
➤ Italian forces
◆ Positions reached by morning 2 July

Miles
0   5   10

— ARTHUR BANKS —

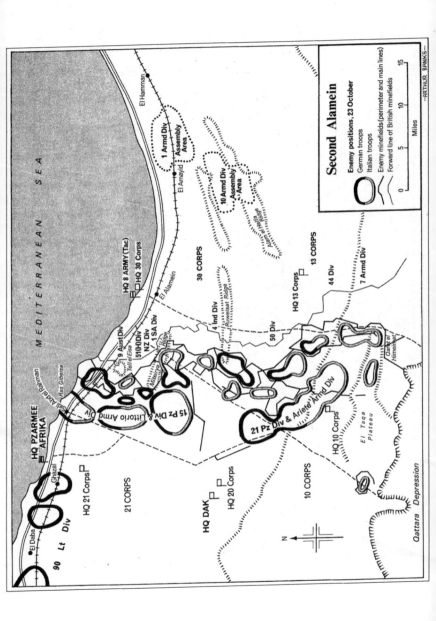

Second Alamein

Enemy positions, 23 October
German troops
Italian troops
Enemy minefields (perimeter and main lines)
Forward line of British minefields

Miles
0   5   10   15

—ARTHUR BANKS—

MEDITERRANEAN SEA

El Hamman

1 Armd Div Assembly Area

El Amayid

10 Armd Div Assembly Area

Alam el Halfa
Alam el Halfa Ridge

HQ 8 ARMY (Tac)
HQ 30 Corps

El Alamein

30 CORPS

13 CORPS

4 Ind Div

Ruweisat Ridge

HQ 13 Corps

50 Div

44 Div

7 Armd Div

9 Aust Div
51(H) Div
NZ Div
1 SA Div
Miteirya Ridge
Tell el Eisa

HQ PZARMEE AFRIKA

Sidi Abd el Rahman
Ras Gibeisa

15 Pz Div & Littorio Armd Div

21 Pz Div & Ariete Armd Div

Qara el Himeimat

HQ 10 Corps

El Taqa Plateau

Ghazal

HQ 21 Corps

21 CORPS

HQ DAK

HQ 20 Corps

10 CORPS

N

Qattara Depression

El Daba

90 Lt Div

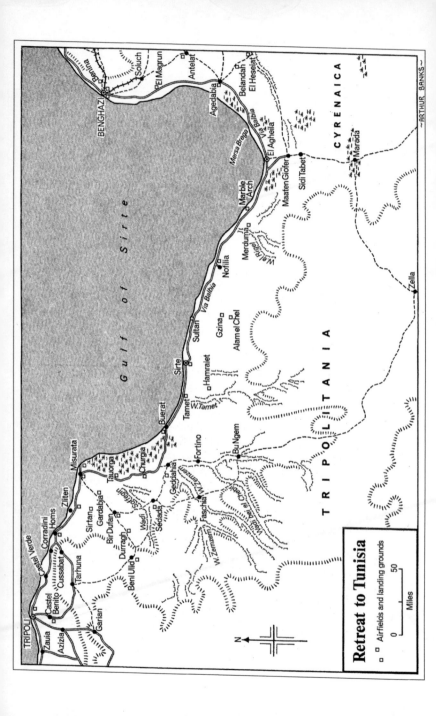

Retreat to Tunisia

□ Airfields and landing grounds

0   50

Miles

N

~ARTHUR BANKS~

CYRENAICA

TRIPOLITANIA

Gulf of Sirte

TRIPOLI
Zauia
Azizia
Castel Verde
Castel Benito
Corradini
Homs
Zliten
Cussabat
Tarhuna
Garian
Beni Ullid
Durragh
Bir Dufan
Gardabia
Sirtana
Tauorga
Churgia
Misurata
Sedada
Geddahia
Fortino
Bu Ngem
W. Tamet
Tamet
Buerat
Sirte
Hamraiet
Sultan
Gzina
Alam el Chel
Nofilia
Zella
Marble Arch
Mersa Brega
El Agheila
Maaten Giofer
Sidi Tabet
Marada
Merduma
W. el Rigel
Benghazi
El Magrun
Soluch
Antelat
Agedabia
Belandah
El Heseiat
Via Balbia
Via Balbia

Wadi Zemzem
W. Zemzem
W. bel el Chebir
Faschia

I

Birth of a Field-Marshal

The genesis of a successful military commander is unpredictable. Some—Wolseley and Roberts, Haig and Ludendorff, Montgomery and Macarthur—perfect a life-long professionalism. Others—Napoleon is a supreme example—during their youth immediately discover their destiny. Then there are those who, like Cromwell, meet war in middle age and find it their *métier*. There is also a special class, quiet academics and executives, men like Monash or T. E. Lawrence, who leave study or office for the battlefield to find that they can match the professionals at their own game. Commanders in this class are unusual, in the first class more frequent: the second order is reserved for a small number whose innate military genius is phenomenal.

Erwin Johannes Eugen Rommel, born at Heidenheim near Ulm on 15 November 1891, was a professional soldier who discovered his destiny while he was young. He devoted his life to the theory and practice of war. But there was nothing in his family tradition to suggest that he might emerge as one of its masters: his roots struck deep into the German provincial middle class, and—setting his military gifts apart—he remained a *bourgeois* until he died. This was in character: he was a Württemberger from Swabia—dour, self-reliant, unsophisticated.

Such a background offered no promise for a professional soldier in Germany before the First World War. So it is important to note that Rommel neither had nor sought any affiliation with the closed order of the General Staff and the Prussian aristocracy which—self-sufficient, self-complacent and self-perpetuating—dominated the German Army before and during the First World War; and which, between the wars and even during the Second World War (though Hitler provided other avenues of military advancement) kept a grasp on many of the main controls. Indeed, Rommel's later disagreements during his African campaigns with O.K.H.* and O.K.W. largely derived from a feeling in their higher echelons that he was an under-educated upstart. Noble names often occur in the roll of Rommel's generals, but his relationship with the 'vons' he commanded never went much beyond the limits of normal military association. He stood aloof. During the 'thirties he even turned down an opportunity of going to the Staff College and thus being initiated into the magic circle. Later, as will be seen, Hitler gave him an opening at a crucial point in his career; but otherwise Rommel owed his promotions to nobody but himself.

His father and grandfather were schoolmasters: and though his father married in 1886 the eldest daughter of the President of the Government of Württemberg, the Rommels remained provincials. In 1898 his father was appointed Direktor of the *Realgymnasium* at Aalen, where Rommel spent his childhood—years which tell one nothing about his inherent powers. It was the outbreak of war in 1914 which released them—immediately: as if, like one of those Japanese flowers whose petals expand when immersed in water, Erwin Rommel could only discover himself in action. He had made a start by joining 124 Infantry Regiment as an officer cadet in July 1910. For a young regimental officer in peace-time his performance was entirely undistinguished; but, as Desmond Young says in his biography, 'from the moment that he first came under fire he stood out as the perfect fighting animal, cold, cunning, ruthless, untiring, quick of decision, incredibly brave'. Though Rommel's fame derives from his achievements during the Second World War, these will nevertheless be better understood if one remembers that in his early twenties he was recommended for the Iron Cross Class II before the end of 1914; awarded the Iron Cross Class I early in 1915; and by 1918 had been decorated with the *Pour le Mérite*, a medal which, when granted to a junior officer in the German Army, was comparable to the Victoria Cross.

Rommel's aptitudes as a young officer on the Western, the Rumanian and the Italian fronts may be assessed (like so many of his operations) from his own words. This Swabian was articulate: he had a particular gift for analysing and describing his battles, large or small. In the latter 'thirties he produced a training manual, *Infanterie Greift An* (which was to have an important

---

* O.K.H., *Oberkommando des Heeres*, was the traditional Army High Command. When Hitler sacked von Blomberg and von Fritsch in 1938 he announced that 'henceforth, command over the entire Armed Forces will be exercised directly by me personally'. He then set up O.K.W., *Oberkommando der Wehrmacht*, 'directly under my command as my military staff'. During the Second World War O.K.W. was usually the executive authority: as Chester Wilmot puts it, 'the separation of O.K.W. and O.K.H. was so strict that even the transfer of a regiment from the East to the West had to be referred to Hitler personally'.

bearing on his future career), wherein he looked back on the individual actions in which he had been engaged during the First World War, described them in simple terms, and annotated them from the point of view of 'lessons to be learned'. Designed as a straightforward treatise for tactical education, it tells one much about the young Rommel's cast of mind and those rudimentary ideas which, without any basic change, he elaborated in a more sophisticated fashion during the Second World War.

Take one instance. During the German thrust into France Rommel suffered some gastric disorder (see p. 153), was continually on the move, and approached a point of total exhaustion. Nevertheless (as he describes), in the early hours of 22 August 1914 he was sent forward in fog on a reconnaissance patrol to explore a French position at Bleid, a village near Longwy. He found the French and drew their fire. Then, reconnoitring further—himself and three men—he turned a corner and ran into a larger group of the enemy. Rommel attacked without hesitation, routed the French and then proceeded to move through the village, setting light to the houses one by one; a small but a significant affair. By late September he was out of action for three months, wounded, but in January 1915 he signalised his return by a classic little affray, well presented in his training manual, which involved penetrating a French stronghold by crawling with his platoon through a deep belt of wire, mastering several block-houses, repelling a counter-attack, and then successfully withdrawing with few casualties. Such forays were, of course, made many times by urgent young officers on both sides, but in Rommel's case his tireless repetition of them led to his being selected for transfer to an élite battalion in which his unusual qualities were given a further chance to flower.

Rommel's *Record of Service* (v. Appendix One) shows that from 4 October 1915 to 10 January 1918 he was an officer in the *Württembergische Gebirgsbataillon*. This was a mountain unit formed in 1915 for exceptionally difficult missions, to be used rather like a modern British Commando battalion or brigade: that is to say, it was intended to be normally employed not as a whole, but in sub-divisions to which special tasks were allocated—battlegroups operating with great freedom of action. Such groups might vary in strength from a company to the whole battalion: an unusual concept in the First World War. It was an ideal opportunity for Rommel to exercise and develop his gifts for independent command, and when his battalion was posted to the *Alpenkorps* on the Rumanian front in 1917 he made his mark immediately. His *Infanterie Greift An* must have had a propaganda purpose, but there is no reason to doubt that Rommel's recollections of his actions are substantially accurate; they cohere precisely with his later performance. This,

3

one feels, is how the young Rommel *must* have behaved—in general if not in detail.

The engagements he describes during his Carpathian period brought his infantry technique to a pitch of perfection which he was to apply consummately in Italy. But, more importantly, he was rehearsing and refining certain fundamental methods which he transferred effortlessly to the management of armour in 1940. First, he insisted on leading an attack himself, and on sharing the utmost hardship of his troops (in January 1917 he captured a village, Gagesti, by lying up during the night in a temperature well below freezing point, attacking when the Rumanians were asleep, and thus taking 400 prisoners). Secondly, in this mountain warfare he made constant use of movement to a flank: by out-manœuvring his enemy he was often able to penetrate to the rear, and then to exploit surprise. All these concepts— control from the front, keeping the battle fluid, indirect approach round a flank, the decisively unexpected thrust—provided a recipe for his victories in 1941–42 in North Africa. 'Where Rommel is, there the front is' was a saying at this time as it was a quarter of a century later. But, as Desmond Young points out, 'he was a young man of twenty-five, looking even younger than his age, and in rank only an *Oberleutnant* from a not particularly distinguished line regiment . . .': and yet his seniors looked to him for guidance.

The scene now changes: on 26 August the Austrian Emperor sent to the German Emperor a plea for help in Italy, which began: 'Dear Friend, the experience we have acquired in the eleventh battle has led me to believe that we should fare far worse in a twelfth.' The twelfth began on 24 October, and Rommel was there. This was because, after various discussions, the Germans transferred six of their divisions to the Italian front—including the *Alpenkorps*. Rommel's battalion, which had suffered heavy casualties in the Carpathians, was sent south on 18 October by a series of forced marches carried out by night. 'The accommodations were miserable, the rain was frequent, and the food was inadequate.' During the night of the 22nd the battalion occupied its assembly area for the attack, dodging searchlights and harassing fire. 'During this advance', says Rommel, 'we all received the impression of having come into the effective range of an exceptionally active and well-equipped enemy.' This was a false impression.

In the Caporetto battle which began on the 24th the *Alpenkorps* was in the southern sector of the Austro-German front. The Württemberg battalion was given as its objective a long and formidable ridge, which rose to three peaks, Matajur, Kuk and Hum. Here the Italians had established the third of their lines of defence. The battalion's mission was a covering one—to secure the right flank of the Bavarian Life Guards and to capture artillery positions. Rommel, however, made of it a great deal more.

Advance was swift in the early stages, and soon Rommel had obtained a foothold (50 yards of trench) in the Italian second line, by sending nine of his men in the guise of retiring Italians down a camouflaged path which linked the front with the reserve line. The Life Guards had been stopped: and at dusk their commanding officer, Count Bothmer, ordered Rommel not to act independently but to maintain support for his Guards. Rommel reacted like a Swabian. 'I took the liberty of remarking that I took my orders from Major Sprösser, who, so far as I knew, was senior to the commander of the Life Guards.' Before dawn on the 25th he was again on the move, slipping from cover to cover, and he ended the day by capturing 12 officers and 200 men. Next morning he pressed forward towards the peak of Matajur, tirelessly forcing his men onwards. Of this day Cyril Falls in his study of Caporetto remarks that 'the facts which he presents in his narrative cannot be disputed and are as extraordinary an example of skill and daring as can be found in the annals of modern warfare'. By the evening the whole Italian position was in Rommel's hands. He reckoned that since his attack started he had accepted the surrender of 150 officers, 9000 men and 81 guns. For Rommel this success had a twofold significance. It established him as a personality and, more importantly, it fixed his attitude towards the Italian army. The Italian troops, he considered, were let down by the incompetence of their officers. His later relations with the Italians in Africa were certainly conditioned by Caporetto.

More fighting in the mountains followed, to be crowned by Rommel's success at Longarone on the Piave front. Here he caught an Italian column passing through the town and took many prisoners. His unit was the first into the town, and the booty was enormous. Some 10,000 Italians with 20 guns and a transport column were captured. By noon Longarone was so full of German and Austrian troops that Rommel posted sentries with fixed bayonets to maintain possession of the quarters they had taken over on arrival!

He was now sent to a staff appointment, which he held until the end of the war—much to his disgust. But in France, Rumania and Italy he had learned how to be a general. During Rommel's African campaigns he gives the impression of a commander whose mind is fresh, uninhibited, experimental, untrammelled by precedent. This freedom of thought owes much to his good fortune during the First World War. An analysis of his front line service shows that it was always in an area where the front was relatively open and where the Germans were dominant. For about a year after its formation, it is true, his Württemberg mountain battalion was left in a peaceful sector of the

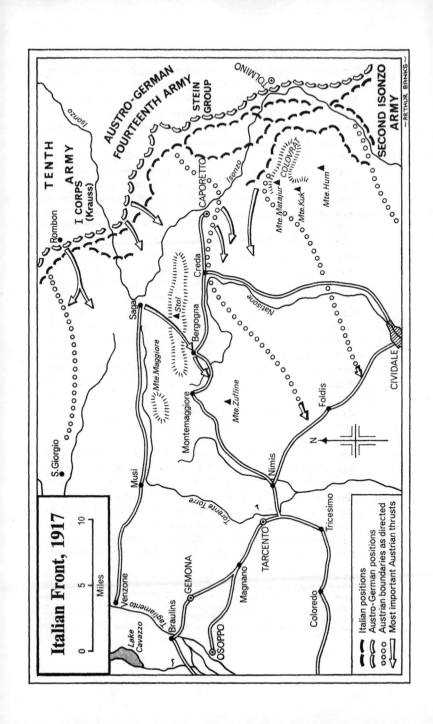

Italian Front, 1917

Miles
0   5   10

S.Giorgio
Rombon
TENTH ARMY
I CORPS (Krauss)
AUSTRO-GERMAN FOURTEENTH ARMY
STEIN GROUP
TOLMINO
SECOND ISONZO ARMY
Isonzo
Saga
CAPORETTO
Mte.Matajur
COLOVRAT
Mte.Kuk
Mte.Hum
Stol
Creda
Bergogna
Mte.Maggiore
Montemaggiore
Mte.Zufline
Natisone
Foldis
CIVIDALE
Musi
Venzone
Nimis
Torrente Torre
TARCENTO
Tricesimo
Magnano
Coloredo
GEMONA
Braulins
OSOPPO
Lake Cavazzo
Tagliamento
N

~ARTHUR BANKS~

Italian positions
Austro-German positions
Austrian boundaries as directed
Most important Austrian thrusts

Vosges; but where Rommel actually saw fighting—in France during the autumn of 1914 and in Rumania and Italy in 1917—mobility and enterprise were always possible. It is an intriguing but academic question to ask what Rommel would have been like had he endured the erosion of hope, the carnage and the slow tempo of the Somme, Verdun, Passchendaele, and the final retreat after March 1918: academic because, with so aggressive a temperament, Rommel would almost certainly have been killed.

But he missed the Western front; and this is an important factor in an interpretation of his personality and his method of command. Because his practical experience was gained in mobile operations with infantry, he found no difficulty in adjusting later to mobile operations with armour. Because he escaped the trenches in the West, he was never affected by that 'siege warfare' mentality which, consciously or subconsciously, distracted commanders in the Second World War who had been junior officers in Flanders. (Montgomery's battles, for all his disclaimers, bear the stamp of a man conditioned by this ordeal.) And, finally, because Rommel went through neither the western holocaust nor the humiliation of retreat in 1918, he emerged from his first war—unlike, say, Hitler or Göring—without neurosis or embitterment: his personality kept stable and balanced—certainly not the stuff from which the street gangs and the Free Corps of the early 'twenties were formed.

It might, therefore, be useful as a background to the rest of this study to define here Rommel's attitude towards the society in which he lived and for which he fought during two World Wars. He was a patriot: country counted for him more than any individual creed. He was never a Nazi; indeed, he increasingly deplored Nazism and its manifestations. It is important to establish this fact firmly, for Rommel's allegiance has often been misunderstood, and from time to time he is referred to as if he was a committed party man. He was not. Such allegations owe much to the efforts of Goebbels and his machine in their exploitation of Rommel's African victories for propaganda purposes, suggesting that they were won by a member of the Nazi 'old guard'. They were fabrications. Even in the 'thirties Rommel was capable of taking as firm a stand against the S.A. and the S.S. as he did against the latter's excesses in Italy and France during 1943 and 1944.*

The acid test in regard to Rommel and Nazism is the decision by the men who organised the July 1944 plot against Hitler (v. Chapter XIV) to replace

---

* Nor could he be bought. Hitler tried to purchase Rommel, as he successfully bought other officers in the German Army, by offering him an estate. Rommel refused to be caught by a dictator's ploy as old as the Roman empire: Gibbon observes of Caracalla that 'the vigour of the soldiers, instead of being confirmed by the severe discipline of camp, melted away in the luxury of cities. The excessive increase of their pay and donations exhausted the state to enrich the military order, whose modesty in peace, and service in war, is best secured by an honourable poverty.'

7

the Führer by Rommel as head of the German state. This was a matter of life or death. Though in many ways the plotters fumbled and mismanaged, it is hardly conceivable that they would have selected Rommel for such a function had they thought him to be tainted by suspicion of subservience to, or sympathy with, Nazism. During the 'thirties Rommel cannot have been unaware of what was 'going on in Germany'; but von Seeckt's determination to insulate the army from politics and Rommel's own preference for a quiet, disengaged life produced a man who was politically naïve. He failed to see the truth about Hitler even when he commanded the Führer's bodyguard during the invasions of Czechoslovakia and Poland. But when the truth dawned, later in the war, his reaction was uncompromising and his death was the consequence. On this his record stands.

The defeat of Germany in 1918 produced problems for both Rommel and the army. For Rommel the solution was simple. His skills were military, and he had a wife to support (on 27 November 1916 he married Lucie Maria Mollin: their only child, Manfred, was born on Christmas Eve 1928). Rommel therefore decided to stay in the army, whose own problem was more complicated, but was equally resolved in a simple way by President Ebert's appointment in the spring of 1920 of General von Seeckt to steer the German forces through the aftermath of Versailles. Von Seeckt's organisation of the minimal German Army allowed by the Peace Treaty is a separate story: for Rommel what mattered was that he was selected as one of the 4000 officers whom the Germans were allowed to retain, hand-picked men. Wheeler-Bennett says of von Seeckt that 'he singled out moderate and responsible types who were capable of adapting themselves not only to modern conditions of warfare but to the modern conditions of society in which they had to live'. This is a good description of Rommel at this time; he comfortably accepted the principles on which von Seeckt based his revolution. The coarse distinction between officer and man must end. The new army must be a force capable of immediate expansion. Its ideology was defined by von Seeckt in his 1921 memorandum on *Basic Ideas for the Reconstruction of Our Armed Forces*: 'The whole future of warfare appears to me to be in the employment of mobile armies, relatively small but of high quality, and rendered distinctively more effective by the addition of aircraft. . . .'

It would be pleasant to disclose that between the two World Wars Rommel elaborated von Seeckt's doctrines about mobility, or to be able to say that he was involved in arguments about the use of armour akin to those customary, during these years, on Salisbury Plain. The fact is that, between the two wars, Rommel was lying fallow. In action he thought creatively; in peace he was at ease.

His record during these years of peace is one of steady but conventional progress. His own regiment, 124, was abolished in the re-shaping of the army, and in 1921 he joined 13 Regiment at Stuttgart, with whom he remained in the rank of Captain for nine years. Then, in October 1929, he went as Instructor to the Infantry School at Dresden, and it was not until 1933 that he obtained his first command, a mountain battalion. During this period he first met Hitler, who inspected his troops in 1935 and seems to have formed a favourable impression. This was the occasion when the S.S. tried to place a row of their own men in front of Rommel's parade as a protection for the Führer, and Rommel—with great courage—refused to turn out his battalion on the ground that it was being insulted. It is easy to forget in the 'sixties what strength of will such a decision required in the Germany of the 'thirties. Himmler and Goebbels were present, and in the face of Rommel's bold stand they cancelled the order. This was certainly not the act of a lackey of Nazism.

Later in 1935 Rommel was sent as an Instructor, in the rank of Colonel, to the War Academy at Potsdam. Here he again had an experience which diminishes doubt as to his commitment to Nazism. He was selected—presumably as a 'safe' officer with a war-hero's glamour—to supervise the military training of the *Hitler Jugend*. He very soon found himself disagreeing with Baldur von Schirach, the *Jugend*'s leader, and was returned to duty. And then, in November 1938, he was put in charge of the War Academy at Wiener Neustadt. Between 1918 and 1938, therefore, Rommel's *dossier* might be described as sound but not spectacular.

But before he joined the War Academy two important events had occurred. First, Hitler had read and approved of his *Infanterie Greift An*. And so, when the Sudetenland was entered in October 1938, Hitler personally selected Rommel to command the *Führergleitbataillon*, his bodyguard. He was given a similar task when in March 1939 the Germans marched into Prague, and in August he was promoted to Major-General on the staff of Hitler's H.Q. —the officer responsible for the Führer's protection during the invasion of Poland. This was a critical step. It confirmed Hitler's confidence in him and enabled him to see from a central point how a *Blitzkrieg* could function. He was thus well poised for his next appointment which, it might be said, started him off on the road to both death and glory.

II

Blitzkrieg

1940

After securing the Führer's safety in Poland Rommel requested a post of danger for himself. He asked for a Panzer command, and was offered 7 Panzer Division, which he took over at Godesberg on 15 February 1940. Hitler's perception in promoting this infantryman to such a command was rewarded by Rommel's achievements in Europe and Africa: it matched Churchill's intuition when the Prime Minister picked out from the Home Guard in the Cotswold village of Chipping Campden General Hobart—the pioneer of armoured warfare who had been rejected by the British military establishment and who, thanks to Churchill,* came back to create 79 Armoured Division, without whose specialised tanks D-Day might have been a disaster.

By a curious coincidence Rommel's predecessor in command of 7 Panzer, General Stumme, was the man he was to succeed at Alamein. It was also a coincidence that the armoured division Rommel was now to lead had the same number as the British division which in Africa was (Shakespeare's phrase) his 'loathly opposite'—7 Armoured, the Desert Rats. Rommel too, by his exploits in 1940, acquired a nickname for his men: the 'Ghost Division'. His victories during the German invasion of France demonstrate Rommel's capacity in the conduct of a *Blitzkrieg* as convincingly as do his African campaigns. It is therefore worth noting that until the spring of 1940 he had no experience of directing tanks in action†—though during

---

* Churchill, and the public, were perhaps moved by some articles by Liddell Hart on 'the waste of brains', which specifically mentioned Hobart.

† Nor, because of his service elsewhere, had he had any opportunity of assessing from personal observation the contribution (unequalled by the Germans) of British armour to the final collapse of his country in 1918.

the German occupation of other countries in 1938 and 1939 he had been an intelligent eyewitness of the movement, deployment and engagement of armour.

But Rommel is one of the Great Captains whose ideas and actions are all of a piece throughout. His way of making war in France in 1914 and in the Italian mountains in 1917 was not, basically, different from the tactical principles and method of command he employed in France in 1940, and later in the desert.

As a young officer he grasped the fundamental concepts which were later expounded and accepted as the doctrine of armoured warfare—the need to thrust deep into the enemy's rear, to disregard one's own flanks and attack the enemy's, and always to maintain momentum. Even in the 'thirties these were considered revolutionary notions by most of the British Army: but Rommel's operations on the Italian front in 1917 reveal that he not only understood them but was already putting them into practice. Now he was to apply them with greater skill in France. Just as a study of Napoleon in Italy or Stonewall Jackson in the Mexican War illuminates their later achievements, so a review of Rommel's methods in France in 1940, considered as a continuation of his performance between 1914 and 1918, is instructive for an assessment of his mature handling of the later battles along the Mediterranean shore. His ideas about leadership never changed, essentially: they were always aggressive, dynamic, unpredictable, and founded on the principle that the place of a commander is at the front. Like Guderian, by 1940 he was a natural exponent of the theory of armoured operations which had been evolved between the wars by some of the best military thinkers in Britain and disregarded by Whitehall. These ideas conformed with Rommel's earlier practice on the Western and Italian fronts and with his later cogitations. In the spring of 1940, therefore, he brought both experience and reflection to a command for which his whole life had been an instinctive preparation.

When the Germans moved into France, Rommel's 'Ghost Division' was part of Hoth's Panzer Corps, which in turn was part of von Rundstedt's Army Group 'A'. This included seven of the ten available panzer divisions. Its astonishing success flowed from the imaginative suggestion of Manstein, von Rundstedt's Chief of Staff, that the original plan of attack, a variant of von Schlieffen's scheme for a thrust through Belgium in 1914, should be modified: Manstein proposed that the main weight of the German armour should be driven through the Ardennes in spite of the professional judgement, accepted on both sides, that the valleys were impenetrable by tanks. (In his memoirs Guderian says that 'at that time nobody believed in a successful outcome, apart from Hitler, Manstein and myself'.)

On the right of the long German line which moved forward on 10 May von Bock's Army Group 'B' was to advance into northern Belgium waving what Liddell Hart calls 'the matador's cloak'—enticing the willing British and French to rush forward into Belgium like an enraged bull past the northern tip of the Maginot Line. Since this was what the Allies had already decided to do, Bock without difficulty drew them forward into a vast and indefensible pocket, and persuaded them to extend their communications dangerously as they took up their ill-prepared positions. The German hammer-blow, meanwhile, struck across the Meuse: its full weight came from von Rundstedt's Army Group 'A', but within this von Kleist's Panzer Group was the implement. As his panzers broke out from the Ardennes to breast the river they had three tasks. Guderian's Panzer Corps (of three divisions) made the main thrust across the Meuse and through Sedan; von Reinhardt, further north, was to make another crossing with his two panzer divisions; and on the right Hoth with 5 and Rommel's 7 Panzer Divisions was to defend their flank. In this invasion Rommel's place was subsidiary: but as usual, by ruthless exploitation of his opportunities, he made of them something at once more dramatic and more effective than his mission required.

This *Blitzkrieg*, designed to drive irresistibly westwards and then to curve to the north across the rear of the British and French, was christened the *Sichelschnitt*, the scythe's sweep. It was a demonstration by their enemy of the theories and techniques painfully evolved and successfully exercised by the British in 1914–18: techniques and theories which had been further developed in Britain by a few pioneers between the wars in spite of cheeseparing and contumely. For them, and for all who understood their ideas, the conquest of France by German armour was the nadir; however, recovery (with set-backs) would be gradual but continuous until British and American tanks dominated western Europe in 1944–45 (though it should be remembered that in the greatest armoured battle, at Kursk, it was the Russians who won).

The *Official History* concludes its preface to an account of the German attack with words which have always heralded a British defeat: 'a lovely spring had succeeded the bitter winter, leave was open in the British Expeditionary Force, and the troops were in good heart.' Optimism might have been less had the Force realised that in the face of ten German armoured divisions (whose officers and men had in many cases had combat experience in Spain and Poland, and whose staffs had rehearsed the complicated—and so far unpractised—problem of moving masses of armour during the occupation of Czechoslovakia and Austria) the Allies could expect the Belgians and Dutch to provide only an insignificant armoured element, while the British themselves could produce no more than one army tank brigade—the infantry tanks of 4 and 7 R.T.R. (the latter only arrived in France on 1 May)—and seven cavalry regiments of light tanks.

The French had a large array; some 3000 machines. But the French were still obsessed by the First World War. Like the British they did not understand the implications of a *Blitzkrieg*—which included the idea of penetration by massed tanks, as Rommel and his colleagues were shortly to demonstrate. (When von Bock heard of the crossings of the Meuse he remarked: 'the French seem to have taken leave of their senses, otherwise they would have prevented it at all costs.') In the spring of 1940, therefore, their considerable armoured resources were dissipated along the front line to provide small and insufficient local support for their infantry divisions—a fallacy to which the British were so often to succumb in the desert during 1941 and 1942—and Churchill's hope, as the Battle of France progressed, that the French might provide an armoured *masse de manœuvre* could never have been fulfilled. The French (de Gaulle an exception) were not thinking in these terms. And so, when Rommel led his division into the assault, he was faced by one adversary whose trivial armoured contingent was partially supported by a modern concept of war, and another whose large stock of tanks was scattered because of an outmoded belief about the use of armour. It is not surprising, therefore, that in Rommel's notes about his first day's fighting one reads 'at our first clash with French mechanised forces, prompt opening fire on our part led to hasty French retreat'. Before the battle began, Rommel and the other German armoured commanders already possessed that moral and technical superiority which make a *Blitzkrieg* possible.

The division Rommel was to lead across France from the Ardennes to Cherbourg was a recently converted 'light' division. Instead of the normal two tank regiments it had only one, extra-large, with a complement of 218 tanks. There was also a reconnaissance and a motor-cycle battalion, two regiments of motorised infantry, three battalions of field artillery (36 guns in all), and an anti-tank battalion, with the usual ancillary services of Engineers, Signals and Supply. It was a balanced force (there was nothing comparable in the French or British Armies) in which were all the units necessary for tackling the variety of obstructions to be overcome at speed if the spear was to be driven home.

After advancing rapidly from the 10 May start-line and brushing aside weak opposition in the Ardennes, the division reached the Meuse at Dinant during the afternoon of 12 May, and found that the French had blown the bridges at Dinant and Houx. Rommel was now faced with one of the most challenging of all military operations—a hurried assault-crossing of a river in the face of substantial opposition (provided, in this case, by the French

18 Infantry and 1 Cavalry Divisions: the former, however, had only just reached Dinant after a lengthy approach march, and the latter had been bruised in the Ardennes). Still, their occupation of houses and emplacements on the west bank of the Meuse presented a formidable problem—which Rommel resolved in a characteristic way.

His men were disconcerted by the French resistance. When Rommel examined the situation on the east bank in the early hours of 13 May he found that artillery and small arms fire were harassing his troops, and collapsing the rubber boats in which they were attempting to cross. 'A smoke screen in the Meuse valley would have prevented these infantry doing much harm. But we had no smoke unit. So I now gave orders for a number of houses in the valley to be set alight in order to supply the smoke we lacked.' North of Dinant his motor-cycle battalion had crossed the river and taken the village of Grange. Rommel ordered them to start mopping up the French positions along the western bank: he then drove down in a tank to the southern front. The tank was fired on several times and Rommel's staff officer, Schraepler, was wounded by splinters. (During their return journey they were bombed by the *Luftwaffe*.) On this left flank a rifle company had been pushed over the river, but there were many wounded, and the bridgehead could not be supported. Rommel's attempt to rush over the Meuse had been decisively stopped.

His reaction was equally decisive. He got his tanks into positions along the eastern bank from which they could neutralise the French fire-points, and 'I now took over personal command of the 2 Battalion of 7 Rifle Regiment and for some time directed operations myself'. Rommel's ardour and expertise re-started the crossing: boats, and later a pontoon ferry, got to work, and in this second wave Rommel was among the first to move over the Meuse. Thereafter he was continually active in the bridgehead. On the 14th he had a narrow escape when his tank slid over on its side down a slope 500 yards from a French battery. Rommel was wounded by a splinter. He tried to fire his 37-mm. gun, but because of the slope he was unable to aim. The subaltern in charge of his supporting tanks reported: 'Herr General, my left arm has been shot off.' 'We clambered up through the sandy pit, shells crashing and splintering all round.' But in the end the bridgehead and the crossing were firmly secured.

It is interesting to note what Rommel thought about this operation. 'A tight combat control west of the Meuse, and flexibility to meet the changing situation, were only made possible by the fact that the divisional commander with his signals troop kept on the move and was able to give his orders direct to the regimental commanders in the forward line. Wireless alone—due to the necessity for encoding—would have taken far too long, first to get the situation reports back to Division and then for Division to issue its orders. Continuous wireless contact was maintained with the division's operations staff, which remained in the rear, and a detailed exchange of views took place early each morning and each afternoon between the divisional commander and his Ia. This method of command proved extremely effective.' It was a personal success. By his presence in the bridgehead Rommel had provided assurance, practical advice, and above all a demonstration to his division in its first large action that the General was more at home in the front line than in his office.

There would be more rivers—the Somme, the Seine. But in Rommel's *dossier* the passage of the Meuse has a special significance: it was here that he proved himself in command of a large force, and in particular of an armoured force. Von Rundstedt's Army Group made bridgeheads at three points: but whereas Reinhardt's crossing at Monthermé was on a very narrow front and was strongly opposed—his tanks did not get over until the 15th—and Guderian's corps was not west of the Meuse in full strength until the afternoon of the 14th, Rommel in the north made an immediate impact. As Liddell Hart puts it in his commentary on the *Rommel Papers*, 'by his advance that day Rommel had created a breach which had momentous consequences, particularly by its effect on the mind of General Corap, the commander of the French 9 Army'. (This psychological blow must have been reinforced, of course, by such intelligence as Corap was receiving about the general progress of the Panzer Groups.) Corap certainly ordered the line of the Meuse to be abandoned; and as Guderian was about to shatter the left wing of Huntzinger's 2 Army on Corap's right, Huntzinger independently came to the same decision. Miserably seeking guidance about the right line of retreat, he tried unsuccessfully to speak to General Georges (the commander of the French North-East Theatre of Operations, which included the B.E.F.) and finally got a reply: 'do the best you can.' He decided to swing back southwards on to the main Maginot Line, while Corap was ordering a retirement on to a theoretical 'stop-line' west of the Meuse. A large gap therefore opened between the French 2 and 9 Armies. By the evening of the 15th Guderian had smashed through into *rase campagne*, and the breach now yawned 60 miles wide.

Rommel exploited this French collapse remorselessly: but to convey the pace and panache of his advance in a condensed study is not easy. He communicates the feeling incomparably in his own *Papers*. No senior commander in the Second World War has been more successful than Rommel in capturing, by his description of his advance from the Meuse to Cherbourg, the tension and the drama of a *Blitzkrieg*. Slim, in his account of his army's break-out into Burma, gets near to Rommel's immediacy and sense of forward motion; but Slim was at too high a level to catch the continuous sensation of personal involvement which makes Rommel's narrative compelling. Liddell Hart puts the point well in his introduction to the *Papers*: 'Rommel carries the reader along with him in his command vehicle.'

Any summary of his subsequent operations can be no more than the bare bones of the story: his own full description gives it the breath of reality. If one compares the records of such leaders on Rommel's own side as von Rundstedt, Guderian and Kesselring, or on the side of the Allies, Montgomery, Alexander, Slim or Bradley (and they all went through the cauldron of battle as well as the calm offices of the highest command), none transmits the exhilaration and anxieties of a general in a mobile action more articulately than Rommel. Liddell Hart is right when he says 'he was a born writer as well as a born fighter. The same expressive gift and urge can be seen in the way he sketched on paper, with pencil or coloured chalks, the operations he planned or even imagined.' But this aesthetic ability (abnormal in generals) did not impair his military capacity in the way, as is sometimes suggested, that Ian Hamilton's powers of command at Gallipoli were softened by his sensibility. In Rommel's case sensibility and service were indivisible. The man in a tent or an office was the same as the one in a tank or armoured car: the thoughts and sensations he put on paper were a transcript of what he felt as he fought.

By 20 May the *Sichelschnitt* plan was consummated. On the 15th Reinhardt's corps broke away westwards from the Meuse and by the evening had reached Montcornet, an advance of 37 miles. Corap was sacked: 'I left at 1400 hours on the 16th, heart-broken.' Guderian's corps swept onwards to the Channel coast, and by the 20th tanks of 2 Panzer Division were at Abbeville, 6 Panzer was thrusting through on their right flank, while further north 8 Panzer was pushing past Montreuil in the direction of the vital Channel ports—Boulogne, Calais and Dunkirk.

These penetrations were not entirely welcome to Hitler and his Higher Command. They could not believe in their success. They began to think in terms of 'the worst case', and their reaction to the events of these crucial days affected their interpretation of Rommel's battle with the British at Arras on 21 May—a conflict whose course has been clouded by mythology but whose consequences were enormous: won by the Germans on the field (because of Rommel), but a psychological defeat. Nevertheless, though Hitler's fatal decision to stop his tanks from moving into the Dunkirk *enceinte* was certainly stiffened by what happened at Arras, it stemmed in fact from his present concern about Guderian's progress. Such a response by the Führer and his staff to the first results of the *Blitzkrieg* is understandable, even if it must be condemned. They had never expected that the gallop through Poland would be repeated. And so, as the armour rushed ahead, they became more and more unhappy about flanks, communications and infantry support—the natural reaction of veterans of the First World War who recalled the capacities of their opponents. Staffs tend to work by precedent: the Germans remembered the Marne.

Guderian was therefore ordered by von Kleist to halt. He argued—indeed he asked to resign, and von Kleist accepted his resignation. It was pressure from von Rundstedt, among others, which persuaded Guderian to remain at his post. (Hindsight reveals that in Germany, as in Britain, the pioneers and protagonists of armoured warfare had their critics; their enemies; and their honest opponents within the military establishment who simply failed to grasp what they were talking about.) In the end Guderian got permission to keep going for the next 24 hours, and his instinct that the momentum should be maintained carried him to the Channel.

Kleist's order derived from Hitler's fear that French tanks might cut his supply lines: the Führer still understood no more than the French or the British what total *Blitzkrieg* could encompass, nor had his intuition pierced into the heart of his enemy's demoralisation. He was more in sympathy than Whitehall with the concept of the *Blitzkrieg*—but he shivered as he saw what he had started. He had neither assessed properly the errors in the Allied strategy nor understood the shock effect of his panzers and Stukas. Halder noted in his diary that at a conference on the 17th 'the Führer is excessively nervous. He mistrusts his own success; he's afraid to take risks; he'd really like to stop now. His excuse is anxiety about our left flank.' By the 18th Hitler was 'raving' and 'bellowing', and alleging that his generals were 'well on the way to spoiling the whole operation and even risking the dangers of defeat'.

As he thrust from the Meuse to Arras Rommel had no notion of these dubieties. He was wholeheartedly concerned with victory. By the early hours of 17 May he had forced a column through to Le Cateau—an advance of 50 miles in 24 hours, which included a drive by tanks through the night. (At this stage in the war such a use of tanks was generally considered unlikely or impossible.) His map of his advance, reproduced in his *Papers*, demonstrates how daringly he thrust beyond the main front of the Panzer Groups, and how his nocturnal initiative put his division at the point of the German spear.

The result was that by now, for the loss of 94 killed and wounded, he was credited with some 10,000 prisoners, 100 tanks, 30 armoured cars and 27 guns—though *pro rata* this was a less remarkable yield than that produced by his detachment of Württembergers at Monte Matajur in October 1917

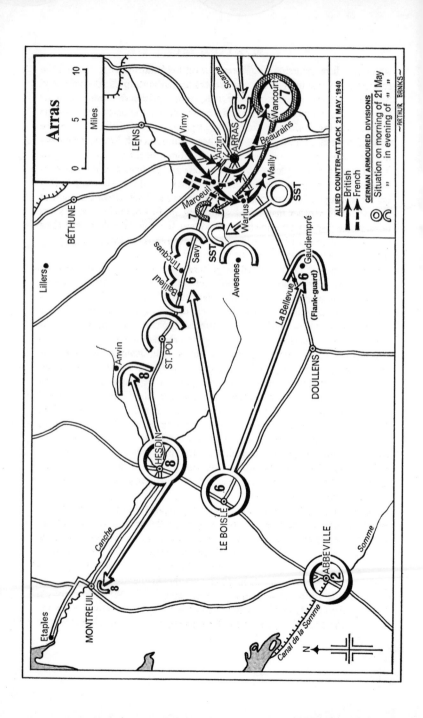

Arras

Miles
0 5 10

LENS

Scarpe

Vimy

Anzin

ARRAS 5

Wancourt 7

Beaurains

Wailly

SST

BÉTHUNE

Maroeuil

Warlus

SST

Lillers

Tincques

Savy

Bailleul

6

SST

Avesnes

Gaudiempré

La Belleue

6

(Flank-guard)

Anvin

ST. POL

8

DOULLENS

HESDIN 8

LE BOISLE 6

Canche

Etaples

MONTREUIL 8

ABBEVILLE 2

Somme

Canal de la Somme

N

ALLIED COUNTER-ATTACK 21 MAY, 1940

British

French

GERMAN ARMOURED DIVISIONS
Situation on morning of **21 May**
" " in evening of " "

~ARTHUR BANKS~

when, it will be remembered, Rommel with his handful of men forced the surrender of some 150 officers, 9000 troops and 81 guns of the Italian Army. Still, his advance maintained its *brio*; more prisoners were acquired; Rommel was awarded the Knight's Cross: and by the early hours of the 20th he was south of Arras, having swept past Cambrai where, in 1917, the first substantial armoured action in history had occurred. Rommel's energy during these days can only be appreciated from a reading of his *Papers*, for it was a matter of myriad decisions, actions and movements. He was constantly in passage from front to rear, whipping forward his reserves, spurring on his leading tanks, exposing himself to danger and acting with the sort of fury which in another man might seem frenetic. In Rommel's case this was normal: he was robust enough in mind and body to be able to sustain a tempo of command which most generals—even those hardened in battle— would find exhausting.

During the 20th his forward units came to a stop. 37 Reconnaissance Battalion was pushed away from Achicourt and other points south of Arras, and when six of his tanks put in an attack near the Arras railway station it was firmly repulsed. These operations were part of Rommel's plan which, on the 19th, he had persuaded Hoth to accept, for a further advance whereby he would establish his division on the ridges to the south-east of Arras. Hoth felt that Rommel's men were too exhausted. But Rommel replied: 'the troops have been 20 hours in the same place, and a night attack during moonlight will result in fewer losses.' Hoth accepted the argument, and at 0140 on the 20th Rommel pushed his tanks forward, accompanying them himself. By 0600 the main force was at Beaurains, two and a half miles to the south of Arras; but his supporting infantry was lethargic in its follow-up, Rommel himself was nearly caught by French tanks at Vis-en-Artois, and he had to pause to restore a situation in which for the first time since the dash from the Ardennes he found himself unbalanced and exposed. The next day's battle would further underline his weakness—for it was the occasion of the historic British 'counter-attack'.

To understand the events of the 21st a perspective is necessary. As the British Expeditionary Force pulled back from Belgium to the line of the Escaut, Gort foresaw the need for a firm bastion on his southern flank. He therefore ordered Major-General Petre, commander of 12 Division, to establish in and around Arras a group to be called *Petreforce*—scraped together from base units and field guns from the Artillery depot, a few light tanks from an ordnance store, and the solid nucleus of 1 Welsh Guards. On 20 May, the day Rommel attacked without success, Gort was visited by the Chief of the Imperial General Staff, Ironside, and handed a directive 'to move southwards upon Amiens attacking all enemy forces encountered and to take station on the left of the French Army'. Gort had in fact anticipated this order by creating another *ad hoc* group, *Frankforce*, under Major-General Franklyn of 5 Division, to 'support the garrison in Arras and block the roads south of Arras'. Franklyn was to make contact with the French. He therefore moved to the Vimy Ridge area north of Arras and joined up with 50 Division and 1 Army Tank Brigade. Out of these movements and directives the so-called British counter-attack on the 21st was born. As at first envisaged it was menacing for Rommel.

When Franklyn visited General Prioux, the commander of the French Cavalry Corps, he found him in a conference with other senior French officers of which the upshot was an understanding that the French would attack southwards in strength against the extended German right flank, while *Frankforce* supported this enterprise (directed on Cambrai) by 'blocking the routes south of Arras'. The French attack was, not surprisingly, postponed. Franklyn nevertheless proceeded with his own plan, because it fitted his broad directive and, for his part, was not thought of so much as a major onslaught as what the *Official History* calls 'a large-scale mopping-up operation'.

Myth and fact now part company. The British attack to the west and south-west of Arras, so often applauded, is actually a model of how not to launch a combined infantry/armoured assault. Franklyn's intention (a petty version of the original grandiose idea for a Franco–British swathe to be cut through the German flank) was for two columns to advance from Vimy Ridge in a curve round the west of the Arras strong-point, and sweep to the south-east of this pivot of manœuvre. Before the beginning of this move his columns were feeble, and they became weaker as the attack developed. The right or westerly combination was made up from the 8th Battalion of the Durham Light Infantry and 7 R.T.R.: the left from 6 D.L.I. and 4 R.T.R. They were driven precipitately into action by an impatient commander: because of Gort's instructions, Franklyn felt he was under pressure. There was little liaison between the Durhams and the armour; the infantry were late on their start line; and the tanks (though this was not Franklyn's fault) were unable to communicate between themselves; there was also a problem about the 'netting' of the tanks' wireless sets, which was not resolved at the time. So the only British armoured brigade, desperately weak by comparison with the powerful Tank Groups the Germans had passed over the Meuse, was sent into attack at Arras almost unsupported.

In the battle that followed Rommel sustained severe shocks, learned several lessons about armoured warfare which he was to apply later in his career with great profit—and emerged master of the field. Unaware of the British plans, and influenced by his rebuff on the 20th, he decided that on the 21st he would by-pass Arras to the south and then swing northwards—the classic Rommel finesse. This centre-line for his 7 Panzer and S.S. Totenkopf Divisions took them on a course parallel to and partly in the face of *Frank-force*. Before the tanks of the British easterly column had even reached their start line they were involved with Rommel's 6 Rifle Regiment. Already their own infantry had failed to keep pace with them; but 6 D.L.I. pressed forward, and were able to do something to stabilise the result of what turned out to be a rapid reversal of fortune.

At first the Germans were thrown into disorder. Their anti-tank guns proved incapable of penetrating the armour of the Matildas, and for the first time since the *Blitzkrieg* had begun it seemed that there was a possibility of a technological defeat. Then 4 R.T.R. ran on to a line of 105-mm. field guns (*not* anti-tank, it will be noted) and the result is described by a junior officer: 'I went forward through the tanks of "A" and "B" Company and thought it very odd that they were neither moving nor shooting. Then I noticed that there was something odder about them; their guns were pointing at all angles; a number of them had their turret hatches open and some of the crews were half in and half out of the tanks, lying wounded and dead. . . . In that valley, the best of our crews were left behind.' Stukas and the more powerful German artillery were next brought in, and the eastern column was stopped in its tracks.

The fortunes of the column on the British right were worse. 7 R.T.R. took the wrong route, and also became separated from its infantry. There was great confusion, central command broke down, and the battle became a series of improvisations. By the early afternoon this other luckless assembly was struggling only some 1000 yards from where Rommel, as usual at the nerve-centre of the battle, was rallying and driving forward his division. In his *Papers* he describes how with Most, his A.D.C., he ran from gun to gun in his battery positions, pointing them at the British tanks along his front. 'I personally gave each gun its target.' The British attack was beginning to flag when 'suddenly Most sank to the earth behind a 20-mm. gun close beside me. He was mortally wounded, and blood gushed from his mouth.' During this defeat of the second British column the 88-mm. was used for the first time by the Germans in an anti-tank role. And it was naked defeat. 'The whole area to the south of the Scarpe about Arras,' says Major Macksey in his *The Shadow of the Vimy Ridge*, '—and within the city itself—was alight from burning houses, tanks and lorries and from the flash of the guns, shells and bombs. The roar of the battle as it came to its climax was almost continuous, with the rumble and crump from the big guns, the crack of the lighter anti-tank guns, the scream and whine of the Stukas. Numbed by this cacophony, the British began their withdrawal.' The reason was not noise alone: as Montgomery later used to put it, the British had been 'seen off' the battlefield. Early on 22 May *Frankforce* was back where it had started; on Vimy Ridge.

Considering the shock the Germans received, and Rommel's personal involvement in the thick of the fighting, it is not surprising that in his immediate battle report for the 21st he dramatised the encounter. (He had acted with his usual energy; as a divisional commander he had exposed himself in, and indeed directed, his front line; and one of his staff had died at his side.) The report read: 'Between 1530 and 1900 hours heavy fighting took place against *hundreds*' (my italics) 'of enemy tanks and following infantry. Our anti-tank gun (P.A.K.) is not effective against the heavy British tanks, even at close range. The enemy broke through the defensive line formed by our P.A.K., the guns were put out of action or overrun, and most of their crews killed.' Von Rundstedt, von Kluge and von Kleist were similarly scared by what, considered in proportion to the German panzer groups' achievement, was no more than a raid.

Hitler's anxiety about the exposure of his armour was also increased, and in consequence energetic steps were taken to push the laggard infantry forward in support. Without doubt, the abortive 'counter-attack' at Arras paid dividends in its effect on the mind of the German Higher Command, and made its strong contribution to the fatal decision to halt the German armour outside Dunkirk. As to the latter, its effects are imponderable: they will probably be argued by historians in perpetuity. What is certain is that at Arras Rommel learned and never forgot that tanks are not expendable cavalry to be used in Balaclava charges against a gun line, but that in engagements between forces of a comparable size a modern general should lure his enemy's armour on to his own well-established artillery and then—and only then— put his panzers into a counter-attack on their broken opponents. He also learned that if a commander of an armoured force operates in its head rather than its tail he can make instant and much more effective decisions. This had always been his style of fighting. At Arras, as at the Meuse crossings, he found that it worked as effectively in directing a massive armoured division as it had once done when he commanded no more than a small mountain unit.

During the next few days Rommel was in a situation comparable with that of a commander of a British armoured division during the difficult days in the desert: he fought on, unaware of disputes among the staff in the rear or of misunderstandings between his immediate masters and Hitler. These were considerable. The notion that the Germans swept from the Ardennes to the Channel according to a programme fully accepted in advance and continuously endorsed as the *Blitzkrieg* proceeded is inaccurate. In the higher echelons of the German Command, notwithstanding their success, there was now a mixture of doubt and confidence which recalled the first few weeks of the 1914 offensive. No one at the top had any certainty—except Göring, whose advice to Hitler about the capacity of the *Luftwaffe* to demolish the British before they crossed the Channel was one of the main factors which made Dunkirk's miracle possible.

The sickle plan seemed to be supported, but during 23 May O.K.W. decided that changes must be made in the command structure. They ordered that von Rundstedt's 4 Army should be transferred to von Bock, the implication being that responsibility for the annihilation of the B.E.F. would lie not with von Rundstedt but with his more mercurial successor. The former did not find the change 'a particularly fortunate one at the given moment'; the latter wrote: 'it's a pity it wasn't done earlier'. Hitler, learning of the decision on the 24th, immediately cancelled it.

Behind these vacillations lies an uncertainty in the German Command about how to deal with the Dunkirk rearguard—a complicated and shrouded business, only relevant here in that it shows how Rommel's 7 Panzer Division, like the British 7 Armoured in the desert, was not always able to count on either a generally acceptable plan (which they could implement) emerging from the rear, or on an assurance of harmony between the men who directed them militarily and those who directed them politically. In Rommel's story this is a constant theme.

He was not drawn into the Dunkirk battle. On 24 May Hitler ordered his panzers to pause on the general line La Bassée-Béthunes-Gravelines: when he lifted the order on the 26th—as the British were deciding to withdraw on Dunkirk—Rommel, released, thrust for Lille. But crossing the Canal de la Bassée proved difficult, and once again he displayed his exceptional abilities as a leader. Rushing round his units he poured out orders, and then 'under my personal direction 20-mm. A.A. guns and later a Panzer IV were turned on the enemy snipers, who were maintaining a most unpleasant fire from the left and picking off our men one by one. I had every house from 300 to 600 yards west of 2 Battalion's bridging point demolished and the bushes swept with fire. . . .' A bridge was essential. 'I drove the sappers on to their utmost speed and had the pontoons lashed roughly together, in order to get at least a few guns and tanks across.' As at the Meuse, a crossing was attained, and the guns and tanks rumbled forward thanks to Rommel's personal intervention.

Their general was recalled to his H.Q. at midday to be told that he had been given another brigade, 5 Panzer, for his attack on Lille—this was a pre-war unit, the armour of 5 Panzer Division, and it contained as a brigade more tanks than the whole of Rommel's 'light' division. Critics of Rommel the hot-headed should note that after his swift succession of victories he remained cool enough to decide that in the coming attack he ought not to move with his forward units, but should stay back, to co-ordinate his enlarged force. His concern now was with ammunition and petrol, and with preventing his armour from being left (as at Le Cateau) unsupported by his infantry. During the night of 27–28 May his troops penetrated to Lomme, due west of Lille, and by this thrust he was instrumental in cutting off and causing (on 30 May) the surrender of half the French 1 Army. Again Rommel did not win a victory without a narrow escape: 'a hail of shells suddenly began to fall round the panzer regiment's command post. . . . I tried to get to the radio to order the cease fire, but the fire was so thick that it was not easy to reach the signals lorry. . . . I was just making a dash for the signals vehicle, with Major Erdmann running a few yards in front, when a heavy shell landed close by the house door near where the vehicle was standing. When the smoke cleared, Major Erdmann . . . lay face to the ground, dead, with his back shattered. . . . I had escaped unscathed.'

There now followed a few days' relaxation. Rommel wrote to his wife on the 29th that 'we were again the first in the front of the western gate' but that they were now at rest. 'Lieutenant Hanke, acting for the Führer, ceremonially decorated me with the Knight's Cross and gave me the Führer's best regards. . . .' On 2 June Hitler himself came forward. 'The Führer's visit was wonderful. He greeted me with the words: "Rommel, we were very worried about you during the attack." His whole face was radiant and I had to accompany him afterwards. I was the only divisional commander who did.' Quotations like this are essential if Rommel is to be seen as a whole: but he can only be so seen if it is remembered that he was murdered in 1944 because of his revulsion from Hitler's policies. In 1940 Rommel, like Hitler, was radiant because he was a soldier who had achieved a signal success. He had not yet realised (as he was slowly to do) that what he achieved by his personal efforts and the death of his men was only fodder for the appetite of a nihilist prepared to abolish Germany for the sake of himself.

On 5 June Rommel drove for crossings over the Somme and the Seine and then made for the sea. By 12 June he was in St. Valéry . . . 'the French General Ihler came up to me wearing a plain military overcoat. His escort officer fell to the rear as he approached. When I asked the General what division he commanded, he replied in broken German, "No division. I command 9 Corps.'' During this day, 'no less than twelve Generals were brought in as prisoners, among them four divisional commanders. A particular joy for us was the inclusion among them of General Fortune, commander of 51 Highland Division, and his staff.' Rommel's thrust from Lille to the Channel was another perfect example of the *Blitzkrieg* put into practice, and its rewards were commensurate. But once again it is only from a reading of his *Papers* that one can properly appreciate how Rommel's personal contribution made his division's success possible. During these days he was tireless ... and these nights. He seems hardly to have slept: in his tank or half-track he moved around his front remorselessly, encouraging, upbraiding, advising. As usual he lived very close to death. 'My armoured command vehicle was fired on by machine-guns from Hangest. The bullets clanged against its armoured walls but fortunately did not penetrate.'

His operations during this week are impressive because of the flexibility made possible by the balanced structure of his division. A bridge down ... engineers available. A strong-point ahead ... infantry for the attack, with tanks moving effortlessly and instinctively in their support and artillery to back them up. A suspect position ... send in the motor-cycle battalion and reconnaissance troops to investigate and if necessary attack. And in a crisis the *Luftwaffe* could always be summoned. This battle-drill of the Germans was professional and perfected. The French and British had nothing equivalent—in the technique of managing a battlefield the British would not catch up with the Germans until 1942. Rommel was one of its most effective executants; in his account of this week's activity one observes him switching, adjusting, combining, and then personally leading his troops to a triumph.

On 16 June he wrote to his wife that 'the war seems to be gradually becoming a more or less peaceful occupation of all France'. But for Rommel there remained one final and spectacular operation: his division was moved on the 16th to a position east of the Seine and south of Rouen, and then set in motion for a direct drive to the west on Cherbourg. By the evening of the 19th he was addressing the senior French officers available there (for Admiral Abrial, the Commander of the French Channel Fleet, kept out of the way and later told Rommel that the fortress had capitulated without his permission: 'I replied that I took note of his statement') and informing them that he was pleased that Cherbourg had surrendered without bloodshed among the civilian population. In its dash 7 Panzer Division travelled over 150 miles in a single day; 'this,' says Liddell Hart, 'far exceeded any day's advance which had ever been made in warfare.'

The cost-effectiveness of Rommel's march from the Ardennes to Brittany was also exceptional. His expenditure of capital was 42 dead tanks and something under 3000 men killed, wounded or missing. The gain was nearly 100,000 prisoners and more than 300 guns, 450 tanks and armoured cars, and 7000 other forms of transport—trucks, cars and horse-drawn vehicles. At Cap Bon in Tunisia, in the last days in Normandy and the final days of the whole war the Allies would achieve similar returns for their expenditure of men and munitions: but these days were yet to come.

In a footnote to the *Rommel Papers* his son Manfred draws attention to what some consider a flaw and others accept as inevitable in Rommel's system of command—an issue which often became a point of tension in the desert: his treatment of his staff. On 13 June one of his senior staff officers 'submitted a memorandum to my father in which he complained that contact had been broken between the staff and the divisional commander, and that the practical conclusion to be drawn from this fact was that the commander should stay farther to the rear'. Manfred sensibly observes that 'in fact, the principal cause of the crisis which had arisen was that the unit commanders had not been sufficiently familiar with my father's technique of command. He had had far too little opportunity of exercising his division as a formation and with its full complement of weapons. The result, especially at the beginning of the campaign, was a need for repeated makeshift measures, until finally, towards the end, operations went more or less smoothly.' This comment is wise and just, and might equally well be made about Rommel's command of the Afrika Korps during its first campaign. But it is one to which any new commander is inevitably exposed. His troops must have the chance of interpreting his personal touch, and he in turn must have the chance of assessing their calibre.

This criticism of Rommel is, however, recurrent. A staff, of course, always likes things to be tidy, always suspects the individualist, always seeks good communications and copious information. Rommel's way of working was anathema for the traditionally trained staff officer: he broke the rules daily. He did so because he daily took decisions at the front, and in France in 1940, as he himself observed, the method of communication to his rear was inhibiting because cypher was slow. Rommel was not slow. He was 'out there fighting'. War is pragmatic, and for a military commander victory is the justification of his methods. Rommel may have caused his staff some inconvenience, but it was constantly offset by success. This was certainly true in France in 1940, and it would soon be proved to be true in North Africa.

III

African Spring

1941

Rommel reached Africa on 12 February 1941. It is ironical that on the very day of his arrival the circumstances which had caused him to be dispatched so urgently were already dissolving. Brigadier Dorman-Smith, whom Wavell had used for liaison with O'Connor in his recent overwhelming defeat of the Italians, was now sent back from the front to convince Wavell of the case for an immediate advance on Tripoli. Dorman-Smith raced to Cairo, and entered the map room at 10 a.m. on 12 February. The familiar maps of the desert had vanished. Wavell gestured towards the maps of Greece which had replaced them and said: 'You see, Eric, I'm starting my spring campaign.'

On the same day Eden, supported by the C.I.G.S., General Dill, left London for the Middle East to organise succour for Greece against a German attack and to endeavour to bring Yugoslavia and Turkey into the war on the side of the Allies. On 12 February, also, Churchill sent to Wavell a long signal stressing that 'your major effort must now be to aid Greece and/or Turkey. This rules out any serious effort towards Tripoli. . . .' Yet what had caused Rommel's arrival in Africa, and what he found to be a prevalent fear among the Italian command, was the assumption that Wavell would bring Tripoli into danger. This was now impossible. The sudden realignment of Britain's policy in the Mediterranean shifted her strength from Africa to the Balkans, and Rommel's presence was irrelevant. His mission was to provide a blocking detachment (*Sperrverband*): Hitler's Directive No. 22 of 11 January, which stated that 'for strategic, political and psychological reasons Germany must assist Italy in Africa'—the birth certificate of the Afrika Korps—defined as the main objective the defence of Tripolitania. Later, at the Obersalzberg meeting between Hitler and Mussolini on 18 January, Hitler declared that there was no point in committing German troops to months of inaction in Tripoli, and after Beda Fomm Mussolini accepted a 'forward policy' in Africa. This policy, however, was essentially defensive; designed to face a threat which (though the Axis had not grasped the fact) had evaporated. There was nothing to block.

The Germans gave their venture across the Mediterranean the code name *Sonnenblume*. But there was nothing flowery in the orders the general staff issued to govern the direction of their troops in an Italian theatre: in these the staff was realistic. Rommel was to be subordinate to the Italian C.-in-C. in tactical matters, but his men must always be deployed together, a German group; they must not be scattered over the desert in fragments supporting the Italian Army. Any suspicion that Italian instructions to Rommel might impair the Germans' reputation allowed him to refer back to Hitler. There was a similar right of appeal from *Fliegerkorps X* to Göring. These *caveats* are reminiscent of the safeguards the British constantly endeavoured and, in spite of Lloyd George, managed to achieve in their negotiations with the French during the hard last years of the First World War. They meant, nevertheless, that Rommel in Africa, like Haig in France, had to deal with an ally on uneasy terms. In Rommel's case, a doubt deriving from his experiences on the Italian front in the earlier war was enlarged by the reports he received when he landed at Castel Benito aerodrome, near Tripoli, on 12 February. The Liaison Officer of the German General in Rome to the Italian High Command, Lieutenant Heggenreiner, described 'some very unpleasant incidents which had occurred during the retreat, or rather the rout which it had become. Italian troops had thrown away their weapons and ammunition and clambered on to overloaded vehicles in a wild attempt to get away to the West. This had led to some ugly scenes.' Rommel's subsequent attitude towards the Italians in Africa was conditioned both by his memories and by this discouraging welcome.

The new British commitment to the Balkans dissipated O'Connor's victorious and veteran army. It was replaced by men inexperienced in desert warfare—at every level, from private to general. O'Connor himself was pulled back, to become G.O.C. British Troops in Egypt. 7 Armoured also retired, the gap being filled by part of 2 Armoured Division, which had only completed its disembarkation in January. Two of its armoured regiments, which had arrived earlier, had been involved in O'Connor's offensive and had already been withdrawn. The front line in the Western Desert was therefore held by its Support Group, 3 Armoured Brigade (equipped with worn-out*

---

* The 'track life' of a tank was always important in the desert. At this stage the British had few tank transporters: in consequence the tracks of their tanks in this forward zone were aged.

medium and light tanks), and an extra regiment hastily supplied with captured but inefficient Italian tanks. 6 Australian and 2 New Zealand Divisions went to Greece. 9 Australian Division, which took over from 6, also sent two of its brigades to Greece, and their replacements from 7 Australian Division were raw. Nor were they available at the front: maintenance problems were such that two of its brigades had to be spread east of Benghazi, while the third was in Tobruk. Greece also sucked away other specialist units from Wavell's army, and substantially reduced its air cover. In simple terms, Rommel was not faced by the hardened professional army he had been sent out to defeat, but by a soft, ill-equipped, amateur assembly.

Moreover, Wavell chose as a successor to O'Connor a man who was to prove a failure, Lieut.-General Philip Neame, V.C. 'I did not know him well,' Wavell wrote later. '. . . I accepted him as a skilful and educated soldier; and his V.C. was a guarantee of his fighting qualities. He was at this time a great friend of Dick O'Connor's, for whose judgement I had much respect.' But with much respect for Wavell—and his confession is characteristically frank—one must remark that a V.C. is no guarantee of a capacity for high command, and that, as it turned out, this was one of those appointments which bedevilled the British in the desert until the merciless Montgomery arrived.

Neame and his few and diffident troops were no match for a Rommel who, after leaving Catania at 1000 hours on 12 February, at about 1300 hours was conferring with the Italian C.-in-C., Gariboldi, in Tripoli, expounding to him a plan for 'not a step farther back, powerful *Luftwaffe* support and every available man to be thrown in for the defence of the Sirte sector, including the first German contingents as soon as they landed. It was my belief that if the British could detect no opposition they would probably continue their advance, but that if they saw that they were going to have to fight they would not simply attack—which would have been their proper course—but would first want to build up supplies.'

Rommel did not then know about the German plan to invade Greece— this had been carefully withheld—but he had quickly taken the measure of his opponents in Africa. His instant grasp of the battle-picture and his decision 'in view of the tenseness of the situation and the sluggishness of the Italian command, to depart from my instructions to confine myself to a reconnaissance and to take command at the front into my own hands as soon as possible', reminds one of Montgomery's reaction when he too found that he had unexpectedly to fly out from England to take over command in the desert. His swift and self-confident reading of the tactical and strategical

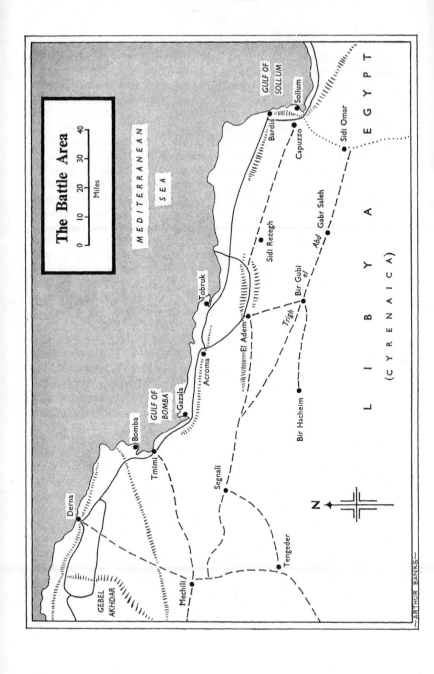

The Battle Area

Miles
0 10 20 30 40

MEDITERRANEAN SEA

GULF OF SOLLUM

GULF OF BOMBA

Bomba

Derma

Tmimi

Gazala

Acroma

Tobruk

El Adem

Sidi Rezegh

Bardia

Sollum

Capuzzo

Sidi Omar

Abd Gabr Saleh

Bir el Gubi

Trigh

Bir Hacheim

Segnali

Tengeder

Mechili

GEBEL AKHDAR

L I B Y A

(C Y R E N A I C A)

E G Y P T

N

~ARTHUR BANKS~

situation has often been commended (though like Rommel he also exceeded his brief. According to his memoirs, on 13 August 1942 'it was with an insubordinate smile that I fell asleep: I was issuing orders to an army which someone else reckoned he commanded'). Just as Rommel decided to 'depart from my instructions', so Montgomery took over 8 Army two days before he was due to do so. The two commanders who, in so many other ways, differed in temperament and battle skill, would at least have this in common when they clashed—a liking for independent action.

Compared with the lethargy and incompetence which the British were soon to display, Rommel's first moves were confident. For a German general in an Italian theatre his support was slim. The first German troops were due in mid-February—but 5 Light Division (which would ultimately become 21 Panzer) was not expected to complete its transfer until mid-April, while 15 Panzer would not arrive until the end of May. Von Rintelen, the German military attaché in Rome, had warned Rommel that he should not pursue too energetic a policy, for 'that was the way to lose both honour and reputation', but on the afternoon of 12 February he was in the air with Colonel Schmundt (one of Hitler's adjutants, who had been attached to him presumably to supply the Führer with private reports) examining what Rommel called 'the soil of Africa'. In their He. 111 they flew over the desert east of Tripoli, 'a belt of sand which had the appearance of being difficult country for either wheeled or tracked vehicles and of thus forming a good natural obstacle in front of Tripoli'. They then looked at the areas around Tarhuna, Homs and Buerat, and finally circled over the Sirte front. 'The flight confirmed me in my plan to fortify Sirte and the country on either side of the coast road and to reserve the motorised forces for the mobile defence.'

This rapid personal reconnaissance was followed by an equally rapid deployment. The Italians, including *Ariete* armoured division, were pressed forward to Sirte, and as the German reinforcements began to disembark at Tripoli on 14 February Rommel insisted that the operation should continue throughout the night, risking the dangers of air attack because of the necessary lights. In consequence 'the men received their tropical kit early next morning, and by eleven o'clock fell in on the square in front of Government House. They radiated complete assurance of victory. . . .' They were 3 Reconnaissance Battalion and an anti-tank battalion: 26 hours later they were at the front. By the 24th the first engagement between German and British forces in Africa had occurred and, symbolically, the British came off the worse. The Germans had no casualties; but the British patrol lost two armoured cars, a lorry and a car, while one officer and two other ranks were taken prisoner. During these days Rommel flew* regularly between Tripoli and the front, familiarising himself with the terrain. He also ordered his workshops to prepare quantities of dummy tanks mounted on *Volkswagen*, which could be used to suggest an impressive armoured strength—the first of those inventive ideas which would later proliferate in Africa and Normandy. 'Speed is the thing that matters here,' he wrote to his wife on 5 March. Rommel had so far not been slow.

Wavell, in assenting to the Greek expedition and withdrawing the best of his troops, was influenced by his appreciation that the Germans, because of Italian naval weakness in the Mediterranean, would not send large quantities of armour to Africa. He correctly estimated the probable German reinforcement during the early spring at about the level of an armoured brigade, and doubted whether, with such resources, the Axis would immediately attempt to recover Benghazi. This was a copybook appreciation; but it omitted that incalculable factor which T. E. Lawrence once described as 'the irrational tenth . . . like a kingfisher flashing across the pool': Rommel.

On 19 March he flew to Hitler's H.Q. to report (and was told by the C.-in-C. of the Army, von Brauchitsch, that 'there was no intention of striking a decisive blow in Africa in the near future'). Brauchitsch and Halder were firmly opposed to the idea of wasting German troops and equipment in Africa. They gave Rommel a tentative permission to try to capture Benghazi once 15 Panzer had arrived; but Rommel properly pointed out that without control of all Cyrenaica it was useless to hold Benghazi—a lesson the Italians had already learned. He returned to his post unhappy about the likelihood that his reinforcements would be few; still convinced, however, that the momentary British weakness in North Africa 'should have been exploited with the utmost energy'.

While Rommel was with Hitler, Wavell was visiting Neame. He found Neame's tactical dispositions, as Wavell himself put it, 'just crazy'. He was alarmed at the state of the cruiser tanks in 2 Armoured Division and the lumbering size of its H.Q. And he was shocked to find that he had not been advised that the escarpment south of Benghazi, unlike that running east from Sollum, was easily penetrable by mobile troops.† 'I came back anxious and

---

* In a private communication Lord Ranfurly (Neame's A.D.C., who was captured with him) has pointed out to me that 'Archie Wavell criticises Neame for not "going forward personally" and in the next breath says there were "no suitable aircraft available". This was so, and made things difficult. Rommel had his *Storch*.'

† This advice came from General Wilson. 'Philip Neame took them up to the escarpment on this occasion specifically in order to convince them that it was not so,' Lord Ranfurly informs me. 'We ate our sandwiches together at the top of the escarpment and it was plain that mobile troops could penetrate in many places.'

depressed from this visit, but there was nothing much I could do about it. The movement to Greece was in full swing and I had nothing left in the bag. But I had forebodings and my confidence in Neame was shaken.' Wavell's instinct was right. As John Connell wrote, Rommel 'returned to Africa with the clearest and most cautious directive from Hitler's headquarters, and proceeded instantly and methodically to disregard it'.

His method of disregard was to attack. Before his visit to Hitler he had instructed 5 Light Division to plan an assault on El Agheila, and on 24 March this went in successfully. It stimulated a signal from Churchill.

Prime Minister to A. P. Wavell   *26 March 1941*

We are naturally concerned at rapid German advance to Agheila. It is their habit to push on whenever they are not resisted. I presume you are only waiting for the tortoise to stick his head out far enough before chopping it off! . . .

But the head was not to be chopped off. On 31 March Rommel started an offensive which, as we now say, was to escalate. 'Our attack moved forward against the British positions at Mersa el Brega, and a fierce engagement took place in the early hours of the morning with British reconnaissance troops at Maaten Brescer.' Neame had warned Cairo of this possibility, but been ignored. On 30 March Wavell signalled, 'I do not believe that he can make any big effort for another month', and added: 'your task for the next two months is to keep enemy from crossing the 150 miles between Agheila and Benghazi without heavy loss to your armoured and mobile troops.' Rommel crossed this space in a few days, shattering in passage his enemy's armour.

If the British could have held the front at Mersa Brega much might have followed. Rommel's doubting masters might have increased their doubt, and the flow of supplies to Africa might have stopped. Rommel himself might have been submerged under a cloud. Wavell—and certainly Churchill—might have been exhilarated by an initial victory in the desert over the Germans. But it turned the other way. '*Luftwaffe* reports clearly showed that the enemy was tending to draw back and this was confirmed by reconnaissance patrols which General Streich had sent out. It was a chance I could not resist. . . .'

Rommel now revealed more convincingly than at any time in his career his possession of that *coup d'œil* which is the Great Commander's gift. His abnormal speed in interpreting the opportunities offered by the ground ahead of him, his quick grasp of the picture provided by his intelligence, and that extra, indefinable quality which is a feeling in the marrow of your bones that 'the show is on', all came together to persuade him not to resist the chance that was offered: he saw that he had his enemy on the run. By 2 April his troops had occupied the area around Agedabia and Rommel had moved his H.Q. into the battle line. Next day he sensed that his opponent 'was now withdrawing generally and seemed to be evacuating Cyrenaica ... so, that afternoon, I decided to stay on the heels of the retreating enemy and make a bid to seize the whole of Cyrenaica at one stroke'. For a man whose previous military experience had been in European theatres, on the downs of France and among the hills and mountains of Italy, and who had been in the African desert for no more than a couple of months, this was an astonishingly rapid appraisal and a remarkably self-confident decision: the more so because it was right.

Part of 2 Armoured Division's Support Group was cut off on the morning of 2 April by Rommel's tanks which, by the afternoon, were grappling with the heart of 3 Armoured Brigade. In this fight five tanks of 5 R.T.R. were destroyed and two more broke down. Gambier-Parry, commanding 2 Armoured, then ordered a withdrawal to Antelat, and Wavell, far away in Cairo, began to realise that something had gone wrong. He first sent a signal.

A. P. Wavell to Chiefs of Staff   *2 April 1941*

... Some forward posts were overrun yesterday.... Losses not serious at present, but the mechanical condition of the Armoured Brigade is causing Neame much concern, and there seem to be many breakdowns. As I can produce no more armoured units for at least three or four weeks, I have warned him to keep three brigades in being, even if it involves considerable withdrawal, possibly even from Benghazi.

That evening, at his 10 p.m. conference at G.H.Q. in Cairo, Wavell decided that it was his duty to examine the situation on the spot. 'I soon realised that Neame had lost control and was making no effort to regain it by the only possible means, going forward personally. I wanted to go forward myself but no suitable aircraft was available, and no one seemed to have much idea where our troops or the enemy were. I sent a message in for Dick O'Connor to come out and take over from Neame.' After only two months on the African shore Rommel had thus got the wise and experienced Wavell 'on the wrong foot', and diminished Wavell's confidence in the general he had himself appointed. (Neame did in fact use a small mobile Battle H.Q., from which he made frequent visits to units: but commanders depend on the impression they create, and Wavell, a not ungenerous superior, was convinced that Neame had lost grip of the battle—as he had.) Rommel's attack also deleted a division from the British order of battle, for after his offensive 2 Armoured Division was not revived. He achieved all this by himself 'going forward personally', and his method is best described in his own words.

'I had been told by the Italian General, Zamboni, that the track from Agedabia to Giof el Matar was an absolute death-trap, and he had done his best to dissuade me from sending troops to Cyrenaica over that route. However, I placed more faith in my own observation and set off with my A.D.C., Lieutenant Aldinger, in the direction of Giof el Matar. After 12 miles we reached the head of the Italian Reconnaissance Battalion. . . . On returning to my H.Q. at about 1600 hours I learnt that the 5 Light Division were saying they needed four days to replenish their petrol. This seemed to me to be utterly excessive and I immediately gave orders for the division to unload all its vehicles and send them off at once to the divisional dump at Arco dei Fileni . . . it meant the division being immobilised for 24 hours, but with the enemy withdrawing this was a risk we could afford to take.' While Wavell and Neame were endeavouring to produce solutions which were out of date by the time they had reached their troops, Rommel was up and down the line issuing orders which could be executed immediately. Yet his feeling that he had done something significant was deflated when he returned to his H.Q. Gariboldi was there, and Gariboldi was furious. He harangued Rommel about his failure to obey the orders from Rome, pointing out that the supply situation was insecure and that there was little possibility of logistic support for a success on the battlefield. 'This brought the argument to a climax.' There then arrived a signal from the German High Command giving Rommel complete freedom of action.

All these Axis operations occurred during 3 April, a day when the British were engaged in self-destruction: destruction virtually without a battle. The graph of the war in the desert has often been compared with a temperature chart: a line which zig-zags between peaks and troughs, with dramatic differences between height and depth. 3 April 1941 provided a deep trough for the British graph. Wavell, up with Neame, appears to have been driven by Rommel's unexpected onslaught, and the realisation that Neame had lost control, into vacillation. Having ordered O'Connor to replace Neame, he now accepted O'Connor's argument that 'changing horses in mid-stream would not really help matters'. O'Connor's view was that new tactics could not be introduced in the middle of a battle. He was unknown to the troops, particularly the Australians; and he would have been far better employed in preparing a defensive position well to the east of Benghazi. 'I therefore decided that I would ask the Chief to reconsider my replacing Neame, and to consider, as an alternative, my remaining with him for a few days, but ultimately returning to organise the defence of Egypt. The Chief agreed to this proposal provided I remained until the situation had stabilised.'

Wavell thus made another mistake. 'Hire or fire' is a good principle when handling generals. Wavell should have backed Neame or dismissed him. To leave O'Connor looking over Neame's shoulder was to prevent a desert-worthy general from exercising effective command, and at the same time to suggest to Neame that he must maintain responsibility for the battle without his C.-in-C.'s full confidence. There is no error a supreme commander can make more grave than to delegate responsibility with obvious doubt. Rommel that evening said to Gariboldi that 'one cannot permit unique opportunities to slip by for the sake of trifles'. Wavell, for the sake of some trifling sense of protocol, failed to grasp the opportunity of replacing the wrong commander with the right one.*

Wavell also interfered with Neame's tactical instructions. Neame wanted Gambier-Parry to use the remains of 3 Armoured Brigade, in a withdrawal eastwards, to block a German advance towards Mechili. Wavell felt that this plan exposed Benghazi to an attack from the south. O'Connor, sitting in the wings, thought Neame's plan 'eminently sound': but Wavell ordered 3 Armoured Brigade, which by now was out of wireless touch with H.Q. 2 Armoured Division, to draw back west and south of the escarpment towards Benghazi. This muddle in the command at the highest level was accompanied by confusion among the fighting units. Nobody seemed to know the location of headquarters. Owing to battery failures and lack of battery-charging facilities, communications were slow and complicated: order followed counter-order. This was a bad day for the British. Unfortunately it is im-possible to register in detail what happened, because all the records of Cyrenaica Command and the H.Q. of 2 Armoured Division were destroyed. But the day's end was decisive. Rommel recorded in his *Papers*: 'Von Wechmar's battalion moved into Benghazi during the night of 3 April, amid great jubilation from the civil population. The British had set fire to all their stores.' And to his wife:

> Dearest Lu,
>
> We've been attacking since the 31st with dazzling success. There'll be con-sternation among our masters in Tripoli and Rome, perhaps in Berlin too. I took the risk against all orders and instructions because the opportunity seemed favourable. No doubt it will all be pronounced good later and they'll all say they'd have done exactly the same in my place. . . .

The drive to the north was three-pronged. On the left Rommel pushed successfully down the coast road to Benghazi. His central line of thrust ran via Antelat and Msus to Mechili, and on the right he sent *Ariete* on a flanking sweep through Tengeder which was also aimed at the vital Mechili area.

---

* In his honest way, Wavell did subsequently record in his papers that 'I think I should have done better to insist on Neame coming back with me' (Connell, *op. cit.*, p. 533).

Converging here, his troops could control the bottleneck through which the British would have to pass in their flight from Cyrenaica. And so it went. On 4 April his advance proceeded on all three fronts with little opposition. (One of the main British mistakes the previous day had been to accept a tactical reconnaissance report that Msus, where the chief supply dumps lay, was threatened by German tanks. The vehicles were in fact a patrol and a section of recovery lorries. But on this day of confusion rumour was enough to cause the guard of the dumps to destroy all the fuel: and in consequence, as Wavell later said in his Despatch, 'from now onwards the movements of the 3 Armoured Brigade were almost entirely dictated by lack of petrol'.)

Those military critics who are inclined to be contemptuous of the performance of the French in the summer of 1940 and of the Americans at Kasserine might well consider how the British response to Rommel's attack in the spring of 1941 provides a classic case of what can happen when inexperienced troops are unexpectedly exposed to a *Blitzkrieg*. A chain reaction occurs. Surprise breeds shock; shock breeds disorganisation and loss of morale; these breed unnecessary errors and the sum is disaster. Because of bad tactical handling, and the decrepit state of its equipment, by the evening of 4 April, the *Rommel Papers* record, 'the British main body was in full retreat and was evacuating Cyrenaica'. Churchill's message to Wavell, which the latter found awaiting him when he got back to Cairo on the evening of the 3rd, was prophetic in a sense which the Prime Minister certainly never intended. 'If this blob which has come forward against you could be cut off you might have prolonged easement. Of course if they succeed in wandering onward they will gradually destroy the effect of your victories.'

The blob wandered onward. Rommel indefatigably pushed his troops forward, flying above and in advance of them in his light aircraft (and dropping down, from time to time, on a unit which had stuck, to force it ahead with his rasping sergeant-major's encouragement). The way he worked is vividly revealed in this passage from his *Papers*: the day is 5 April. 'At about 1400 hours that afternoon I took off in a Junkers and flew to Ben Gania. After landing, I heard from the *Luftwaffe* that there were no longer any British to be seen in the area of Mechili and to its south. Schwerin's column thereupon received the order: "Mechili clear of enemy. Make for it. Drive fast. Rommel." The remainder of our forward troops were also switched to Mechili. I myself flew off with Aldinger in the afternoon to take over personal command of the leading units. Towards evening we flew back to look for 5 Light Division's columns, which we discovered making good speed to the north-east. . . . I now sent the *Storch* back and drove up the track in my "Mammoth" to Ben Gania in order to get my own idea of the difficulty of the march. Two and a half hours later, completely covered in dust, we reached the airfield. . . .'

Neame was baffled by Rommel's speed and assurance. By 7 April the three prongs of Rommel's assault met at Mechili and, like ripe fruit, British generals dropped into his hands. The commander of 3 Armoured Brigade, Rimington, was the first. Then Neame himself, with O'Connor and Brigadier Combe, missed their way in a night drive and were captured. (Ranfurly, who was also captured, says they were taken by 'a small German armoured group . . . they must have been the best part of 50 miles from the last reported German positions.') In the early hours of 8 April Gambier-Parry was also caught, and Wavell himself might later have been taken. Departing from a conference at Tobruk, he was a passenger in a plane which twice failed to take off. At the third attempt it got into the air, but an engine failure forced it down in a stretch of the desert where German patrols were active. Fortunately for Wavell a Sudanese—'his teeth gleamed white in a black face'—picked him up: but Churchill's 'blob' might well have absorbed in its wandering his own Commander-in-Chief.

Rommel himself could have been captured on the 7th. He was flying in an attempt to find and guide one of his columns which had gone astray on its way forward from Msus, and saw below him what he thought were German vehicles: it was only in the split second before landing that he realised that they were British. But sometimes the tide of luck runs at full flood for a commander, and during these spring days it was a spring tide for Rommel. Not only was he out-manoeuvring the enemy and hauling in their generals on his own front: on another front a battle was taking place, in counterpoint with his own, which was of the greatest assistance to him in the sense that it distracted Wavell and Whitehall. The calendar of events in Greece speaks for itself. On 6 April Operation *Marita* starts and Greece and Yugoslavia are invaded. On 8 April the Metaxas Line is turned and in eastern Macedonia the Greek Army surrenders. By 14 April the British and Commonwealth troops have abandoned the Monastir Gap and the Aliakmon Line, and are falling back on Thermopylae. This dismal retreat continues until 28 April, when the final British evacuation from Greece occurs. Happy the commander whose opponent, like Wavell, has to deal with concurrent disasters!

'The reconquest of Cyrenaica was now complete. However, it still seemed to me very important to remain on the enemy's heels.' Rommel's triumphant entry in his *Papers* is countered by Churchill's message:

Prime Minister to A. P. Wavell   *10 April 1941, 2330 hours*
We all cordially endorse your decision to hold Tobruk and will do all in our power to bring you aid.

Here now was the centre-piece of the desert war. Rommel on the 10th told his staff that the Suez Canal was his objective, but that Tobruk must first be taken. The British had already appreciated the point: as early as the 7th an Australian infantry brigade and some tanks were being moved up westwards by sea. 9 Australian Division was in Tobruk by the 10th: a scurry of other units occurred, and Wavell found in the Australian, Major-General Morshead, a man with the temperament to endure a siege. By the 11th both manning and investment were complete. 'Stukas', Rommel wrote, 'attacked the defence works, the layout of which was still completely unknown to us. More troops arrived on the 12 April and it was decided to open the first major attack on the stronghold that afternoon.'

Rommel's luck now ended. It was ominous that General von Prittwitz, who arrived in advance of the 15 Panzer Division he was to command, was killed by a direct hit from an anti-tank gun during the opening phase of the attack. Between 10 and 12 April, as is clear from his *Papers*, Rommel was a gadfly around the Tobruk perimeter, encouraging, advising and condemning: but he was too late. Within the perimeter were four Australian brigades, an assortment of tanks, some anti-aircraft guns, and a resolute commander. And on the Egyptian frontier the British were evolving under Brigadier Gott an improvisation of small harassing columns, congenial to a nation which created the Commandos, the Long Range Desert Group and Wingate's Chindits in Burma. Here was a moment when, as in the Battle for Britain, two ideologies came face to face. The German was cocksure (until he hit the defences of Tobruk Rommel *was* cocksure), but he met at Tobruk Australians whose philosophy was 'give it a go', and whose spirit could not be quenched by a siege: and outside Tobruk the British, exploiting a situation in the desert which allowed them to make much of their gift, developed over the centuries, for providing young officers with an independent command. Morshead told his men in Tobruk, 'There'll be no Dunkirk here. If we should have to get out, we shall have to fight our way out.' Rommel saw the situation in the same intense, dramatic light. His *Papers* covering these mid-April days are full of such sentences as 'I drove north in my Mammoth behind the tanks. . . . I drove up to a point about 100 yards south of the wire to see for myself how the operation was developing . . . we were forced to withdraw after the aerial of our signals vehicle had been cut through by a splinter. . . . I spurred the division to the utmost speed. . . . I now drove off with three anti-tank guns in order to save what was left . . . the driver of the Mammoth was wounded by a bullet which came through the visor. . . . I climbed into the driving seat and drove myself . . . it was a pitch-black night and we tried to navigate by the stars . . . machine-gun fire was reported from in front of Acroma. At this news I drove across there as fast as I could go. . . .'

Apart from the furious energy which Brigadier Jock Campbell was to display on Sidi Rezegh airfield during the *Crusader* battle, no commander 'led from the front' with more dynamism than Rommel revealed in his attempt to rush the defenders of Tobruk. He was everywhere, doing everything—exhorting, instructing, expostulating, planning and leading: it was an astonishing example of courage, confidence and competence. But he was thwarted. He failed to take Tobruk. And he summarised the reason exactly when describing 5 Light's inadequacies: 'the division's command had not mastered the art of concentrating its strength at one point, forcing a breakthrough, rolling up and securing the flanks on either side, and then penetrating like lightning, before the enemy has had time to react, deep into his rear.' As Liddell Hart observes, the *Blitzkrieg* method could not be better epitomised in a sentence. Of course, when he wrote it Rommel had hindsight. But this, undoubtedly, was the technique he was trying to apply at Tobruk, and he was robbed of success by four factors: the *brio* of the Australians, the fact that he had had no opportunity to train the German troops in his methods since their arrival in Africa, the simple cowardice of the Italians, and lack of information about Tobruk's defences—though he mounted several assaults during April, it was not till the 19th that the detailed maps of the fortifications of Tobruk filtered through from the Italian High Command. (The British, however, were no better. General Holden of the R.T.R., who was in all the battles for Tobruk, tells me that during the final collapse of the fortress a year later the minefield maps in use were utterly out of date.) On the 23rd Rommel had a meeting with Gariboldi and Roatta, the Italian Chief of Staff, at which 'I was ceremonially awarded the Italian "Medal for Bravery". I am also supposed to be getting the Italian "Pour le Mérite".' But, as he wrote to his wife, 'what a trivial business it all is at a time like this'.

The pressure on the perimeter of Tobruk was steadily maintained by Rommel until he had to face a moment of truth. By 2 May he accepted that 'we were not strong enough to mount the large-scale attack necessary to take the fortress'. He would have to live with an ulcer in his side. Behind him, in Germany, doubt was developing in a way which supports the argument that if he had failed earlier at Mersa el Brega he might have been sacrificed. Halder now wrote in his diary: 'Reports from officers coming from this theatre as well as a personal letter show that Rommel is in no way equal to his task. He rushes about the whole day between the widely scattered units, stages reconnaissance raids and fritters away his forces. No one has any idea of their dispositions and battle strength. The only certainty is that the troops are widely dispersed and their battle strength reduced.' Halder had, of course, no notion of what command in the desert involved.

It is an odd coincidence that the man he now sent out to report on Rommel's failure to capture Tobruk was in due course to surrender Stalingrad—von Paulus. In Halder's view Paulus was 'perhaps the only man with sufficient personal influence to head off this soldier gone stark mad'. Paulus watched one more abortive attack on Tobruk, assessed Rommel, and reported—as any objective critic would have done—that Rommel was weak logistically; not enough could be got across the Mediterranean to keep him going; and therefore there was no point in reinforcing him further. He also set an embargo on further attacks towards Egypt. His report to the German High Command was forwarded in a code which had been broken: and it was quickly deciphered. This started a flow of messages between London and Cairo.

Churchill to Wavell   *5 May 1941, 0405 hours*

Have you read my telegram of 4th inst.? Presume you realise the highly secret and authoritative character of this information? Actual text is more impressive than paraphrases showing enemy 'thoroughly exhausted' unable pending arrival of 15 Armoured Division to do more than hold ground gained at Tobruk and assigning as main task of Africa Corps retention of Cyrenaica with or without Tobruk, Sollum, Bardia. . . .

Wavell to Churchill   *5 May 1941, 1405 hours*

I saw the secret message yesterday. . . . I have already issued orders for offensive in Western Desert at earliest possible date to be prepared on assumption *Tiger* successful.

Churchill to Wavell   *7 May 1941, 2340 hours*

I told them to send by the most secret method the actual text of the message . . . if *Tiger* comes through it will be a moment to do and dare.

Though this knowledge of how the Germans were privately thinking was obviously valuable for Wavell, the references to *Tiger* were the beginning of his end in the desert. The Prime Minister, ardent to retrieve a defeat, had already signalled on 22 April '. . . you will, I am sure, be glad to know that we are sending 307 of our best tanks through the Mediterranean . . . you should furnish us with your plan for bringing these vehicles into action at the very earliest. . . .' Thereafter Churchill's concern about the content of a convoy which he had bravely and rightly forced on a reluctant Admiralty urged Wavell, against his better judgement, into premature attack. The *Tiger* convoy passed Gibraltar on 6 May and docked at Alexandria on 12 May in spite of air attacks by day and night. Some of its tanks had already been ear-marked by Wavell for Crete (an example of the current distractions of his manifold command), but in Churchill's mind his 'Tiger-cubs' were all that was necessary to defeat Rommel. He never grasped that a tank in the desert in the 1940s was something different from his horse at Omdurman: that technical alterations of many kinds were essential before a disembarked tank (especially one sent from England to Egypt in 1941) could function efficiently in the sand. This failure in technical comprehension, added to his fury when he found that Wavell had properly prepared a 'worst case' plan for evacuating Egypt, and his later rage about Wavell's intransigence over Iraq and Syria, destroyed the C.-in-C. Compared with all this the Paulus report on Rommel was insignificant.

In assessing a commander it is well to understand his opponent's problems. How cheered Rommel would have been if he could now have looked at 'the other side of the hill'! During May and June 1941 he certainly had his own difficulties: the aftermath of victory—tired and disorganised troops, all the uncertainty about supply which followed a swift advance in the desert, a sense that what he had done was undervalued and misinterpreted in Germany. But once again he was lucky, in that the distractions with which Wavell had to deal were incomparably larger. Rommel was never in danger of that counter-offensive which might have caught him at his most vulnerable: the Allies' defeat on his own front was but a small part of their disasters.

The time-table of Wavell's preoccupations during these weeks is indeed staggering. To the south-east, the Abyssinian campaign was still running its course; Haile Selassie did not enter Addis Ababa until 5 May, and the Duke of Aosta did not surrender at Amba Alagi until 17 May. On 20 May the German invasion of Crete began, and until the final evacuation on 31 May Wavell was daily, and often hourly, concerned with instructions and rein-forcements for Freyberg on the island, and with initiating and answering signals for Churchill and the Chiefs of Staff. He was also observing the disappearance of the Royal Navy in the Mediterranean: the disappearance, too, of any immediate hope of more 'Tiger-cubs'. The bill for the Navy was a total loss of three cruisers and six destroyers, and damage (often serious) to an aircraft carrier, three battleships, six cruisers, and seven destroyers. Raschid Ali in Iraq simultaneously created a diversion. On 29 April his troops surrounded the British base at Habbaniyah, and it was not until 30 May, as Crete was being evacuated, that terms of armistice, after anxious consultations and grave dangers, were agreed. Meanwhile the presence of German bombers in Syria, and evident collusion between the Vichy régime and the Axis, provided a disturbing prelude to the Allied invasion of Syria which was to be successfully concluded in June.

In the centre of this panorama, skeleton forces faced one another on the Egyptian frontier. Rommel's policy was to maintain the investment of Tobruk, hold Bardia, and with a mobile group defend the line Sollum–Sidi Omar. Colonel Herff, commanding this group, took the Halfaya Pass in a sudden attack, which strengthened the concept of a 'forward' defence. But Rommel was a realist. He appreciated that he had little time to develop these open positions into anything like a strong defensive line before the offensive which, he assumed, the British would soon launch. Had he been able to read the Churchill–Wavell correspondence, he would have been convinced. He therefore ordered a line of retirement to be prepared at Gazala—which was to be useful to him in 1942—based on what he had learned about the defences of Tobruk. For the rest, he hoped that his thin screen would do what it could in the event of an attack, remembering that so far as the embryonic Gazala Line was concerned 'how to withdraw the non-motorised German and Italian forces to that line remained, of course, a problem'. The irony of command is perennially instructive. Here was Rommel on the verge of a victory, obsessed with problems of holding a line and then withdrawing, while Wavell, driven onward by his Prime Minister, had to apply his mind, among his many preoccupations with defence, to a premature offensive.

Rommel had a foretaste of what he was expecting when, on 15 May, Gott put in a quick thrust and captured Sollum and Capuzzo; but Rommel reinforced with a battalion of panzers, and the battle fizzled out, the British withdrawing from all points except the Halfaya Pass: on 18 May, Rommel noted, 'we were, with that exception, back where we started'. Wavell's star was now fading: on 19 May Churchill told Dill that he proposed to sack him, and substitute Auchinleck. During the next month the Prime Minister pressed Wavell hard to use his 'Tiger-cubs' SOONEST while Wavell maintained his determination not to commit his new tanks until they were ready for action. By the time Churchill's gift was available at the front, however, Rommel had been reinforced by 15 Panzer, and all the hopes vested in the famous convoy were to be shattered.

On 26 May, Herff's mobile force attacked the British troops on the escarpment in strength, and by dawn on the 27th Gott had agreed to a withdrawal. Rommel in his *Papers* exaggerates the defeat when he says that the Coldstream Guards and their supporting troops and armour 'were soon driven out and fled in panic to the east, leaving considerable booty and material of all kinds in our hands': the loss was in fact 173 men, four field guns, eight anti-tank guns and five 'I' tanks. But the psychological defeat was what

43

mattered. This was not at all what Churchill wanted. Rommel had created a situation in which the Prime Minister's confidence in his C.-in-C. collapsed. On 28 May Churchill sent Wavell a long and critical signal, in which he snarled: 'as I try to support you and your army in every way and especially in adversity, I feel sure that you will not resent these observations which I feel it my duty to make.' Dill, the C.I.G.S., tried to soften the blow by an immediate personal letter to Churchill, beginning, '*My dear Prime Minister*, I have of course despatched your telegram of today to Wavell. At the same time I feel I should let you know that there is much in it that I do not like.' But by now the damage that Rommel had caused could not be repaired, and on the same day Wavell, acting under extreme pressure, sent up into the desert his instructions for *Battleaxe*; instructions which produced the final cause for his dismissal. Rommel had won the first round—in so far as the desert campaigns can be envisaged as a conflict between two commanders in an enclosed ring.

For a time, there was equilibrium. Rommel held Halfaya Pass: Commonwealth troops held Tobruk. Each of these positions promised a tactical opportunity, and the question was—who would strike first? Rommel energetically developed the defences of Halfaya to anticipate a move by Wavell, and was especially active in dealing with the vast amount of Italian equipment which he had recaptured. This he reconditioned; and when Gariboldi tried to reclaim the arms his own troops had abandoned, Rommel firmly snubbed him. But during this period of waiting the most important act of the Afrika Korps was to prepare dug-in positions at Halfaya for their 88-mm. A.A. guns in an anti-tank role: 'so that with their barrels horizontal,' as Rommel put it, 'there was practically nothing to be seen above ground. I had great hopes of the effectiveness of this arrangement.'

It was one of the most important tactical inventions during the war in Africa,* disastrous for the British, and infinitely rewarding for the Germans. During the *Battleaxe* operation which was to follow, the Germans had only 13 88-mm. A.A. guns, but their employment in this new role was decisive; it left a legacy of doubt in the British tank units about their relative effectiveness which would not be dispelled until the arrival of the Sherman tank from America and the victories at Alam Halfa and Alamein, in the autumn of 1942. Indeed, it might be said that Rommel's exploitation of his 88s was a battle-winning device akin to the introduction of tanks by the British on the Western front in 1916: the difference being that the British mismanaged their invention, and failed to gain real benefit from it until the latter months of 1918,

---

* 88s had indeed been used in this role at Arras in 1940; but it was in Africa that Rommel developed an idea into a technique.

whereas Rommel progressively and profitably applied and elaborated this new use for an old weapon. On the other hand, the conservatism of the British was rarely revealed more starkly than in their failure to make use of their own 3·7 A.A. gun in a similar role. It was in fact suggested; the gun was tried in the desert for this purpose—and rejected. During the Second World War the British were generally superior to the Germans in their creative use of artillery, but in this particular respect they were quite unnecessarily out-distanced. In defence, and at a later stage in attack, Rommel's army perfected with artistry the use of the A.A. gun in an armoured engagement.

The tanks that were to attack Rommel's guns were also imperfect. For an understanding of the coming battle this signal is significant:

A. P. Wavell to C.I.G.S.   *30 May 1941*

State of Tiger cubs on arrival Egypt.
    Light tanks Mark VI. Eight out of the 21 require complete overhaul.
    Cruiser Mark IVA 15, average mileage 700 or half their life.
    Cruiser Mark VI 67, in good order.
    Infantry tanks, first 69 ready on 28 May required average 48 man-hours each in shops. Examples of heavier repairs are: two gear boxes, cracked and faulty, required exchange, broken sprockets, rackham clutches slipping, unserviceable tracks, one left-hand engine seized, top rollers seized, two engines over-heating and lacking power require top overhaul.
    Had cubs only required to be fitted with desert equipment and camouflage painted, all would have been ready for operations by 31 May.

Nevertheless, on 15 June Wavell launched the offensive which Churchill desired and Rommel expected (for his wireless interception, always better than that of the British in the early days in the desert, benefited from the British lack of security on the air). Its plan was normal. Like the Western front in the First World War, the Western Desert imposed on the commanders of both sides an inescapable condition—the terrain. It was usually impossible to do other than push with infantry along the coast and try to achieve a hook with armour around the southern flank. Such now was Wavell's intention: he set it out in a telegram to the C.I.G.S. on 10 June. Part of 4 Indian Division (now commanded by Messervy) would move between the sea and the escarpment: another 4 Indian group in the centre would move against the Halfaya-Capuzzo area: and 7 Armoured Division (under O'Moore Creagh, operating freely in the south, was to swing round the pivot of Sidi Omar and sweep northwards through the enemy's rear. (It would be less 4 Armoured Brigade, which was to support 22 Guards Brigade in its attack on Capuzzo and then revert to 7 Armoured.) This move in the south would, it was hoped, lead to a clash between the main armoured forces. But its success depended on the new 'Crusader' tanks. Their deficiencies had already been reported, and because of their defects they were subsequently to cause constant trouble: too many of them had been produced too soon. So Wavell's May signal to Whitehall about the proposed battle was now to be justified: 'I think it right to inform you that the measure of success which will attend this operation is in my opinion doubtful.'

Both sides were deluded about their opponent's strength. Rommel, however, was genuinely strong: strong in dispositions, strong in intelligence, relatively strong in tanks and anti-tank guns—but weak in fuel. He had anticipated an attack early in June, and when, during the afternoon of 14 June, the British began to move forward under the command of Beresford-Peirse, Rommel must have had a sense of poise. He had 15 Panzer sitting opposite the Capuzzo-Sollum front, nicely blocking any drive along the coast: and his reserve, 5 Light, which he had so far held back to the south of Tobruk, was alerted by him at 2100 hours on 14 June and was soon on the move to cover his right flank. So when, in the early hours of the 15th, the British began their assault, they achieved neither surprise nor success. On the coastal flank the Indians made little progress. In the centre the 88s at Halfaya destroyed 11 out of 12 Matildas as they groped forward, and four out of six of their followers were mined. On the left 7 Armoured (adding up their 'Crusader' breakdowns and their own casualties from 88s) were cut down to 48 tanks. By comparison Rommel's loss of Capuzzo to the Guards' Brigade was insignificant.

In this battle, as in his spring offensive and as he would contrive in the months to come, Rommel made the British exhaust their armour prematurely; thus enabling him to inject, in the later phase, counter-attacks which could not be resisted by an enemy short of tanks, whose infantry also lacked satisfactory and sufficient anti-tank guns. During the 16th this attrition continued.

In comparing the plans of the two sides for the next day it is clear that Rommel was far the superior in his more rapid assimilation of the facts, his more rapid decision about what to do, and the drive behind his command which forced his troops to success. The British idea was to slog on, hoping that 4 Armoured Brigade could be detached from the infantry in the north (which never happened) to support the armour in the south. Rommel, on the other hand, was thinking forcefully and swiftly: 'I planned to concentrate both armoured divisions suddenly into one focus and thus deal the enemy an unexpected blow in his most sensitive spot.' This was a classic manœuvre: and Rommel's subsequent comment that 'it is often possible to decide the issue of a battle merely by making an unexpected shift of one's own weight' reminds one of those eighteenth-century captains who pared the principles of command down to the essentials—of Marlborough the practitioner and

Saxe the theorist. Beresford-Peirse and his divisional commanders were not fighting the battle with this kind of sophistication.*

At dawn on the 17th Rommel's pincers began to converge, and his plan started to achieve its success. Once again he put his opponents on the run. In his *Papers* he noted: 'The commander of 7 Armoured Division sent a request to the Commander-in-Chief of the desert force to come to his headquarters. It sounded suspiciously as though the British commander no longer felt himself capable of handling the situation. It being now obvious that in their present bewildered state the British would not start anything for the time being, I decided to pull the net tight by going on to Halfaya.' Messervy's headquarters were nearly overrun (as Churchill put it, 'everything went wrong') and 4 Armoured Brigade was now disintegrating. By 0930 the message which Rommel had intercepted was filtering through the malfunctioning wireless net from 7 Armoured to Beresford-Peirse and Wavell, the 'distinguished visitor' who Beresford-Peirse said he would now bring forward. By midday on the 17th, when Wavell and his generals reached the H.Q. of 7 Armoured, Messervy of 4 Indian had already ordered a retreat in the north. Wavell therefore instructed Creagh to conform. 'He flew back at once to Cairo,' John Connell records in his biography, 'and that afternoon signalled Dill a full account of the battle from the time of his arrival at Sidi Barrani. Its opening words were: " I regret to report the failure of *Battleaxe*." '

Dearest Lu,   *18 June 1941*

The three-day battle has ended in complete victory. I'm going to go round the troops today to thank them and issue orders. . . . I've been three days on the road going round the battlefield. The joy of the 'Afrika' troops over this latest victory is tremendous.

For Churchill this was a disaster. Rommel had been in Africa for only a few months, but he had shattered the morale of the Grand Old Man. In the third volume of his war memoirs Churchill wrote: 'success in the Desert would have meant the destruction of Rommel's audacious force. . . . No news had reached me of the events of the 17th, and, knowing that the result must soon come in, I went down to Chartwell, which was all shut up, wishing to be alone. Here I got the reports of what had happened. I wandered about the valley disconsolately for some hours.'

The Prime Minister soon recovered, and Rommel's first adversary was driven out of the ring.

---

* But it should be noted that the German tanks, when separated from their 88s, were, according to British armoured commanders, sometimes very inept in *Battleaxe*. 15 Panzer was, of course, still inexperienced in the desert.

Prime Minister to A. P. Wavell   *21 June 1941*

I have come to the conclusion that public interest will best be served by appointment of General Auchinleck to relieve you in command of armies of Middle East. . . .

At St. Valéry in 1940 Rommel had accepted the surrender of 51 Highland Division: now, in the summer of 1941, Wavell of *The Black Watch* was in effect handing in his surrender, defeated by Rommel on the battlefield and discharged by his Prime Minister. During the spring and summer of this year, whatever O.K.W. and O.K.H. might think, Rommel had beaten the best the British could put into the field and effectively humiliated the man who had so far proved their most capable Theatre Commander. Churchill remembered that he said at the time, 'Rommel has torn the new-won laurels from Wavell's brow and thrown them in the sand.' He also noted that 'this was not a true thought, but only a passing pang'. For the time being, however, the laurels were with Rommel.

IV

Plans and Preparations

Summer and Autumn 1941

Tobruk was now Rommel's* chief concern. His front line had been flung far forward, and he realised that until Tobruk was captured his army would be exposed to an attack launched simultaneously from the fortress and the frontier. He considered this to be unlikely so long as there was a chance that the Germans might break through the Caucasus, but estimated that with the approach of winter a British offensive could be mounted in November. He determined to forestall it. In the meantime, he took the precaution of disposing his forces so that no spoiling thrust from Egypt could interfere with his arrangements for investing and finally overwhelming the garrison of Tobruk.

This concern would certainly have been increased if he had been able to follow the interchange of communications between Churchill and Auchinleck. From the moment the latter reached Cairo he was put on the rack.

Prime Minister to General Auchinleck   *1 July 1941*

You take up your great command at a period of crisis. . . . You should have regard especially to the situation at Tobruk and the process of enemy reinforcement in Libya and temporary German preoccupation in their invasion of Russia. . . . The urgency of these issues will naturally impress itself upon you.

Pressure on Auchinleck to attack Rommel at the earliest possible moment never ceased until *Crusader* started in November. Even after that victory Churchill was unrepentant. In *The Second World War* he states that 'General

---

* There is a gap in Rommel's *Papers* after his account of *Battleaxe*. His own narrative starts again in the spring of 1942. But the Chief of Staff of the Afrika Korps, General Bayerlein, has filled this gap with a personal review of Rommel's actions and attitudes during these crucial months, and from this and other sources a definite picture emerges.

Auchinleck's four and a half months' delay in engaging the enemy was alike a mistake and a misfortune'. The strategic facts alone justified Rommel's pre-occupation: but had he been faced by a Commander-in-Chief less obdurate in his resistance to Churchill's demands he might well have had to deal with an attempt to relieve Tobruk at a much earlier stage (and might well have defeated it).

Rommel's success in *Battleaxe* did not alter the priorities of the German High Command: Russia remained all-important. Guderian, indeed, at his headquarters on the Dnieper, noted on 13 July that 'on this same day the O.K.H. was also preoccupied with the strategy of Rommel's African campaign and future operations in Libya: these were to be co-ordinated with an attack on the Suez Canal, through Turkey and Syria. Preliminary studies for an operation through the Caucasus, towards the Persian Gulf, were also started.' But this was long-term thinking. And though General Roatta came over from Italy to tell Rommel that the Italians were in favour of reinforcing the African Army, and that they envisaged bringing the German element up to four mechanised divisions, while the Italian was to have an armoured corps of three divisions as well as two or three motorised divisions, 'their zeal', Rommel observed, 'did not last long'. However, he was promoted to Panzer-General, and wrote to his wife on 3 July, 'of course I've heard nothing official yet, but I understand it's been announced on the radio'.

His own ambitions were vast and precise. He calculated that with proper re-inforcements he could rebuff a British attack during the winter, reach the Canal in the spring, and then drive for Iraq with the objective of seizing Basra and severing the supply route to Russia. He recorded these thoughts in his *Papers*, and von Ravenstein has confirmed that they were in his mind. Rommel believed that if he could thrust eastwards beyond the Canal his supplies could be forwarded through Syria, and that his own advance, combined with successes in Russia, might persuade Turkey to join the Axis. In the winter of 1941–42 the general weakness of the Allies in the Mediterranean and the Middle East—in Iraq and Iran, on Cyprus, in Syria—was so great that a powerful German thrust along the African shore, accompanied by an attack on Malta, might have reached these objectives. Indeed, such a possibility was the permanent nightmare of the Chiefs of Staff and the Middle East Command. Like Wavell, Auchinleck was sensitive to the dangers and keenly aware of his responsibility: in October, for example, General de Guingand (at that time a colonel on the Joint Planning Staff), was sent at the head of an interservice team from G.H.Q. Cairo on a round of visits to the commands in Syria, Palestine, Iraq and Iran to co-ordinate plans for meeting a German penetration into these territories. Withdrawals, demolitions, a 'scorched earth' policy, enlistment of tribesmen for guerilla action on the German lines of communication were all being seriously considered.

But though Rommel's strategic assessment was matched by this British concern, his ideas were not welcomed: General Halder, for example, considered that he ignored the realities of the supply problem, and observed: 'Rommel cannot compete with the situation.' Nevertheless, the Germans' early successes in the Russian campaign had led their High Command to contemplate the possible subjection of the Middle East, and to agree that, at least, the conquest of Tobruk was an essential step towards the conquest of Egypt. O.K.W. was conscious of the growing strength of the British, and decided, in early October, that their opponents' strategy would be first to relieve Tobruk and then to switch their augmented forces to the Caucasus. (The Italians naturally assumed that the British objective would be the occupation of Libya. *Comando Supremo* warned Bastico on 20 October that an offensive was about to start, but he and Rommel disregarded the warning —convinced that their troops, in their present positions, could counter any British advance.)

As Hitler was still unwilling to try to capture Malta these strategic ideas of Rommel were certainly too large, and O.K.W. was right to be dubious, for interruption of the supply line across the Mediterranean and up into the desert was continuous and effective between the end of *Battleaxe* and the beginning of *Crusader*. Bayerlein records that in September the Panzer Group received only a third of the troops and a seventh of the supplies that were needed. A letter from Rommel to his wife on 29 September is significant because of its tone of relief: 'The last few days have been exciting. A large shipment arrived for us at Benghazi. It took 40 hours to unload. All went well. You can imagine how pleased I was. With things as they are in the Mediterranean it's not easy to get anything across. For the moment we're only stepchildren and must make the most of it.' Between July and November, in fact, 48 Axis ships were sunk: they carried 200,000 tons of supplies. By October the British had been able to gather together a surface striking force (the cruisers *Aurora* and *Penelope* and the destroyers *Lance* and *Lively*) which, called Force K, was based on Malta as a reinforcement for the submarines and aircraft still operating from the undefeated island. It is a measure of the insecurity of Rommel's supply line that on 9 November this small force was able to destroy completely the *Duisburg* convoy (seven merchantmen, a total of 40,000 tons), in spite of its cover of two 8-in. cruisers and several destroyers. Such was the prevailing pattern. Though Rommel insisted, in September, that he would be unable to attack without better protection in the air, and though instructions were given to *Fliegerkorps X* to concentrate on guarding the convoys to Derna and Benghazi, the British for the time being maintained their predominance in the Mediterranean. Rommel's demand for more air cover for the Tripoli convoys was refused because of the overriding requirements of the Russian front.

But he also needed more support in the air because the Western Desert Air Force was joining in the destruction of his supplies. Air Vice-Marshal Coningham had evolved a strong and flexible organisation for the support of 8 Army, and behind him Air Marshal Tedder was improving the system for repair and maintenance of aircraft and expediting the flow of reinforcements. The R.A.F., in fact, was now in good shape in the Middle East: it was working on a carefully planned scheme for attacking Rommel's lines of communication all the way from the docks where supplies were loaded and unloaded right up to the points where they were stock-piled behind his front line. Naples, Brindisi, Tripoli and Benghazi were regularly bombed, and the seaways were steadily attacked—in September six ships were sunk by aircraft on the North Africa run, and five more in October. As the date for *Crusader* approached, the intensity of operations over Rommel's land-line also increased. During the first week of November, for example, some 200 tons of bombs fell on Benghazi, and between 4 November and 13 November there was a daily average of nine aircraft over the depots at Derna.

The refusal of O.K.W. to make a major commitment in Africa, and these attacks by the Navy and the R.A.F., meant that in the autumn of 1941 Rommel failed to receive the substantial reinforcements on which his broad strategic plan had been based. He was limited both by policy and expediency to the single problem of the conquest of Tobruk. But this does not mean that his strategic ideas were inaccurate or excessive. The tendency of some military critics to place Rommel's military capabilities at no higher a level than that of a good commander of an armoured corps must be qualified by the fact that he was capable—during this summer and autumn, as at other times—of looking ahead and 'thinking big'.* T. E. Lawrence said of his own desert war, 'the chief agent had to be the general's head'. Rommel's intellectual grasp of the possibilities now open to the Axis in the Mediterranean and the Middle East was more profound than that of his superiors at O.K.H. and the circle surrounding Hitler.

The reinforcement of armour which reached him enabled him to strengthen the regiments in his command. The 5 Light Division was now renamed 21 Panzer, and a Special Service Africa Division (*Division Afrika zur besonderen*

* In one of his *Papers* written shortly before his death Rommel remarked that 'anyone who fights a whole world must think in continents'.

Verfügung, or *Div. z.b.V.*) was also formed from various independent units already in Africa and troops ferried over by air transport. But this (soon to be known as 90 Light Division) had no tanks: by November it was composed of seven infantry battalions and a strong artillery group. For the assault of Tobruk a siege train was built up under the command of General Böttcher— Artillery Command 104—and gradually enlarged until it included nine 210-mm. howitzers, 38 150-mm. and 12 105-mm. Rommel's concentration of this powerful force under one command was to pay dividends in *Crusader* and in the battle next summer at Gazala. He personally controlled its deployment from time to time, and it provided him with a mass of fire-power which the British would not begin to equal until the conflicts of July 1942 or to surpass until Alam Halfa and Alamein. Once again Rommel had initiated an important tactical development: it was simple in conception, but as Clausewitz wrote, 'everything is simple in war, but the simplest thing is difficult'. (It is sometimes argued that at this stage in the desert the British were unable to concentrate their artillery because the weakness of their anti-tank equipment caused them to dissipate their field artillery in anti-tank roles, and this indeed happened. But the truth is that, at this time, the idea of effective concentration and deployment *en masse* was neither understood nor implemented by the Desert Army.) Each of Rommel's armoured divisions contained a panzer regiment of two battalions, though by November one company of each battalion—i.e. 21 tanks—was still in Germany, and these did not reach Africa until the following spring. In addition there was a motorised infantry regiment, an artillery regiment and an anti-tank battalion, an armoured reconnaissance unit, a machine-gun battalion and the usual ancillaries.

During these autumn months Rommel's structure of command was also re-organised. O.K.H. despatched General Gause to act as a liaison officer with *Comando Supremo*, and gave him a large staff: but Rommel, characteristically, would have none of this. 'General Gause had received explicit instructions not to place himself under my command, but did in fact do so after I had told him categorically that the command of all troops in Africa was vested in me alone.' He was, of course, exceeding his authority; but, relying on Hitler's support, and backed by Cavallero, he demanded that the German and Italian forces in Africa should be unified in a *Panzergruppe* which he himself would command: he won. On 21 August he wrote to his wife: 'I'm very pleased about my new appointment. Everybody else in that position is a Colonel-General. If things go here as I should like them, I, too, will probably get that rank after the war's over.' Gause had to abandon his independent role and become Rommel's Chief of Staff in the new Panzer

Group, while Rommel got control of all troops east of 'the Bulge', except for Gambara's 20 Italian Corps. The command structure, therefore, displayed diagrammatically was now:

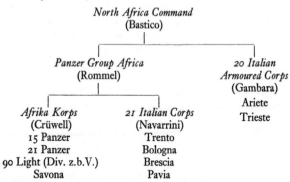

At the end of October there was another important alteration in the chain of command. Hitler decided that he must place German officers in more of the key positions on the Mediterranean front, and in spite of Italian objections insisted on the appointment of Field-Marshal Kesselring as Commander-in-Chief, South (*Oberbefehlshaber Süd*). Kesselring was ordered to get control of the air and the sea between Italy and Africa. He took over *Fliegerkorps X*, commanded from Greece by General Geisler, and the 5 Italian *Squadra* in Libya: but Hitler also proposed to transfer from Russia *Fliegerkorps II*—the Russian winter reducing activity in the air. Rommel was still to be directly responsible to Bastico; but the introduction of a German Field-Marshal into the Mediterranean command inevitably altered the balance of power. Kesselring's growing dismay, as he came to comprehend the incompetence and lethargy of the Italians, underlines the difficulties with which Rommel had to contend. The Field-Marshal criticised the Italian will to make war: the half-heartedness of their mobilisation: the state of training of their troops: their deficiencies of equipment and the unsatisfactory relations between officers and men. Their convoy system, he thought, was ineffective; loading and off-loading in their ports was dilatory and anti-aircraft protection was inadequate. And yet, as Kesselring wrote in his memoirs, 'Tripolitania stood or fell with its supplies.'

Nevertheless, as the autumn advanced, Rommel was in a better posture. His grip on the African Army had been confirmed, and though he had received no complete new divisions he was now commanding a compact and well-knit force. By November there was a hope that Kesselring might stiffen the organisation in his rear, and a promise that his protection in the air would eventually improve. His autumn arrangements might well come to fruition.

These were threefold. First, he had so disposed the Axis forces that they could be used flexibly to stop any British attack on his rear while he tackled Tobruk. Between Halfaya and Sidi Omar he deployed the Savona Division, strengthened by groups of German infantry and armour. Von Mellenthin says that he 'worked feverishly' at improving his positions on the frontier, and that a formidable mine barrier grew up between Sidi Omar and Sollum. Rommel used to be in his Armoured Command Vehicle by 5 a.m., studying situation reports, and then he would tour his front all day (often navigating himself), in spite of the summer heat which could reach a shade temperature of 110°. His lunch would be a few sandwiches and his evening meal would be equally meagre. 'During his visits to the front he saw everything. When a gun was inadequately camouflaged, when mines were laid in insufficient number, or when a standing patrol did not have enough ammunition, Rommel would see to it. Everywhere he convinced himself personally that his orders were being carried out. While very popular with young soldiers and N.C.O.s, with whom he cracked many a joke, he could become most outspoken and offensive to commanders of troops if he did not approve of their measures.' He also paid close attention to the investment of Tobruk, whose garrison was contained by infantry of 21 Corps, by a continual planting of minefields round the perimeter, and by air attack on the harbour and administrative quarters at the rate of some 500 sorties per month between July and October.

The Afrika Korps was moved to the coast between Tobruk and the eastern flank, and put through a rigorous course of training. This, the second of Rommel's arrangements, was of the utmost significance. The training was based on close co-operation between tanks and anti-tank guns in the assault— both the new 50-mm. and the 88s which had been so devastating in *Battleaxe*. Artillery and armour were drilled to work together. Two techniques— bringing anti-tank guns boldly forward into the front line of the armoured battle, and using an anti-tank gun line, carefully camouflaged, as a defensive surprise on to which the panzers might lure the British armour—were now being elaborated by the Germans. The tactical ideas of the Afrika Korps were in advance of those of the British, and would justify themselves during the next 12 months. Rommel's informed, persistent, professional attention to detail coupled with his fertility in tactical invention were now producing an army which could act in any situation with speed, flexibility and assurance: and it is these qualities which, because they have been possessed by only a limited number of commanders, make it possible to think of Rommel as similar in calibre to Marlborough and Wellington, if not as their equal in distinction or range of capacity.

From 1914 onwards Rommel always emphasised the co-ordinated and immediate use of all arms in both attack and defence: in 1941 the Germans, compared with the Desert Army, were distinguished by the smoothness of their battle drill. Sir Francis Tuker, who commanded 4 Indian Division during *Crusader*, made a relevant comment on an attack his division had to repel during the later stages of the battle: 'the swift preparation and laying-on of this attack by the Germans was the outcome of constant training, of the perfecting of a battle drill which is not learnt on the square . . . we were at a disadvantage, for we were preparing an attack and were disposing ourselves for it; but perhaps we were working in the old style of careful, detailed staging, instead of in the new style of automatic deployment followed by a concentrated stroke at speed at the point selected for outflanking or penetration.' This principle—'a concentrated stroke at speed'—was the one on which Rommel had acted throughout his military career, and his capacity as a trainer of men is demonstrated by the way he imbued the Afrika Korps with his doctrine. They acquired an ideology—attack, but wherever possible concentrate all available arms before attacking. The British would not elaborate and diffuse such a doctrine until the autumn of 1942.

On 14 September Rommel despatched 21 Panzer Division on an operation which, somewhat inappropriately, was called *Midsummer Night's Dream*. Its original objective was a suspected group of British dumps near to the frontier at Bir el Khireigat. The dumps, it was found, did not exist, but the raid was nevertheless mounted with the secondary objective of destroying any enemy forces in the area. Under the mid-September moon the panzers attacked with strong bomber and fighter support. But the operation was abortive. 7 Support Group, under Brigadier Jock Campbell, had orders not to get committed, and it successfully disengaged, while two squadrons of the South African Air Force caught the Germans refuelling. One result of this failure was that the number of 'runners' in the tank units of 21 Panzer fell from 110 on 11 September to 43 on 20 September, and it was not until 12 November that these casualties were replaced. But the consequences of the raid (which may have been intended as a practical exercise to conclude the panzer divisions' training) were far more important than a mere loss of tanks. It confirmed Rommel's view that the British were not yet ready to attack, and suggested that the region into which his armour had thrust was of no significance. But this was the very area where 8 Army was shortly to establish the enormous forward dumps on which *Crusader* was to be based. The final effect of

Rommel's misunderstanding will be seen when his famous 'dash to the wire' is discussed.

Lulled into a false sense of security, and increasingly obsessed by a desire to deal with Tobruk, on 26 October Rommel issued orders for an offensive: it was scheduled to take place between 15 November and 20 November. The third of his autumn preoccupations—planning the break-in—could now begin to bear fruit. His aim was to pierce Tobruk's defences on the eastern flank with the z.b.V. Division and 15 Panzer, holding the rest of the perimeter with the infantry of the Italian 21 Corps. To the south he placed 20 Corps, to baulk any attempt at an encirclement of his forces on the frontier, while 21 Panzer, south-east of Gambut, was held available for a counterattack. This concentration of his mind on Tobruk temporarily warped Rommel's judgement, for he became more and more unwilling to consider any evidence that a British offensive was imminent. Bastico argued for delay—he wanted the supply situation to improve and another Italian armoured division to arrive before Rommel committed himself; indeed he thought that the British were only waiting for Rommel to get involved at Tobruk before moving themselves. O.K.W. also expressed doubts, but Rommel was adamant. Von Ravenstein remembers how, when *Luftwaffe* photographs were produced of the British extension of their railway westwards from Matruh, Rommel threw them on the ground, saying, 'I will not look at them.' He also brushed aside intelligence reports from Admiral Canaris (Head of the *Abwehr*) and when he visited Rome early in November to discuss supplies he personally rang up Jodl at O.K.W. to complain, 'I hear that you wish me to give up the attack on Tobruk. I am completely disgusted.' Jodl succumbed, in the face of Rommel's guarantee that 21 Panzer could handle any British advance. But the most partial critic could not maintain that during these weeks before his intended attack Rommel was functioning with a clear mind.

There is, indeed, another possible interpretation. In *Panzer Battles* General von Mellenthin (who at this time was serving as a Colonel on the staff of Rommel's *Panzergruppe*) states that Rommel's dismissal of the possibility of a British offensive was a calculated device to allay Italian fears—what the *Secunda Offensiva Britannica* volume in the Italian official history describes as 'an excessive Latin nervousness'. Von Mellenthin says that Rommel ordered his staff to assume an air of confidence when talking to the Italians—and Cavallero, in his memoirs, records that when he asked Rommel during his November visit to Rome whether the enemy might make a large-scale enveloping attack Rommel replied that he only foresaw an action by small forces. Von Mellenthin argues that Rommel was aware (from the reports, for example, of his Wireless Interception Service) that the British were on the verge of an attack, but did not wish his own plans for an assault on Tobruk to be delayed by an Italian demand that the Panzer Group should be deployed for a defensive battle. The available evidence suggests that this is too subtle an interpretation; Rommel's reactions during the first phase of *Crusader* were not those of a man alert in the conviction that an Allied offensive was imminent.

He was, in fact, now confused by the error of 'making a picture' of his enemy, and was incapable of being objective. His wife and Countess Ravenstein joined the two generals in Rome, and it was during this visit that the interpreter Dollman, who acted as an *entrepreneur* in Italy between Italian and German diplomats and military V.I.P.s, observed that: 'I soon clashed with Field-Marshal Rommel, who took an immediate dislike to me and whose attitude to the Italians encouraged me to believe—erroneously, as history has since demonstrated—that he was an out-and-out Nazi.' Rommel's obsession with the attack he was planning is illustrated by a story told by Desmond Young in his biography. After the wives had spent a morning in St. Peter's, Rommel listened to their lunch-time account of their expedition in silence and then turned to von Ravenstein and said, 'You know, I have been thinking again about what we ought to do with those two infantry battalions.' This is not surprising because, like many others in his profession, Rommel never developed an aesthetic sense. Blumentritt in 1944 observed, 'no landscape, no historic building interested him; he was just a soldier'. (He also saw in Rome the Italian film, *On From Benghazi*, which managed to depict his triumph in the spring without including a single German. 'Very instructive,' Rommel commented, with his nice sense of irony, 'I often wondered what happened in that battle.')

The battle which Rommel would soon be fighting had been planned more carefully and prepared more elaborately by the British than any previous engagement in the desert war. Wavell's defeat of the Italians, crowned by O'Connor's victory at Beda Fomm, had been achieved by brilliant improvisation following a bold attack with undefined objectives. In *Crusader* the British objectives were definite: the intention was to destroy Rommel's armour and to relieve Tobruk.

Like the Axis, the British took advantage of the summer pause to reorganise and enlarge the structure of their command. Auchinleck, having noted the performance of General Sir Alan Cunningham in his defeat of the Italians on the East African front, demanded and obtained him as the C.-in-C. of what, after 26 September, was to be known as 'Eighth Army'—because, he said, 'I was impressed by his rapid and vigorous command in Abyssinia and his obvious leaning towards swift mobile action. I wanted to get away from the idea, which seemed to be prevalent, of clinging to the coastal strip, and to move freely and widely against the enemy's flank and communications.' Cunningham established his H.Q. in the desert on 9 September, knowing that two corps were forming to constitute his Army and that he had been charged by Auchinleck to examine two possible schemes for the defeat of Rommel. 30 Corps was envisaged as an armoured counterpart of the Afrika Korps, and would comprise 7 Armoured Division, 1 South African Division and 22 Guards' Brigade. 13 Corps would consist of infantry (the New Zealand Division, and 4 Indian, supported by Matilda and Valentine 'I' tanks). The light 4 Armoured Brigade with its new Stuart tanks from the U.S.A. would also be available. Reinforcements were now flowing steadily to equip these formations. (By the end of October, the *Official History* records, 300 British cruisers, 300 Stuarts, 170 'I' tanks, 34,000 lorries, 600 field guns, 80 heavy and 160 light A.A. guns, 200 anti-tank guns and 900 mortars had arrived.)

For 30 Corps the commander was intended to be Vivian Pope, a brilliant tank expert, latterly Director of Armoured Fighting Vehicles at the War Office; but on 5 October he and his two senior staff officers were killed in an air crash. One of the many imponderables about *Crusader* is whether Pope would have provided that constructive leadership of the British armour which, in the event, was noticeably lacking. Pope was replaced by Willoughby Norrie, commander of 1 Armoured Division, which was at present in convoy from Britain. General Godwin-Austen was to command 13 Corps. Had he been able to appreciate these appointments Rommel would have been encouraged; for whereas his own leaders—men like Bayerlein, Crüwell, von Ravenstein—were now acclimatised to the special requirements of the desert campaign, Cunningham's victories had been gained over ground of an entirely different character, which had given him no experience of handling large formations—especially of armour. Godwin-Austen had been serving with Cunningham, in command of 12 African Division, while Norrie was fresh from home. This confrontation of relative novices by relative veterans would be an important factor in the fighting which was to follow: it was certainly a considerable asset for Rommel.

After examining the alternatives offered to him Cunningham rejected the plan for an advance on his southern flank, via Jarabub and Jalo, aimed at severing Rommel's supply line in the Benghazi area. He was wise. The going was uncertain; to support the advance would have presented a formidable administrative problem, and his columns would have been moving far away from the substantial forces he would still have had to maintain in the north, to mask the Italians and Germans on the frontier. In any case, there was no guarantee that Rommel would not react by counter-attacking towards Alexandria. The second plan was for a drive westwards down the coast, accompanied by feints further south. This Cunningham also rejected, substituting a scheme for an advance by 30 Corps across the frontier between Maddalena and Sidi Omar to a position some 30 miles to the west at Gabr Saleh. Here the British armour was to wait for Rommel to show his hand, while on its right 13 Corps would outflank and contain the enemy's frontier posts. Between the two Corps 4 Armoured Brigade would move as a flank guard for 13 and a reinforcement for 30. A small diversionary force would work towards Jalo and the west.

The essence of this third plan, which was accepted as the basis for *Crusader*, was that 30 Corps would cause an armoured battle to happen in which the Afrika Korps would be destroyed, and *only* then was an attempt to relieve Tobruk to be synchronised with a break-out by the garrison. The moment of synchronisation was to be selected by Norrie who, it was presumed, would be in the best position to judge when his armour had dominated the battlefield. This plan was probably better than either of those rejected by Cunningham, but it was subsequently compromised by two mistakes. The intention to halt at Gabr Saleh, after the initial sweep forward, handed the initiative over to Rommel before the battle had even started; and the original idea, to force the Germans into a decisive action with a concentrated 30 Corps, was rapidly dissipated. Still, this was the plan approved for an encounter which 8 Army approached with a high heart and a confidence stimulated by the sight of their massive reinforcements.

The apparent strength of this mass, however, was greater than the reality. Auchinleck and Cunningham had many difficulties to overcome in mounting their offensive, and not all were resolved in time. A long debate between London and the Australian Government about the replacement of 9 Australian Division in Tobruk, for example, ended with an uncompromising demand from the Australian Prime Minister that the relief should take place, whatever the effect on the coming offensive might be. The Chiefs of Staff ordered this to happen on 15 September; its execution diverted a considerable air and naval effort from the main task of preparing *Crusader*. Again, 1 South African Division, placed in 30 Corps because its infantry battalions were lorried, had not been severely tested in Abyssinia and had since been employed in preparing defences at Mersa Matruh. It therefore needed careful training for its mobile role: but delays in the arrival of its transport hampered this so much that by 15 November, the proposed date for *Crusader*, its commander, General Brink, refused to move. Auchinleck was compelled to postpone the offensive until 18 November. His attention was also distracted by the need to satisfy the New Zealand Government (who were pressing the Cabinet on this point) that there would be a sufficient air support for the offensive. All these matters illustrate one of Rommel's great advantages. While he had to handle his own allies, the Italians, with some show of formal consideration, he could usually be ruthless in disregarding their point of view: but the British C.-in-C. Middle East could never treat his Commonwealth divisions so casually. Each of their commanders had direct access to his own Government, and Churchill was more anxious to conciliate the Commonwealth than Hitler was to appease Mussolini.

There were also technical problems. The supply of water in the forward areas was paramount, but though 160 miles of pipe were laid, and seven pumping stations and nine reservoirs built, an air attack on Fuka on 11 October caused the loss of almost all the water which had been accumulated in the west: vigorous action only just restored the situation by mid-November. And 22 Armoured Brigade (which was to be part of 7 Armoured Division) was late in arriving and did not disembark until 14 October, when it was discovered that its cruiser tanks were mechanically unsound. The need for their repair left this inexperienced territorial Brigade with only a month to become 'desert-worthy' before D-Day. It was for these and similar reasons that, in spite of his reinforcements, Auchinleck felt 'we were working to very close margins as regards equipment and training'. But his doubts were hidden from his troops, and their morale was unimpaired.

Not surprisingly, since the preparations for his offensive were unprecedented. The dumping of supplies in the forward areas was so thorough that at one time, according to the *Official History*, the transport involved was consuming 180,000 gallons of petrol a day. Careful security, wireless discipline, and the current superiority of the Desert Air Force concealed from the Germans the detailed intelligence which could have warned them of an imminent offensive, and when Rommel returned from Rome on 18 November he was still bemused by his *Midsummer Night's Dream*. He reckoned, in his headquarters at Gambut, that 7 Armoured Division, the New Zealanders and the South Africans (as well as 50 Division, which was actually in Cyprus) were all stationed far to the east around Mersa Matruh.

On the previous night, while Rommel was still in Athens on his return journey, a commando group under Colonel Keyes was put ashore by submarine near Apollonia to attack the house where, it was thought, Rommel was living. This was an application of the wasp's technique: a sting at the nerve-centre of the enemy. But though Rommel had once occupied the house which the commandos assaulted, it was now only used by his Quartermaster's staff. Colonel Keyes was killed in this mis-judged attack and was awarded a posthumous V.C.: but his gallantry, unfortunately, had no effect on *Crusader*.

In the early hours of 18 November, therefore, as 30 Corps, unseen and unsuspected, surged westwards beyond the frontier and 13 Corps moved into positions south of the Savona Division, the situation was that Rommel, commanding a competent army without reserves, still looked towards Tobruk: while Cunningham (to implement a plan which was inherently weak) was moving towards him with an exhilarated but largely untrained force, with senior officers lacking experience of the desert, but with an abundance of equipment and a good stock of reserves. These, as the battle developed, would stand 8 Army in good stead.

Crusader was primarily a clash of armour. The total number of tanks in the opposing armies, and their distribution between divisions and brigades, are calculated differently by different authorities. Bayerlein, in his contribution to the *Rommel Papers*, says that the Panzer Group included 260 German and 154 Italian tanks: of the Germans he counted 15 Panzer I, 40 Panzer II, 150 Panzer III and 55 Panzer IV. The *Official History*, based on a wider review of the relevant information, gives Rommel a total of 390 tanks, broken down as follows: 70 Panzer II, 130 Panzer III, 35 Panzer IV, and 146 Italian M 13/40 in the Ariete Division. 8 Army disposed in 30 Corps of 94 of the earlier marks of cruiser, 210 Crusaders, and 173 Stuarts—a total of 477, which does not include those in 13 Corps' Army Tank Brigades: 135 in the 1st and 126 in the 2nd (of which most were Matildas or Valentines). But behind Rommel's front line lay little in the way of armoured reserves: behind Cunningham, in the workshops and the depots, were over 250 tanks of various types, while convoy W.S. 12, already on its way, was transporting to him 124 Crusaders, 60 Stuarts, and 52 'I' tanks. (But Rommel had one superiority. At this stage in the desert war the Germans were far ahead of the British in the technique of tank recovery. The British had a theoretical knowledge of how the job should be done. The Germans had some suitable vehicles.) In the air the British started with 550 planes in action out of a total of some 650, and Rommel with 342 out of a total of 536. The British also had 66 serviceable planes in Malta—but the Germans, if circumstances allowed, might be able to draw on 750 aircraft of all types which at present were scattered around the Mediterranean in Greece, Crete, Sicily and other bases.

Such were the strengths and weaknesses of the plans and armies which, under rain and thunder and lightning, were now moving into conflict on the morning of 18 November, 1941, and were to produce armoured battles unsurpassed in violence during the whole of the African campaign.

V

Crusader: The Winter Battle

1941

Auchinleck and Cunningham achieved their first objective—complete surprise. Violent rainstorms had turned the German airstrips into seas of muddy water, and the grounded Luftwaffe was helpless. Reconnaissance Unit 33 reported to Rommel that there was activity in the area of the Trigh el Abd, but by the morning of 18 November the first forward move of 8 Army, carried out under wireless silence, was completed without causing alarm. 30 Corps was now west of the wire, and 13 Corps had worked its way to the south of the Savona Division. By 0900 the tanks of 30 Corps were refuelling at the dumps which had been secretly established beyond the frontier.

Rommel's first reaction to the signals from his armoured cars was that this was no more than a reconnaissance in force. His staff was mainly concerned with planning the attack on Tobruk, and when Crüwell (who throughout *Crusader* appreciated the changing situation with more realism than Rommel) visited *Panzergruppe* H.Q. in the evening to say that von Ravenstein was unhappy about the day's developments and wanted to move an armoured group towards Gabr Saleh, Rommel told him that 'we must not lose our nerve', and refused to confirm von Ravenstein's orders. During *Crusader* many errors of judgement occurred; Rommel had already made two. He had not appreciated correctly the evidence of a British offensive, and therefore failed to make the immediate concentration of his armour which (as Cunningham developed his attack) might have had a decisive effect in the early stages of the battle. The Savona Division had obtained from a prisoner a detailed picture of Cunningham's plans, but Rommel rejected this as unreliable, and during 18 November his attention was still devoted to Tobruk.

On the 19th it was Cunningham's turn to err. He succumbed to the temptation which so often seduced British commanders in the desert. Puzzled by Rommel's failure to respond to his appearance at Gabr Saleh, he disregarded his main objective—the defeat of the German armour by a solid 30 Corps—and started to fragment his force. 'Mercifully for us,' as von Mellenthin puts it, 'he sent 22 Armoured Brigade off to Bir el Gubi to attack Ariete Division.' (Von Mellenthin, writing as an eye-witness at Rommel's H.Q., provides in his *Panzer Battles* a particularly valuable account of *Crusader* from the German point of view.) The raw troops attacked with *élan*, but with the support of only one field battery, and the head-on assault of the yeomanry regiments was decisively repelled by the Italians. Meanwhile 7 Armoured Brigade was pushed up to Sidi Rezegh, and 4 Armoured remained at Gabr Saleh to keep contact with the left flank of 30 Corps.

Rommel was now slowly beginning to face the facts. At midday Crüwell contacted him, and by 1230 von Ravenstein's idea of sending a strong battle-group southwards to Gabr Saleh was accepted. A force of some 120 tanks, with artillery support, was assembled, under the able Colonel Stephan, and at 1430 Rommel arrived to watch its advance. By dusk it had mauled two regiments of 4 Armoured Brigade. This was something—but it was essentially a deviation from what Rommel should have been attempting: by now he should have been drawing his panzer divisions together.

However, although his own mind was still not entirely engaged his doctrines were at work among his subordinates. During the evening of the 19th von Ravenstein rang Crüwell to propose that 15 and 21 Panzer should be united. Crüwell's Chief of Staff, Bayerlein, spoke to *Panzergruppe*, and Rommel replied by giving Crüwell a free hand with a directive to 'destroy the enemy battle groups in the Bardia-Tobruk-Sidi Omar area before they can offer any serious threat to Tobruk'. Cunningham, on the other hand, was continuing his dispersion. He ordered 7 Support Group to join 7 Armoured Brigade at Sidi Rezegh, and moved 1 South African Division towards Bir el Gubi, north of which 22 Armoured Brigade was operating, while he continued to hold 4 Armoured back at Gabr Saleh.

But next day the united Afrika Korps was employed in the pursuit of a ghost. During the 19th the King's Dragoon Guards had chased Reconnaissance Unit 3 over the Trigh Capuzzo towards Sidi Azeiz, and 3 Royal Tanks had been sent to their support. Crüwell identified this as a large-scale manoeuvre, and on the 20th he ordered the Afrika Korps to deal with it. But the British had vanished, and 21 Panzer was soon stranded near Sidi Omar, out of petrol. 'Frantic appeals', says von Mellenthin, 'arrived at *Panzergruppe* Headquarters, asking for petrol to be flown in by air.' While this was going on the British had been strengthening their hold on Sidi Rezegh, and as the German armour was apparently committed elsewhere it seemed to General Gott, who commanded 7 Armoured Division, that the time had come to order the Tobruk garrison to start their break-out. After some hesitation Cunningham ordered that this should begin on the morning of the 21st.

Here was a further departure from the original British plan. The German armour had not yet been brought to battle and destroyed: now the Tobruk garrison was being ordered to move before this destruction had been achieved. But *Crusader* was a tangle of errors. Von Mellenthin observes that 'there is no doubt that we missed a great opportunity on 20 November. Cunningham had been obliging enough to scatter 7 Armoured Division all over the desert, and we had failed to exploit his generosity.'

There had in fact been confusion on both sides. During the night of 19-20 November Cunningham was embarrassed by a breakdown on 8 Army's wireless net, and he left Norrie's H.Q. at 30 Corps to return to his army command post at Maddalena: but the only information his staff could give him was that the R.A.F. had seen German transport moving in a westerly direction. There were still no signs of Rommel's anticipated reaction with his armour—Crüwell, of course, was now away on his wild-goose chase. The confusion, however, was soon ended, for Crüwell, realising his mistake, stopped his vain pursuit and began to swing the Afrika Korps back to the west. The result was that in the late afternoon 15 Panzer met and savaged 4 Armoured Brigade. 22 Armoured had been ordered to move to its support, but it had been disorganised by its attack on Ariete and failed to arrive until dusk, when Neumann-Silkow, 15 Panzer's commander, broke off the action. The Germans leaguered on the battlefield.

Nevertheless Cunningham was not dismayed. Misled by optimistic reports about the destruction of German tanks, he thought that the conflict between 4 Armoured Brigade and 15 Panzer represented the decisive action envisaged in his original plan. And 4 and 22 Brigades were now re-united. The code word authorising a break-out had been sent to Tobruk's commander, General Scobie, and Gott had ordered Brigadier Campbell, with 7 Support Group, to assist Scobie's attempt by securing the Sidi Rezegh ridge early on the 21st. 5 South African Brigade was directed to Sidi Rezegh in support. It was on its way by 5 p.m., but it halted during the night because the divisional commander considered that his men were not sufficiently trained to make a night march.

Before the end of the day, however, Rommel had at last appreciated that the British were in earnest. Crüwell visited him during the evening, and was told that next morning the Afrika Korps must 'attack and destroy the enemy force which has advanced on Tobruk'. It is possible (but not certain) that Rommel's appreciation was aided by the B.B.C.'s 9 p.m. news bulletin, which announced that 'Eighth Army with about 75,000 men excellently armed and equipped had started a general offensive in the Western Desert with the aim of destroying the German-Italian forces in Africa'. Whatever the reason, Rommel's energies were now released. At 0400 on the 21st he sent a message to Crüwell emphasising that 'the situation in this whole theatre is very critical' and pressing the Afrika Korps to 'get going in good time'.

Cunningham and Rommel had set the scene for a clash of armour which, starting at Sidi Rezegh on 21 November, was to continue for three days and, in the words of the *Official History*, was 'the fiercest yet seen in the desert'. If awards for gallantry are an index of the intensity of an action, it may be noted that during these days no less than four Victoria Crosses were won. But neither side had a monopoly of valour. Sidi Rezegh was a true 'soldier's battle', in which the tank crews and infantry of the Afrika Korps displayed as much courage and endurance as their opponents of 8 Army.

The airfield at Sidi Rezegh had been occupied by Brigadier Davy's 7 Armoured Brigade on the afternoon of the 19th. At 1630 his tanks rushed it while planes were still taking off. The airfield lay in a slight depression, overlooked by higher ground to the south and the Sidi Rezegh escarpment to the north. Early on the 20th Sümmermann's Afrika Division, trying to extend their hold on this escarpment and at Belhamed, had attacked at dawn and again at 0800. Their attacks had been successfully repulsed, and during the day British optimism increased. It was in this spirit that Campbell was ordered by Gott to seize the northern ridge in the early hours of the 21st—to conform with the sortie from Tobruk: for Scobie's aim was to reach El Duda, some four miles to the north-west of Campbell's objective. Here there was a pincer-movement of which Rommel would have approved, and when it began the drive from the north made progress. Units of the Royal Tanks lost half their equipment, and 2 Black Watch, in an attack on the strong-point called *Tiger*, lost three-quarters of their men, but a sally-port from Tobruk was opening—some 4000 yards broad and deep. The southern half of the pincer, however, failed to close. At 0830 on the 21st Campbell advanced with 6 Royal Tanks and a reinforced battalion of the K.R.R.C.: they took some 800 prisoners and captured a few more miles of the open escarpment, but their success was soon cancelled, for 6 Royal Tanks, pushing north to El Duda, were almost eliminated. At the same time a new threat had appeared in the south-east, so Davy, leaving the remnants of 6 Royal Tanks with Campbell, moved the two other regiments in his Brigade to meet it. By 1000 most of one of them, 7 Hussars, were in flames. Their colonel was dead, their ammunition nearly exhausted, and their remaining 12 tanks had been hit or damaged during the action.

Rommel and Crüwell had operated independently to produce this new situation at Sidi Rezegh. For Crüwell the first problem had been to disengage from the British armour at Gabr Saleh. The battle drill of the Afrika Korps worked successfully, and a screen of anti-tank guns and 88s prevented the British from interfering, so that Crüwell's main body was able to speed towards the airfield and create the threat which Davy proved unable to counter. The destruction of 7 Hussars was crucial. It was followed, during the morning, by severe losses to 2 Rifle Brigade and a steady attrition of Davy's third Regiment, 2 Royal Tanks. In the maelstrom on the airfield the Germans were only just held back: 4 and 22 Armoured Brigades failed to relieve the strain, but in spite of their losses the British still held their ground. 'The inspiring example set by Brigadier Campbell', Auchinleck wrote in his despatch, 'who led several tank charges in person greatly contributed to this result.' But the Victoria Cross which Campbell won at Sidi Rezegh would not have been gained if Rommel's training of the Afrika Korps had not been so efficient that to defeat them called for such inspiration.

Rommel had nothing to do with this affair. He had sensed the danger of a sally from Tobruk, and when 70 Division and its supporting tanks began the break-out at dawn on the 21st he characteristically took personal command of Reconnaissance Unit 3 and a number of 88s, hurried them to the salient which the Tobruk garrison was creating, and sealed it off—though Scobie's troops took 550 German and 527 Italian prisoners. (It seems possible that it was the 88s led into action by Rommel which also shot 6 Royal Tanks to pieces.)

'The situation', says the *Official History*, 'was now so extraordinary that a brief summary will not be out of place. Over the 20 or so miles of country from the front of the Tobruk sortie to the open desert south-east of Sidi Rezegh airfield the forces of both sides were sandwiched like the layers of a Neapolitan ice. In turn, starting from the north, there were (a) the troops of the 70th Division who had broken out, opposed by (b) German and Italian troops facing north and west; (c) a layer of Axis troops facing south, opposing (d) part of the 7 Support Group north of the Sidi Rezegh airfield; the rest of 7 Support Group and 7 Armoured Brigade facing south to oppose (e) the bulk of D.A.K. heading north, pursued by (f) the 4 and 22 Armoured Brigades. To complete the picture there were troops of the 361 *Afrika* Regiment on Point 175 to the east of Sidi Rezegh airfield, and the whole of the 155 Regiment to the west. A complicated situation indeed, which, if suggested for the setting of a training exercise, must have been rejected for the reason that in real life these things simply could not happen.'

By the evening of the 21st the German command was uneasy. Crüwell wanted to disengage his armour and pull back to Gambut: Neumann-Silkow wanted to attack again. At 2130 Rommel (still ignorant of the true situation at Sidi Rezegh) sent orders to Crüwell to prevent a link-up between Scobie's troops and 30 Corps. Crüwell compromised by moving 21 Panzer to Belhamed, and drawing 15 Panzer back to regroup south of Gambut (without informing Rommel). He thus separated his two divisions by an 18-mile gap, and must be considered to have made a major error of judgement.

The British, on the other hand, were scenting victory. Crüwell's westward move towards Sidi Rezegh had been interpreted as a retreat, and Norrie's recommendation to Cunningham that 13 Corps should be ordered to advance from the frontier had been accepted. The New Zealand Division was soon on the move; reports of its advance so disturbed Rommel's *Panzergruppe* H.Q. at Gambut that it was transferred to El Adem during the night.

Neither Cunningham nor Auchinleck had accurately appreciated the day's events. If Rommel during 21 November spent too much time in the front line he had at least been able to organise a decisive success at a decisive point, and he was getting the 'feel' of the battle. Cunningham at Maddalena was thwarted by the weak wireless net of 8 Army: he was short of up-to-date information, and remote from the arena. (It is also worth noting that 8 Army had not yet evolved the system of liaison officers which, developed by Montgomery, was to prove so valuable in Africa and N.W. Europe.) The consequence was an unjustified mood of elation at the headquarters of 8 Army and in Cairo, shared by Churchill in London.

Prime Minister to General Auchinleck   *22 November 1941*
Thank you for the very full information now flowing. I might perhaps broadcast Sunday night if it seems expedient, so please let me have anything that comes to hand. What I will say will be on most general lines like my statement in the House of Commons. I am most anxious however to make any success tell fully over the world. . . .

But no such message of success could yet be sent to Churchill, for even while his signal was being transmitted on the 22nd 8 Army was facing fresh disasters—and for these Rommel was directly responsible.

On 22 November the British situation at Sidi Rezegh seemed to be strong. At 1030 5 South African Brigade was moving north, and promised a valuable reinforcement of infantry: 7 Armoured Division was now more closely concentrated and the New Zealand Division was forcing its way to the west. But once again Rommel and Crüwell, by independent and perhaps instinctive action, contrived a victory—working together in sympathy like Marlborough and Prince Eugene at Blenheim. During the afternoon of the 22nd Crüwell attacked the eastern flank of 7 Armoured Division with 15 Panzer. Meanwhile Rommel devised the kind of improvisation which will always justify him when his critics condemn his practice of commanding from the front of the battle. At midday he conferred with von Ravenstein, and ordered him to attack southwards with the infantry and most of the artillery of 21 Panzer into the area of the Sidi Rezegh escarpment while Panzer Regiment 5, with 88s in support, made a wide turning movement to the north. The tanks were to slip past Belhamed, use the by-pass road to El Duda, keep away from the Sidi Rezegh escarpment and force their way into the airfield from the west. Rommel's grouping of his heavy artillery under Böttcher for the siege of Tobruk was also used, by another improvisation, to support 21 Panzer's manœuvre. Its gun positions were in the centre of the arc which von Ravenstein's turning movement was about to define, and Böttcher was thus well placed to support with heavy concentrations of fire the whole of von Ravenstein's deployment.

This was successful. As 22 Armoured Brigade advanced on to the airfield the tanks of 21 Panzer burst in from the west, taking by surprise the remnants of Davy's 7 Armoured Brigade and 7 Support Group. The shroud of dust and smoke was so thick that Gatehouse, watching from the east with 4 Armoured Brigade, was unwilling to commit his tanks to a blindfold battle. A troop of 3 Royal Tanks was pushed into the fog to investigate, and 'Jock Campbell, who had been an inspiring figure to all, driving about the airfield in his open truck and shouting himself hoarse', led the troop, according to Auchinleck's despatch, 'straight across the the western flank before they could discover what was happening'. The confusion was so great that Gott ordered 7 Armoured Division to fall back southwards on to the South Africans, and the Afrika Korps was left in control of the airfield.

8 Army then suffered another misfortune. At dusk 15 Panzer, moving to the support of 21, crashed into the H.Q. of 4 Armoured Brigade and 8 Hussars. At about 1900 hours 8 Panzer Regiment surrounded their leaguer, switched on head-lights and began to round up prisoners. 'It was,' says von Mellenthin, 'a crushing blow to the best armoured formation in 7 Armoured Division': the Germans claimed 267 prisoners and some 50 tanks. Their brigade commander, Gatehouse, escaped capture, because he was on his way back from a conference with Gott, but for the time being 4 Armoured Brigade had been neutralised. It still had about 100 tanks, but its nerve-centre was dead.

In the early hours of the 23rd Rommel signalled to Rome to point out that

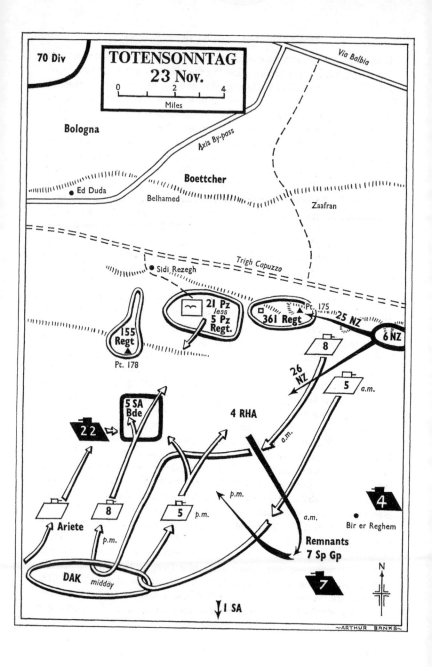

all the Axis forces should now be brought under a single commander. Mussolini agreed to his request, and Gambara's 20 Corps was transferred to the *Panzergruppe*, though Rommel was still left subordinate to Bastico. The 23rd was a symbolic day for his army. It was *Totensonntag*, the Day of the Dead when the Germans solemnly remembered their losses in the First World War. Another Day of the Dead was now dawning.

Rommel's battle-plan was one of his favourite manoeuvres. He ordered Crüwell to attack the rear of 30 Corps at 0700 and the Ariete Division to advance towards Crüwell at 0800, thus catching Norrie's troops in a vice. These orders, however, did not reach Crüwell until the afternoon. Rommel's movements during the 23rd are in fact obscure, and his commanders had once again to act on their own initiative. According to von Mellenthin he left *Panzergruppe* H.Q. early in the morning to visit Afrika Korps, but was delayed by, and then involved in, the westward advance of 6 New Zealand Brigade.

The New Zealanders were trying to work their way to the aid of 30 Corps by moving forward to the south of, but parallel with, the Trigh Capuzzo. They had good luck at dawn, for they surprised the Afrika Korps H.Q., missing Crüwell but capturing most of his staff, documents and headquarters equipment. During the day first one and then a second battalion of the brigade was drawn into an attack on Point 175, and before nightfall 450 casualties had been inflicted—the highest rate of loss in the New Zealand Division so far, whether in Greece, Crete or the desert. The third battalion, 26, managed to push south and by midday was in sight of 5 South African Brigade. Rommel may or may not have been trapped by these operations, but he certainly did not reach his headquarters again until the evening of the 23rd, and by this time much else had happened—in particular to the South Africans.

This was because Crüwell had made his own battle-plan and acted on it. Leaving 21 Panzer's infantry to sit on the high ground south of Sidi Rezegh, he ordered 5 Panzer Regiment to join 15 Panzer Division in a curving manœuvre to the south-west which would link them with the tanks of Ariete. The Germans and Italians were then to turn together to the north, and in a simultaneous attack press 30 Corps on to the guns and infantry of 21 Panzer waiting for them at Sidi Rezegh. During the early morning of the 23rd there was a heavy mist over the desert, but as it lifted Crüwell's columns found themselves among the soft transport of 7 Armoured Division and the South Africans. In the chaos that followed it was once again Brigadier Campbell, with his Support Group, who tried to establish order and stop the Germans. This was the famous occasion when Campbell, sitting exposed on the top of his command vehicle and rallying his men with 'Stop' and 'Go' flags made from his own scarves, shouted to an artillery troop: 'Expect no orders. Stick to me. I shall advance soon!'

Neumann-Silkow wished to exploit this success with 15 Panzer and to pursue the stampeding transport, but Crüwell insisted on joining Ariete. The south-westerly movement therefore continued, and the Italians were contacted. Crüwell then formed up his armour and motorised infantry as if on a parade-ground, and drove north-east, straight at 5 South African Brigade. Such a cavalry charge was what von Mellenthin coolly describes as 'an innovation in German tactics'. It was certainly costly, for most of the officers and N.C.O.s in the lorried infantry units were killed: but it was successful. By nightfall the South Africans were finished. Heavy casualties, 3394, meant that they could no longer function as a Brigade, and though Crüwell had lost some 60–70 tanks as well as his infantry leaders, and had narrowly avoided capture himself, he was master of the battlefield.

And Rommel was now nearly master of 8 Army, for on 23 November Cunningham lost his nerve. He had been under an enormous strain—conducting a vital offensive in conditions and with a staff and army to which he was a stranger. He was also a heavy smoker, and before *Crusader* started he had been advised, because of an eye infection, to stop his smoking: which, it has been suggested, added to the strain. But this is irrelevant: no psychological subtleties are needed to explain his feelings on the 23rd. He had at last realised how the rate at which he was losing tanks might affect the defence of Egypt, and he was oppressed by the thought that the Afrika Korps might outflank and overrun his naked infantry divisions. In this mood of doubt and uncertainty he quite properly asked Auchinleck to join him in conference, and the Commander-in-Chief, with Air Marshal Tedder, arrived at 8 Army's H.Q. that evening. 'I was in no doubt myself at any time as to the right course', Auchinleck wrote in his despatch, 'and at once instructed General Cunningham to continue his offensive.'

Rommel's mood was now the exact opposite of Cunningham's. He returned to *Panzergruppe* H.Q. at El Adem 'in a state', says von Mellenthin, 'of excited exultation'. This cannot have been due to a realistic appraisal of his situation, for whether or not he had (as seems probable) been occupied during the day in helping to repel the New Zealanders at Point 175, he was certainly ill-informed about what had happened south of Sidi Rezegh. There, Bayerlein recalls, 'twilight came, but the battle was still not over. Hundreds of burning vehicles, tanks and guns lit up the field of that *Totensonntag*. It was long after midnight before we could get any sort of picture of the day's events, organise our force, count our losses and gains and form an appreciation of the general situation.' Nor had Rommel had any contact with Crüwell, who spent hours during the darkness searching for Neumann–Silkow and von Ravenstein. Yet at midnight he sent a signal to Berlin: 'Intention for 24 November (a) to complete destruction of 7 Armoured Division (b) to advance with elements of forces towards Sidi Omar with a view to attacking enemy on Sollum front.' Item (b) was the prelude to the most controversial act in the whole of his military career.

The orders to execute it were given by Rommel to Neumann–Silkow at 0400 in 15 Panzer's headquarters and at 0600 to Crüwell, who at last caught up with his commander on the Tobruk by-pass. First, the coast road eastwards from Tobruk would be kept open by the lightly equipped Reconnaissance Unit 3 (though Rommel's staff warned him of an increasing threat from the advancing New Zealand Division). Second, Rommel would place himself at the head of the Afrika Korps, with Ariete (now under his direct authority) moving on his right flank, and in a wide sweep to the south and east would encircle 13 Corps and relieve his forces on the frontier. He told Westphal, who was to remain at El Adem, that he hoped to be back 'by the evening of the 24th or next morning'. He had set his hopes, as the South African *Official History* puts it, 'on a spectacular *coup* which would finish the campaign with a single stroke'. According to von Mellenthin he was not interested in 8 Army's supply dumps: his aim was to annihilate his enemy, by cutting off the retreat of 30 Corps and driving 13 Corps back on to the minefields at Sollum. Indeed he said to von Ravenstein as he gave him his orders: 'You have the chance of ending this campaign tonight.'

It took time to reorganise the panzer divisions after their experience of the last three days, and Rommel was so impatient to start his 'dash to the wire' that he set off about 1030 at the head of 5 Panzer Regiment, leaving the rest to follow. He pulled his Chief of Staff, General Gause, into his car and departed at so furious a pace that his wireless truck, delayed in a soft patch of sand, was left behind. And so, in a foray which recalled to Churchill 'Jeb Stuart's ride round McClellan in 1862 on the York Town Peninsula in the American Civil War', the Commander and Chief of Staff of the Axis Panzer Group had no means of communication with their rear H.Q. However, by the end of the afternoon they were on the frontier, having travelled 60 miles in six hours and produced the chaos which it had been part of Rommel's purpose to create. Moreover, they had fatally weakened Cunningham's morale.

Rommel's route to the east had taken him through the dispersed headquarter and supply areas of 7 Armoured Division, the South Africans and 30 Corps. He had been followed by 15 Panzer at midday and later by Ariete, though the latter were soon blocked by the South Africans. The effect of this stream of armour rolling through parks of soft-skinned transport was immediate. Staff, water, petrol and other stores were captured, and an automatic retreat by the supply echelons was started whose impetus increased as the day ran on and rumour spread. Cunningham was also affected, for he was on a visit to 7 Armoured Division just before noon when news of Rommel's approach was received, and was rushed back to his airstrip by Brigadier Clifton, Chief Engineer of 30 Corps, who has described graphically how 'almost unopposed, driving everything ahead like sheep, about 20 German tanks rolled eastwards, completely disintegrating our rear organisation . . .'. Cunningham's Blenheim was actually shelled as it took off—narrowly avoiding a three-ton lorry! When he reached Maddalena he was handed a written directive by Auchinleck, stating that 'you will continue to attack the enemy relentlessly using all your resources even to the last tank'. Auchinleck was becoming more and more concerned about Cunningham's determination to fight to the finish—which was not increased during the afternoon, as Cunningham flew over to 13 Corps and saw a tank battle occurring between the headquarters of 13 Corps and those of his Army.

The next day, after returning to Cairo, Auchinleck sent Cunningham a message dismissing him from his command. In a sense, therefore, Rommel had won the moral victory which was one of his objectives. It was only afterwards that he would learn how this victory had turned to his disadvantage: how Auchinleck, having replaced Cunningham by Ritchie, was to take a firm and decisive grip of the battle: and how the British will for victory remained unshaken.

On the afternoon of the 24th Rommel was still bursting with confidence. He realised that his rout of the British transport had left untouched the hard centre of 13 Corps—4 Indian Division and the New Zealanders. The next step would be to smash it: at 1600, therefore, he ordered von Ravenstein to hasten northwards to the Halfaya area, even though the main body of his division was still in transit. At 1700 Crüwell reached him, and was given orders for Afrika Korps' operations on the 25th. Rommel's idea was that 21 Panzer should cross the frontier and then, turning left, attack the Indians from their rear while 15 Panzer, astride the frontier, moved in from the south. Gambara's Ariete and Trieste Divisions were to conform from the east (Trieste, apparently, never received this order). And thus the Indians would be encircled: it was a conception typical of Rommel, but Crüwell disliked it. It was too ambitious: it was also based on ignorance of the true positions of 13 Corps. Crüwell was worried, too, about his supplies and dispersion of the Afrika Korps in their sudden swoop forward. (His supply situation would have been transformed if the Germans had spotted two vast dumps, each six miles square, which had only 22 Guards Brigade to protect them—a mistake which was possibly a by-product of the abortive *Midsummer Night's Dream*, and certainly a result of careful camouflage and the R.A.F.'s command of the air.) But Crüwell was overruled, and went off to feel his way through the Indian Division's posts to make contact with von Ravenstein.

Returning in the darkness, he and Bayerlein came across Rommel and Gause sitting in a broken-down truck. It was the kind of coincidence which was normal in the desert. Rommel was shivering with cold. His party was crowded into Crüwell's A.C.V., which drifted along the frontier wire in search of a gap. Finally a furious Rommel dismissed the A.D.C. from the driver's seat and took over himself: but even he could do no better, and the Commander-in-Chief of the *Panzergruppe* with his senior staff (ten officers and five men) spent the night in a solitary truck on the frontier of Egypt while British tanks, lorries and despatch riders drove within yards of them: somehow they escaped.

25 November produced a picture as complicated as the scenes at Sidi Rezegh. Ariete was unable to disengage from the South Africans. Rommel therefore changed his mind and ordered Crüwell to attack on his own, eastwards between Sidi Omar and Sidi Azeiz with 15 Panzer and westwards from Halfaya with 21. Orders were then followed by counter-orders. Throughout the day a series of disjointed actions developed, in which 4 Indian Division's field artillery fought defiantly in defence of their infantry, and destroyed many German tanks. The R.A.F. bombed continuously. 'Heavy losses among our troops', the diary of the Afrika Korps noted. 'Where are the German fighters?' (These had in fact been driven back from their landing-grounds at Gambut by the advancing New Zealand Division.) An attempt by Reconnaissance Unit 33 to raid Habata and the British supply line was broken up by the R.A.F. before it had even started. 'In short,' von Mellenthin observed, '25 November was a thoroughly unsatisfactory day in which we suffered heavy losses for little result.'

At Sidi Rezegh Rommel had made firm and constructive decisions, but during this period on the frontier his control of the battle—if it can be said to be a control—was ill-considered, impetuous and erratic. It is hard not to feel sympathy for Crüwell as he watched the dissipation and destruction of his precious tanks. Rommel's powers of endurance were exceptional: but since he arrived in Africa on the 18th he had been continuously engaged in action, often in the dual role of Army Commander and combatant, and on the 25th he behaved like a tired man unsure of himself. He would soon recover his 'touch', with disastrous results for 8 Army. But a period was still to follow during which the Afrika Korps suffered vague and indecisive direction; a period which can only be understood in relation to what had been happening along the coast and to the west of Rommel's sortie, the theme of the next chapter.

Here, then, is an appropriate point at which to ask whether Rommel's 'dash to the wire' was justifiable. In war there are certain acts and decisions which can be described as absolutely right or absolutely wrong. Rommel's decision and action fall into neither of these categories: they will be the subject of perennial debate by military critics. Is Liddell Hart correct in saying that 'Rommel's raid resulted in more forfeit than gain. When the raid started, he had almost won the battle. When the raid ended, the scales had tilted against him. But the margin was very narrow, not only psychologically but physically . . . the course that he actually took might be condemned by cautiously conventional doctrine, but it was in accord with the classic ideas of generalship as applied by the "Great Captains" of History'? Is General Carver (who served as a staff officer close to Willoughby Norrie) correct in treating Rommel's raid, in his admirable book on *Tobruk*, with undisguised contempt? Is the *Official History* fair in stating that 'it is hard to avoid the conclusion that if Rommel had behaved on this occasion more like *le bon général ordinaire*, and less like the impulsive leader who was accustomed to see his exploits succeed provided they were bold enough, matters might have turned out worse for the British'? Or does Desmond Young make a shrewd point in his biography of Rommel when he observes that had the raid succeeded it would have been rated as a masterpiece?

Rommel's defence is probably contained in an observation by the cynical Count Ciano that defeat is an orphan, whereas victory has many godparents, or, as Admiral Mahan put it, 'Defeat cries aloud for explanation; whereas success, like charity, covers a multitude of sins.' His impulsive action might well have produced a victory, and the hindsight of critics would then have had a different focus. His drive through France in 1940 and his thrust from Agheila in 1941 had shown him what might be achieved if an armoured spearhead could puncture the soft-skinned administrative areas of an army, and his experiences in the First World War had proved that daring paid dividends. He certainly succeeded in undermining Cunningham's morale, and he could not have foreseen, when planning his attack, that Cunningham's uncertainty would be replaced by the self-assurance of Auchinleck. With luck, moreover, the Afrika Korps might have overrun the British dumps. It is therefore not unreasonable to imagine a situation in which, by his raid, Rommel had demoralised the British High Command, captured its main supplies, and created overwhelming 'alarm and despondency'. This kind of operation will always be condemned if it fails and praised if it succeeds. Grant's eastward move across the Mississippi at Vicksburg, and his subsequent manœuvres which ended in Pemberton's encirclement, illustrate the risk Rommel took. Grant succeeded: Rommel failed. But had Grant failed and Rommel succeeded the verdict on their efforts would now be different.

Rommel's certainly failed in the practical execution of his plan. A raid or conclusive thrust such as he envisaged depended, in the desert, on efficiency of communications: but at the beginning of his attack he committed himself to wireless silence, and his subsequent behaviour kept him out of touch with his headquarters at El Adem, and also, from time to time, with his divisional commanders: yet it was pointless for the head of a panzer force to lead his troops in the field if he could not communicate with their generals, a lesson Rommel had himself learned in France in 1940. In the execution of his plan he was also misled by an inadequate appreciation of his enemy's positions. Historians will argue for ever about the validity of Rommel's strategic purpose: but there can be no argument about his tactical arrangements in that phase of the Winter Battle when the 'dash to the wire' followed the Day of the Dead. They were bad.

A justification of Rommel's 'dash' such as I have put forward leaves unanswered the question, was there a better alternative? Crüwell certainly seems to have had an alternative plan in mind: concentration of the Afrika Korps against the British forces outside the Tobruk perimeter. Throughout the battle it is clear that he saw this as the main German objective, though to what extent he was able to press his views on Rommel is uncertain. At their meeting at 0600 on the Tobruk by-pass Rommel was already committed to a move which, depending on one's view-point, was either brilliant or stupid. The battle had developed rapidly, and from the beginning there had been little opportunity either for careful thought or for an exchange of views: when they met, Crüwell was seeking to consummate the considerable success of his corps and Rommel was perhaps seeking that 'something different' which it was in his nature to require when he found himself caught in anything akin to positional warfare. He lacked the composure of the general who can win the 'set battle'. He was a Jeb Stuart rather than a Grant, and in this respect Montgomery was always his superior. Caught in a clinch, Rommel's instinct was to strike out—if possible, unexpectedly: in France and Italy in the First World War and, especially, in France in 1940, this had been his way, and it may well be an explanation of his refusal to accept Crüwell's request for a renewal of the assault on Tobruk. His staff, certainly, disapproved of his decision. Von Mellenthin writes: 'it is my conviction that if we had kept the Afrika Korps in the Sidi Rezegh area, we would have won the *Crusader* battle.'

Commanders must always, at some time or another, make questionable decisions. If they did not do so the function of a military historian would become tediously descriptive: it would not remain, as it does, perennially interesting because it involves appraisal and the asking of questions. Rommel's 'dash to the wire', like the Somme, and Passchendaele, provides an eternally debatable subject—debatable because, for example, it is an open question whether by rushing to the east he thus enabled the British, in spite of their rudimentary system of recovery, to regain enough of their tanks from the battlefield to make it possible for them, with reinforcements, to re-enter the arena.

VI

Advance and Retreat

1941–42

While Rommel was racing to the frontier of Egypt, and involving the Afrika Korps in a series of ineffective engagements, his staff, unable to make contact with him, became more and more concerned as they read the battle. 'Huddled in our greatcoats', von Mellenthin writes, 'in the wooden huts which served as our Headquarters at El Adem, Westphal and I viewed the situation with increasing anxiety.' This was primarily the result of the moves of 2 New Zealand Division.

Two Brigades of the Division, 4 and 6, had started westwards from the area of 13 Corps on 21 November, and by the 23rd 6 Brigade had reached Point 175, south-west of Tobruk. (The third Brigade, 5, had been held back on the frontier to the north of 4 Indian Division.) Their commander, General Freyberg, kept pressing forward, but he was on his own, for Rommel's sortie had destroyed any hope of protection for his southern flank. He was cut off from his base, short of supplies, and now led a two-brigade division. But Freyberg was Freyberg V.C., and there is a general consensus of opinion that 2 New Zealand Division was one of the most efficient formations in 8 Army. So by the evening of the 23rd 4 Brigade was established in the Gambut area (denying its airfields to the *Luftwaffe*) and Divisional Headquarters had been set up at Bir Chleta. By the next evening Freyberg was signalling to his corps commander: 'we are attacking westward and are now on a line running north and south through Point 175 . . . if we had petrol and ammunition we might have been in Tobruk tomorrow night but impossible to be definite.' Early next morning the New Zealanders justified Freyberg's optimism by attacks whose success made it possible to plan a junction between his division and the Tobruk garrison. This began to be practicable on the night of

26–27 November, and was finally achieved the following day. But these attacks had almost exhausted the division. The New Zealand *Official History* describes their effect on 6 Brigade. 'There was an enormous number of dead and wounded all over the battlefield. A significant feature was the sight of many men who had been hit by solid shot of anti-tank guns fired at point blank range. These projectiles had torn large portions of flesh from the bodies of their unfortunate victims and it would be hard to imagine a more unpleasant sight or a more heavily contested battlefield.'

For Westphal and von Mellenthin, huddled in their huts, there were two other matters of immediate concern. The Italians were becoming nervous and Westphal, only a colonel, had now to deal with agitated—and Latin—corps commanders. But the German staff system indoctrinated its 'chosen few' with the habit of assuming responsibility, and during these testing days Westphal revealed a strength of character and clarity of judgement which justifies it. More importantly, the H.Q. at El Adem was conscious that as the days slipped by the British were being given an opportunity to reinforce and reorganise. As von Mellenthin observes, 'the Afrika Korps had accomplished nothing decisive on the frontier and was only a fraction of the magnificent force which had entered the battle on the 18th. The British armour had been given a respite; many tanks had been salvaged, large tank reserves had been sent up from Egypt, and 4 and 22 Armoured Brigades were again formidable fighting formations. The Royal Air Force dominated the battlefield.' What the worried staff officers at El Adem could not know was that General Ritchie, now in command of 8 Army, had refused to allow himself to be flurried by the complicated and unpromising situation he had inherited. His natural optimism and his lack of imagination, which were to prove disastrous at Gazala next year, were now an advantage: he steadfastly looked on the bright side, and by 27 November was already writing to Auchinleck: 'As I see it the major situation in Cyrenaica as a whole is excellent from our point of view and all indications are that the enemy is getting more and more hard put to it.'

But from the German point of view, also, the situation was improving. This was largely due to Westphal's courage and self-assurance. After vain efforts to contact Rommel or Crüwell (in the latter's defence it must be pointed out that after his H.Q. had been overrun he was functioning with a skeleton staff and signals section) Westphal sent a firm instruction to 21 Panzer Division, cancelling all previous orders and directing it to move westwards towards Tobruk and the rear of the New Zealanders. His appeal was overheard. Auchinleck's despatch observes that 'on 27 November wireless messages for the enemy armoured divisions to return from the frontier were intercepted'.

Rommel also was aware of Westphal's concern, but ignored it in his desire to achieve a conclusive result on the frontier: here confused fighting had continued, especially with 5 New Zealand Brigade. The confusion was not improved by Rommel. On the evening of the 26th, for example, he ordered 15 Panzer to clear up the situation around Sollum and then to return to El Adem. During the night he issued instructions for the Sollum attack to be carried out in the dark, and then cancelled them, with fresh orders for an immediate move to Tobruk. When Neumann-Silkow finally got going, he successfully overran the H.Q. of 5 New Zealand Brigade at Sidi Azeiz: their losses were 44 dead, 49 wounded, and 46 officers and 650 other ranks prisoners. By the evening of the 27th 15 and 21 Panzer Divisions had made contact on the Trigh Capuzzo, the former having driven off, during the afternoon, a two-pronged attack by the revived 4 and 22 Armoured Brigades, who gained a tactical success but threw it away by withdrawing into leaguer as darkness fell.

Westphal at El Adem and Crüwell on the frontier had persisted in the view that Tobruk, and the forces attempting its relief, were the critical centre of the battle. At last Rommel accepted their diagnosis: and as usual, once he had cleared his mind and recognised the realities, he was soon transformed from the muddled and ineffectual leader of the last few days into his urgent and decisive self. German prospects had improved, therefore, because the Afrika Korps was concentrating and preparing to tackle its proper objective, while its commander had come to realise what that objective should be. A final curtain had fallen on Rommel's second *Midsummer Night's Dream*.

During the evening of the 27th he was again in touch with his headquarters: he had reached Gambut, and was able to speak by wireless to El Adem. Westphal explained to him the weakness of the Tobruk front and the despair of the Italians. After a conference with Crüwell Rommel flew, by night, to El Adem. His return was awaited with apprehension—how would he deal with Westphal's assumption of command? One of his A.D.C.s, Lieut. Voss, has described what happened when he arrived. 'Rommel was at first furious at Lieut.-Col. Westphal's independent action in recalling 21 Panzer Division to El Adem. On returning to headquarters he greeted nobody, but stalked silently into the command vehicle and looked at the situation maps. Behind him stood Gause. We tried to signal to Gause that he should talk to Rommel and explain Westphal's decision. But it was not necessary, for Rommel suddenly left the vehicle saying that he was going to lie down. Nobody dared to go to the vehicle where Rommel was sleeping, to report on the situation. Next morning, however, to everybody's relief, the general made no further mention of the incident. He was as friendly as ever and work at headquarters continued smoothly.' This was the Rommel of whom von Mellenthin writes that he 'was not an easy man to serve; he spared those around him as little as he spared himself. An iron constitution and nerves of steel were needed to work with Rommel.' His own attitude was defined on almost the last page of his *Papers*: 'Officers who had too little initiative to get their troops forward or too much reverence for pre-conceived ideas were ruthlessly removed from their posts and, failing all else, sent back to Europe. With the lower-ranking staff-officers, I was less concerned about their knowledge of strategy (for how often does a junior staff officer have to think in terms of strategy?) than that they should bring with them a good grounding in tactics . . . . from my officers, I demanded the utmost self-denial and a continual personal example. . . .' In fact Rommel habitually exercised the necessary rigour of the Great Commander—that rigour which is an acceptance of priorities and a recognition that if his staff, and corps of officers, are inadequate his troops, however fine their quality, will be lost without leadership. No one in Rommel's Panzer Group, from divisional commanders down to the lowest under-officer, was safe from the lash of his tongue. Though both his men and his officers knew this their morale, curiously enough, rarely flagged. (It must be noted that in the Orders of 90 Light Division it was once laid down that to sing 'The Song of the Poor Buggers' would be a court-martial offence. The words were not quoted.)

And yet the tough armour of the Panzer General concealed a tender heart. On 27 November, the day on which he made his grim entry into the El Adem H.Q., he wrote to his wife: 'I'm very well. I've just spent four days in a desert counter-attack with nothing to wash with. We had a splendid success. It's our 25th wedding anniversary today. Perhaps it'll run to a special communiqué. I need not tell you how well we got on together. I want to thank you for all the love and kindness through the years which have passed so quickly. I think, with gratitude to you, of our son, who is a source of great pride to me. . . .'

Moreover, as his army knew, the Panzer General lived hard. Bayerlein has recorded how the commander of the Afrika Korps was summoned to Rommel's forward H.Q. at Gambut for the conference which occurred during the night of the 27-28th. 'After searching for a long time in the darkness they finally discovered a British lorry, which General Crüwell's command car approached with great caution. Inside it, to his good fortune, were no British troops, but Rommel and his Chief of Staff, both of them unshaven, worn with lack of sleep and caked with dust. In the lorry was a heap of straw as a bed, a can of stale water to drink and a few tins of food. Close by were two wireless trucks and a few dispatch riders. Rommel now gave his instructions for the next day's operations.'

Their object was to eliminate the New Zealand Brigades and to close the ring around Tobruk. When the link-up with the garrison had been achieved, Godwin-Austen had signalled to Churchill 'Corridor to Tobruk clear and secure. Tobruk is as relieved as I am.' But Rommel was now determined that this triumph should be short-lived. His intentions were wildly misinterpreted by Ritchie who, in his mood of optimistic aggression, at 1845 on the 27th ordered 30 Corps to prevent the German armour from 'escaping westwards' to the south of Sidi Rezegh!

Rommel's aim was for Crüwell to assemble his armour north of Belhamed, and then strike west and south-west to cut the channel joining the New Zealanders to the Tobruk garrison. But Crüwell had other views. He felt that the lie of the land made a converging attack on Sidi Rezegh more promising. Rommel's plan was the result of his desire to re-invest Tobruk: he was unwilling to allow its defenders to be stiffened by a division for whose capabilities he had the greatest respect. Crüwell seems to have thought that his panzers could smash the New Zealand brigades and then bottle up their survivors in the fortress. He was a strong, independent character (as his actions throughout *Crusader* reveal), and he now decided to go his own way, sending the Panzer Army off on manœuvres which, during 28 November, might gain them start-lines for an offensive nearer to his own concept than to Rommel's. They had some success: for though in the north 21 Panzer was still advancing slowly from the frontier, during the afternoon of the 28th 15 Panzer, with 43 tanks, climbed on to the escarpment from the south-east and pushed for the airfield. In its path lay the main New Zealand dressing station, which was rapidly overrun. This episode was graphically described in his diary by Colonel Kippenberger (who had been wounded in 4 New Zealand Brigade's attack on Belhamed during the night of the 25-26th).

> *Nov. 28th.* General,* Gentry, Maxwell and Kenrick all looked in, very cheery and confident. Gentry says Germans have only fifty tanks left. About five German infantry came in and made us all prisoners. Alan Tennant popped his head in the door and said, 'We're in the bag.' The orderlies all went out with their hands over their heads.

Kippenberger (who on 4 December made a daring and successful escape and went on to command first a brigade and then, in Italy, the New Zealand Division) also noted that '4th, 5th and 6th Field Ambulance, and Mobile

---

* General Freyberg.

Surgical Unit, and about 1200 wounded are prisoners and 900 German prisoners have been released'. Such dramatic reversals were a regular feature of the *va-et-vient* of the desert campaigns.

But Ritchie's notion that the Afrika Korps was retreating, and must be cut off, had no immediate effect on the reconstituted 7 Armoured Division. Apart from the Support Group it now included 4 and 22 Armoured Brigades, both replenished with tanks, and was operating along the southern flank of the Afrika Korp's centre line. But it did little to interfere with the advance of 15 Panzer, and during skirmishes with Germans in the morning and Ariete in the afternoon it lost 22 tanks—failing, at the same time, to help 1 South African Brigade to bring to the hard-pressed New Zealanders the infantry reinforcements they urgently needed. This was not entirely the fault of 7 Armoured, for the South Africans' commander, Pienaar, was crawling forward cautiously, fearing—and fearing with some justice—that his inexperienced brigade might be assaulted by enemy armour in a situation where the tanks of his allies could not protect him. After his snail's progress he therefore halted for the night at Taieb el Essem, 20 miles south-east of Sidi Rezegh.

To the north of the escarpment things went better for 13 Corps during the day: 18 New Zealand Battalion, with infantry tanks from Tobruk, took prisoner 637 men of the German Infantry Regiment 155. But in the south the intrusion of 15 Panzer on to the escarpment could not be ignored, and during the night of the 28th Godwin-Austen, his corps' headquarters, and Freyberg's administrative units all entered the Tobruk *enceinte*, leaving Freyberg himself to face the morning with his battered brigades in their positions at Sidi Rezegh. The latter, still expecting that the South Africans would reach and reinforce them, were refreshed that same night by a remarkable enterprise. Starting from Fort Maddalena a convoy of over 250 lorries, led by Brigadier Clifton and escorted by a handful of light tanks and armoured cars, somehow contrived to cover 40 miles of rough going, in the dark, without interference from Ariete or the German armour through whose leaguer areas they passed, and to deliver at dawn its cargo of water, food and ammunition. War in the desert was often compared with war at sea: this was a daring act of gun-running—like the dashes to Malta of the fast mine-layers, *Abdiel*, *Manxman* and *Welshman*.

But earlier that evening, at 2000, Crüwell had issued orders for an offensive which was to lead to the temporary withdrawal of a decimated New Zealand Division from the desert. His plan was for 21 Panzer to attack Belhamed from the east with the support of 90 Light's artillery, while 15 Panzer curved round the southern flank of Sidi Rezegh and then, swinging right, came in on

El Duda from the south-west. The gap between the two divisions would be filled by Ariete. At 2100 Crüwell received instructions from Rommel to execute the latter's own plan for preventing the New Zealanders from retiring into Tobruk, but either because he preferred his own scheme, or because it was too late to modify his orders, he ignored his superior, and the offensive which started early next morning, 29 November, began on Crüwell's terms.

No significant progress was made on the first day. 15 Panzer, whose westward advance was watched by a group which included Rommel, Crüwell and Bastico, did indeed reach and attack El Duda by early afternoon, gaining a foothold in the position at 1830 in spite of fierce resistance by 1 Essex and 2/13 Australian Battalions of the Tobruk garrison. But a counter-attack at 0130 next morning by a couple of Australian companies and 11 infantry tanks recovered the lost ground: for a time 15 Panzer was also deprived of its 8 Panzer Regiment, which deciphered a message incorrectly and then made off towards El Adem. In the north-east 21 Panzer (with only 20 tanks in action) was even less effective. It began by losing von Ravenstein who, making a reconnaissance, was captured by 21 Battalion of the New Zealanders on Point 175. (He was replaced by General Böttcher: the Böttcher Group, in turn, was taken over by Colonel Mickl.) Moreover, papers taken with von Ravenstein contained valuable intelligence about the German plan. By the evening 21 Panzer had still failed to reach its start-line at Zaafran, due east of Belhamed, and on this exceptional day it was not the Afrika Korps but the Italian Ariete Division which did best.

This was due to a chain reaction started at 1515 by the arrival of a South African armoured car at Freyberg's H.Q. A wireless link with 1 South African Brigade now became available, and Pienaar was ordered by Freyberg to move to Point 175. Ariete, however, had assumed that Point 175 was held by Germans, and their column, as it innocently approached, was interpreted by 21 Battalion to be that of the South Africans. The consequence was that the latter were surprised, overrun, and reduced to a complement of 200. Ariete had also, during the day, successfully held off the tanks of 7 Armoured: and the chain reaction continued when news of the fall of Point 175 reached Pienaar, for in spite of further pressure from Freyberg he was confused by failing wireless communications, was now faced with the probability of meeting opposition if he pushed on through the night, and therefore, exercising his customary caution, decided to halt. He signalled to Norrie that, as a result of the loss of Point 175, Freyberg had stopped his advance—but this was incorrect, and his action must be put down to his state of uncertainty. The result was, however, that though the net had not been drawn as tightly round the New Zealand Division as Crüwell had intended, it had nevertheless suffered further casualties and still awaited reinforcement.

'During this day,' says von Mellenthin, 'Rommel went personally to Afrika Korps Headquarters and insisted that the New Zealand Division should be destroyed in the open field, and not be driven into Tobruk.' This determination to maintain his objective was to bear fruit during the next two days: and it should be remembered that on 29 November Rommel's situation, if not grave, was unpromising. 15 Panzer had been rebuffed; 21 Panzer was weak and lethargic; the Tobruk garrison and the New Zealanders were still fighting hard; and 7 Armoured, though it had achieved no striking success, was still attacking pertinaciously and constantly harassing with its 'Jock columns', while it had a certainty of reinforcement on which the Afrika Korps could no longer rely. 'In the circumstances', one may agree with von Mellenthin, 'Rommel's decision to continue the battle until he had wiped out the New Zealanders is a striking proof of his will-power and determination.'

This was important, because Crüwell was now a pessimist. It was Rommel's tenacity which forced his troops into attack on the 30th. The intention was for Mickl (who had been captured and then quickly escaped) to assault Sidi Rezegh from the south-west: 15 Panzer would come in from the west and 21 Panzer would continue to struggle forward from the east. The morning passed in preparation, which included a steady bombardment of the positions on Sidi Rezegh to which the New Zealanders could not reply effectively because of their shortage of ammunition. The graph of *Crusader* was now approaching one of its critical peaks, and it is interesting to note the scale of the forces involved. 21 Panzer was down to 15 medium and six light tanks. 15 Panzer had 28 medium and 11 light. 7 Armoured, well away from the crucial point, had 120 tanks of all types, now concentrated under the command of Gatehouse. In 6 New Zealand Brigade the four battalions could only muster 26 officers and 829 men. It was a constant characteristic of the desert war that, while armies were engaged, relatively small groups could have a decisive effect by winning or losing some key point. In this minuscule situation, for example, Sidi Rezegh was for 4 and 6 New Zealand Brigades a Waterloo without a Blücher: yet the arrival from their south-east flank of 1 South African Brigade, which never occurred, might have been decisive, especially if it had been accompanied by some of those tanks from 7 Armoured which had at least a numerical superiority over the Afrika Korps.

The wandering regiment of 15 Panzer had been recalled, and during the afternoon the division launched its attack—Rommel having overruled requests for a postponement. The result was immediate: within an hour and a half 6 New Zealand Brigade was destroyed, and as the sun went down 600 of its remaining officers and men were prisoners. The survivors were refused permission to enter Tobruk by Godwin-Austen because a hope still lingered that 1 South African Brigade would take Point 175 during the night, and then march for Sidi Rezegh, while the British armour had been ordered to reinforce at dawn. But the hope was vain. Although a message from Freyberg reached Pienaar telling him that 'Sidi Rezegh was captured this afternoon. Our position is untenable unless you can recapture it before dawn 1 December. You will therefore carry out this task at once'; although 4 Armoured Brigade (which had taken over the remaining tanks of 22 Brigade) gave support to the South Africans; and although Norrie had joined Pienaar and personally ordered him to retake Point 175, the attempt at a breakthrough failed.

Next morning came the turn of 4 New Zealand Brigade. It was over-whelmed at Belhamed, and, though the remnants of 6 Brigade were joined by tanks of 4 Armoured, confusion followed when a signal was received from Gott ordering the New Zealanders to retire. The tank commanders thought they were to cover a withdrawal to the south, but the infantry fell back towards Zaafran and the east. For the time being they were out of the battle: they assembled on the frontier and were then sent up to Syria to rest and re-equip. The intensity of their struggle can be summarised by one fact: before 20 Battalion was overrun at Belhamed shortly after dawn on the 1st, it had had five commanding officers in the last three days. But the efforts and losses of 2 New Zealand Division won their reward. 'Tobruk was again isolated,' von Mellenthin observes, 'and on paper we seemed to have won the *Crusader* battle. But the price paid was too heavy; the *Panzergruppe* had been worn down, and it soon became clear that only one course remained—a general retreat from Cyrenaica.'

It was, however, a course that Rommel was not yet prepared to follow. He was under no illusions about his supplies. With Bastico, on the 30th, he had discussed the problem and they had jointly sent an urgent demand back to Italy for reinforcements—guns, trucks, tanks and signal stores. But both Bastico and Rommel knew that the chances of anything substantial reaching Africa in time to turn the tide of *Crusader* were remote: indeed, their request seems to have been more a diplomatic move, designed to produce pressure on the French to open up the Tunisian ports to the Axis, than a realistic indent. It stirred the Duce to tackle Hitler, and to point out that in November only a third of the requisite stores for the African Army had been shipped across the Mediterranean. But the answer came on 4 December, when a staff officer from *Comando Supremo* was sent by Mussolini to tell Rommel that, apart from his basic requirements of food and ammunition, he could expect nothing more until early January. In the meantime Auchinleck was pushing up reinforcements from the Delta, generously and perhaps dangerously. Apart from the steady flow of armour, 150 Brigade of 50 Division was coming forward from Cyprus, and 38 Indian Brigade from Egypt; but so were units of 1 Armoured Division which had only recently been craned from their convoy, and were in no sense desert-worthy in terms either of their mechanical preparation or their tactical training. Still, these were tanks with men inside them. Rommel, so far, had lost 142 of the 249 tanks with which he had started *Crusader*; in every other respect, of personnel and equipment, his army was irremediably short. At this point in the battle, therefore, the 'staff solution' would have been for him to withdraw and reinforce. He counter-attacked.

This was really a sign of the undiminished pugnacity which later would make Rommel drive the British back to Gazala: not an indication that he had appreciated his weakness *vis-à-vis* Auchinleck. On 2 December he ordered Crüwell to send battle groups from the two armoured divisions eastward; one from 21 Panzer along the Via Balbia and one from 15 Panzer along the Trigh Capuzzo, with the hope of producing some relief for the Axis forces still locked up on the frontier—the forces his 'dash to the wire' had tried to release. Crüwell was still his commander's critic. 'We must not', he said, 'repeat the error of giving up to the enemy a battlefield on which Afrika Korps has won a victory and undertaking another operation some distance away, instead of destroying the enemy utterly.'

Crüwell was right. Most of the few remaining tanks of the Afrika Korps were now in need of rest and repair—as were their crews—and the counter-attack was feeble. It was both hampered and protected by the weather; hampered because movement on the ground was difficult, protected because the superior R.A.F. was inactive. But on 3 December conditions changed sufficiently for the German striking force to be spotted from the air. In consequence one of its columns was virtually wiped out near Bardia by 5 New Zealand Brigade, while the other was strafed, shelled and roughly handled by units of 4 Indian Division. Rommel's hope that he might break through to his beleaguered forces on the frontier and this time drive his enemy on to the Sollum minefields had been thwarted by sheer weakness, and his diminished columns withdrew to Gambut.

On 4 December an attack by 21 Panzer and the Mickl Group on El Duda was equally unsuccessful. And now Ritchie, who on 1 December had been joined at his headquarters by Auchinleck, began to exercise with his reinforced army a pressure that would prove irresistible. His immediate target was El Adem: and though 30 Corps, now more powerful than its opponent, wasted its strength in the characteristic 8 Army way by scrappy and unco-ordinated actions around Bir el Gubi, its operations were menacing enough to give Rommel a final warning. On 4 December he saw the truth of his situation. This was the day when Colonel Montezemolo brought him news from *Comando Supremo* that apart from his minimum requirements of fuel and food Rommel could expect no more stores until the beginning of January, when the reinforced *Luftwaffe*, under Kesselring's impulsion, might enable convoy movements to re-start. Rommel decided on a final and desperate course of action. He must deal with the British at Bir el Gubi, then strike east again, capturing the supply dumps which had now been identified on the Trigh el Abd, and force his way through Sidi Omar to relieve the frontier garrisons. If this proved impossible he saw that he was in danger of being out-flanked, and that his only choice was to withdraw rapidly to the west with his mobile troops and as much of the slow-moving Italian infantry as could be saved.

It did prove impossible. During the afternoon of the 5th Rommel sent the Afrika Korps south towards El Gubi, expecting a clash with 7 Armoured. In fact they hit 11 Indian Brigade, and though it was overrun nothing conclusive followed. The darkness passed in a confusion well described in a passage from *The Tiger Kills*.

> It was the third night there had been no sleep for anyone. The German leaguer flares soared and fell all around; the mutter of motors and sound of digging could be heard on all sides. The remainder of the Mahrattas were completely cut off, but the telephone was not destroyed. It was once cut, but an Indian signaller went out and repaired it within fifty yards of a couple of panzers. Lieut.-Colonel M. P. Lancaster gave a running commentary, in Urdu in case the Germans were listening, telling how his battalion was re-organising, where the enemy were, and what he proposed to do. Suddenly he said to the Brigade Major, 'Keep quiet. There are Germans here.'

Next morning brought more skirmishing, and in a further attack during the afternoon the Afrika Korps was bombed and shelled. In the bombardment Neumann-Silkow was mortally wounded. It was, indeed, no sinecure to hold a high command under Rommel. Von Ravenstein was a prisoner; Neumann-Silkow was now dead; Sümmermann would be killed in an air attack on 9 December; and in 1942 other key men would be removed by capture, wounds or death—Crüwell at Gazala, and von Vaerst, Gause and Westphal; von Bismarck and Nehring at Alam Halfa; Stumme and von Thoma at Alamein.

Rommel now made the unavoidable decision. For 24 hours he resisted Crüwell's desire to withdraw, instructing him to try to advance again on the 7th. But at 0930 that day he was at Crüwell's H.Q., saying, sensibly:

> If the enemy was not beaten today we should have to abandon the Tobruk front and go back to the Gazala position. Preliminary measures for this had been taken the previous night—the heavy artillery had been withdrawn from the Tobruk front, and 90 Light Division and the Italian formations. The Sollum front would also have to be abandoned.... Afrika Korps was to hold out today and keep the enemy off, and to counter-attack if the enemy pressed too hard. During the night it was to withdraw 30-35 km. north-west.

This was the climax of *Crusader*, the moment of truth: for the Afrika Korps, as might have been expected, made no progress during the day, and by the afternoon Rommel finally settled for a fighting retreat to Gazala.

It would not be a withdrawal into a vacuum. When the May assault on Tobruk failed, the line running south from Gazala into the desert was selected as the position where Cyrenaica could be held, whatever might happen to the units on the frontier. By midsummer the line had been partly developed, and now, in December, there was available for Rommel something less than a fortress but more than a stretch of open desert. His retirement is summarised by Bayerlein: 'Withdrawing a step at a time, fighting isolated and sometimes very troublesome actions as they went, all troops reached the Gazala Line by 12 December without the enemy having succeeded, during the withdrawal, in cutting off any sizeable detachments of troops or inflicting any serious casualties.' The significant sentence is 'Rommel's decision found no agreement with his Italian superiors'. In fact the Italians were appalled by it.

Rommel's own diary states:

> I also received a visit from Excellency Bastico in a ravine south-east of Ain el Gazala bay, where we established our H.Q. on 12 December. He is very upset about the way the battle is going and is particularly worried about the Agedabia area, to which he wants to move an Italian division as quickly as possible. It worked up to a very stormy argument, during which I told him, among other things, that I was not going to stand for any of my Italian divisions being taken from me and redisposed by him. I would have no option but to make the retreat through Cyrenaica with the German forces alone, leaving the Italians to their fate.... Excellency Bastico thereupon became more amenable.

This was a reflection of a debate which would continue in one form or another until the spring of 1943. The arguments 'pro' and 'con' derived from Italy's desire to maintain prestige and position in North Africa and Rommel's intention, as a commander in the field, to take decisions which seemed to him to be tactically or strategically correct. In this debate he was at a disadvantage, to some extent, because his military superiors were apathetic about North Africa while Hitler had an ambivalent regard for Mussolini: yet Rommel was always prepared to act independently and to deal with the Italians on the spot as he thought fit, and in the last resort he had Hitler's ear.

It is difficult to assess how, in this complicated diplomatic situation, Kesselring helped Rommel. Two factors were at work. It is clear from his memoirs that Kesselring had a love-hate relationship with Rommel—a mixture of envy and respect for Rommel's achievements and a desire to magnify the results of his own command. It is also clear that he was trying to pour oil on the Axis—to lubricate the relations between Germany and Italy in a way that would produce, in the Mediterranean, effective military co-operation. From Kesselring's point of view, therefore, Rommel was a success-ful nuisance. So while he describes Rommel's decision to retreat from Tobruk and the subsequent counter-attack which carried him back to Gazala in laudatory terms—'both operations were characteristic of Rommel at his best'—in the same paragraph of his memoirs he says that 'a certain willing-ness to meet the Italians halfway, even a formal correctness, would have made the obvious antagonism less acute or less apparent. Rommel's retreat was a blow to the Italian Command in Africa and Rome and—rightly or wrongly—Count Cavallero and Marshal Bastico felt Rommel's decision as a slight to themselves and a danger to the Axis partnership.' These sentences reveal the difference between a man who has to fight a political and a man who has to fight a military battle. Rommel had to think about instant action, this day—or tomorrow. Kesselring's concern was with long-term relationships. Of course he had his own military preoccupations; but in these as in his political concerns Rommel was both a too victorious and a too contumacious colleague.

This crisis in German-Italian relations (and it *was* a crisis: hot words were spoken) raises the question of Rommel's capacity in one of the areas where a military commander must excel: his ability to melt into a homogeneous army a variety of national forces, and to establish a common doctrine, with understanding and without friction, between allies of different temperaments and different war-aims. In this politico-psychological field Eisenhower and Alexander certainly succeeded: Montgomery partially failed. In Africa Rommel failed without question. He never understood the Italians, nor did he carry them with him in his planning. He admired their soldiers but des-pised their officers. And so, lacking the sympathy and tolerance which Eisen-hower and Alexander habitually displayed, he never treated the Italians as 'first class citizens' or welded his Panzer Group into a whole. The result was that when an issue arose like the retreat from Tobruk, which involved Italian prestige as well as a military decision, he acted as a soldier and not as a states-man. He made the decision, in fact, without letting his allies feel it was so inevitable that from their point of view it was politically justifiable. All that is child-like and feminine in the Italian temperament was rejected by Rommel, and all their strong military virtues, as displayed from time to time by the Ariete Division and, for example, their parachute battalions, were never fostered by him or equated, in his mind, with the qualities he ascribed to the Afrika Korps.

The immediate subject of Rommel's debate with the Italians was Cyrenaica. Colonel Montezemolo had reported back to *Comando Supremo* after his visit, and as a result the Italians had accepted the need to abandon Tobruk. But Cyrenaica? Bastico, as has been seen, fought hard to avoid a precipitate retreat. Before his confrontation with Rommel at Gazala he had already made the Italian position clear. On the 8th *Comando Supremo*, in agreement with O.K.H., laid down that Bardia and the frontier garrisons should hold fast, supplied by air and sea. On the 9th Bastico issued a policy statement which put all the forces in Cyrenaica (Italians included) under Rommel's command. But on the 12th he sent a directive to Rommel, based on *Comando Supremo*'s instruction that decisions about Cyrenaica should be left to *il comandante in sito* (who, Bastico assumed, was himself) in which he ordered that Gazala must be the last ditch of defence and withdrawal further west must not be contemplated. Rommel, however, was going his own way: and in the circumstances it was the right one.

He met Bastico's demands to the extent of sending the remains of 90 Light back to Agedabia in case Ritchie tried to copy O'Connor's drive to Beda Fomm—for Bastico was particularly worried about the possibility that the Afrika Korps might suddenly vanish westwards without leaving a firm base on to which his sluggish Italians could fall back. (It was during the move of 90 Light that Sümmermann was killed in an air attack during the night of 9 December.) Meanwhile, without any confidence that the Gazala line was his final destination—for as von Mellenthin says, 'Rommel's main anxiety was that the enemy would make a strong armoured thrust across the desert and get across our main line of retreat'—Rommel managed to break contact with the British sufficiently to emplace his army at Gazala by 11 December and to form a front composed of the Italian infantry in the north, then the Italian Mobile Corps, with the Afrika Korps covering the open flank in the south.

Ritchie had made a curious arrangement whereby 30 Corps (in theory the experts in fast-moving operations) took over responsibility for reducing the Axis strongholds on the frontier while 13 Corps (primarily an infantry command) absorbed 7 Armoured Division and handled the pursuit. Whatever the unorthodoxy of this re-organisation, Godwin-Austen evolved precisely the plan—the inevitable plan—which Rommel feared. He sent 5 New

Zealand Brigade and a Polish Brigade to attack and pin down the Italians while 7 Armoured and 4 Indian made a broad movement south of Rommel's right flank, aimed at Tmimi, Derna and Mechili. The plan failed. The Indian Division, meant to slip round the flank, found itself engaged in a direct and bloody involvement with the Italian 20 Corps; the manœuvres of 7 Armoured in Rommel's rear used up much valuable petrol but missed the enemy; the Poles and New Zealanders were stopped by the Italian infantry; and during the afternoon of 15 December over 1000 men, of 1 Battalion of the Buffs and other troops of 5 Indian Brigade, were killed or captured by 15 Panzer. Moreover indifferent weather, difficulties about fighter escorts and the confused situation on the ground meant that, as the *Official History* records, 'for nearly three days the enemy's troops in the comparatively small area southwest of Gazala had not one bomb dropped on them'. Nevertheless Ritchie's continuing pressure, though it achieved no immediate tactical gains, was enough for Rommel: he decided that he must pull out from the Gazala line during the night of 16-17 December.

The reaction in Italy to the news of the intended withdrawal was instantaneous. Cavallero flew over from Rome with Kesselring, and, the latter says in his memoirs, 'we met in conference at Berta on 17 December 1941. Feathers flew. . . .' At this conference (which in fact opened on the 16th) Cavallero reversed arguments which Rommel had used in the past when attack and not retreat was his purpose. As the *Official History* puts it, Cavallero pointed out 'that events outside the Mediterranean' (he was no doubt thinking of the Far East) 'might influence the campaign and that the one object should therefore be to gain time'. The first stage of the meeting ended with an apparent acceptance by Cavallero of the plan to withdraw from Gazala to Mechili and Tmimi, but air reports of advances by British columns made Rommel decide that he must pull back even further, and without delay. Cavallero was horrified.

'At 2300', Rommel noted in his diary, 'he appeared at my H.Q. again, this time accompanied by Field-Marshal Kesselring, Excellency Bastico and General Gambarra. In a voice charged with emotion, he demanded that the order for the retreat should be withdrawn. He did not see the necessity for it, and in any case feared political difficulties for the Duce if Cyrenaica were lost. Kesselring backed him up strongly and said that it was completely out of the question for him to give up the airfield at Derna. I stood my ground and said that it was too late to alter my decision. The orders had been issued and were in some cases already being executed. Unless the Panzer Group wanted to face complete destruction, it had no choice but to fight its way back through the enemy during the night. I fully realised that this would mean the eventual loss of Cyrenaica and that political difficulties might result. But the choice I was faced with was either to stay where I was and thus sacrifice the Panzer Group to destruction—thereby losing both Cyrenaica and Tripolitania—or to begin the retreat that night, fight my way back through Cyrenaica to the Agedabia area and at least defend Tripolitania. I could only choose the latter. Excellency Bastico and Gambarra behaved so violently in my room that evening that I was finally obliged to ask Bastico how he, as Commander-in-Chief of the North African forces, proposed to handle the situation. Bastico evaded the question, and said that as Commander-in-Chief it was not his business; he could only say that we ought to keep our forces together. Finally, the delegation left my H.Q. having accomplished nothing.'

The logic of the situation was more compulsive than the Italians' emotions. During the evening of 16 December the Afrika Korps and the Italian Mobile Corps, with Crüwell in overall command, started to skirt round the southern edge of the Cyrenaican *massif* while the Italian infantry divisions began their trudge along the coastal lowlands in the north. 'If General Rommel had weakened on this decision', the *Official History* concludes, 'there is little doubt that the Axis forces would have been destroyed and the whole course of the war in the desert changed. He deserves great credit for seeing the issue clearly and for refusing to be shaken from his decision.'

It enabled his army to withdraw, by 22 December, to Beda Fomm and Antelat without suffering the casualties which a less rapid retirement would have produced, for the speed of his retreat surprised the British, and threw them off balance. Ritchie had calculated that things would move more slowly, and the gradual organisation of his pursuit columns was out of date by the time it was effected. 8 Army (and its tanks and transport) was now so weary that its desire to pursue was less powerful than the Axis desire for self-preservation. There were muddles of orders and organisation—too many dissipated and fragmentary units, too many changes of plan, too many problems of supply—and the consequence was that O'Connor's thrust to Beda Fomm was not repeated, while Rommel was already beginning to benefit from the swing of the pendulum. He was now reasonably close to his supply ports, and 8 Army was once again dangling at the end of a long line of communications. The arrival on 19 December of 22 tanks at Benghazi and 23 at Tripoli was an omen: it did not matter that the *Carlo del Greco* with 23 tanks and the *Fabio Filzi* with 22 had both been sunk on the 13th, for events would prove that the logistic balance had at last moved in Rommel's favour. On 25 December he wrote to his wife:

> I opened my Christmas parcel in my caravan yesterday evening and was very pleased with the letters from you and Manfred and the presents. Some of it, like

the bottle of champagne, I took straight across to the Intelligence truck where I sat over it with the Chief, the Ia and the Ic. The night passed quietly. But the Italian divisions give us a lot of worry. There are shocking signs of disintegration and German troops are being forced to the rescue everywhere. . . .

He also wrote that 'I hope we now succeed in making a stand'. His hope was justified by the knowledge not only that his forces were now safely assembled at Agedabia but also that, on 23 and 24 December, attempts by 22 Armoured Brigade and 22 Guards Brigade to harass his rear and strike at his southern flank had failed. Their failure was emphasised on 28 December, when Crüwell exploited the separation of the two brigades and won a significant local victory. Sixty tanks of the Afrika Korps forced 90 tanks of 22 Armoured Brigade to retreat, with the loss of 37 as against seven German casualties.

Crusader now guttered out. In another armoured action on the 30th the result was similar—23 British tanks: seven German. For the rest it was a matter of patrols and skirmishes, while the steady rain falling on the dunes and marshes impeded attack. Throughout 6 January there was a sand-storm, and behind its screen Rommel managed to pull out the rearguards which had been covering his final retreat to Agheila.

10 January 1942

Dearest Lu,

Operations going as planned so far. Our mines and *Luftwaffe* are making things difficult for the enemy pursuit. To think that we've got our forces back 300 miles to a good line, without suffering serious harm, and in spite of the fact that the bulk of it is non-motorised! That our 'unemployed' generals are grousing all the time doesn't surprise me. Criticism doesn't cost much.

The Afrika Korps goes into the second line today, for the first time since 18 November. Crüwell's got a very bad dose of jaundice and it's doubtful if he'll stick it out. I'll soon be the only one of the German officers who's seen the whole thing through from start to finish. . . .

Another letter to his wife, on 17 January, conveyed a hint. 'The situation is developing to our advantage and I'm full of plans that I daren't say anything about round here. They'd think me crazy. But I'm not; I simply see a bit farther than they do. But you know me. I work out my plans early each morning, and how often, during the past year and in France, have they been put into effect within a few hours? That's how it should be and is going to be, in future.'

This was a prelude to a continuous series of victories which would carry Rommel over the whole of the ground he had just surrendered and far beyond it, to El Alamein, the gate to the Middle East.

VII

Benghazi and Beyond

1942

'On 21 January', Auchinleck reported in his despatch, 'the improbable occurred, and without warning the Axis forces began to advance.' The tactical details of this triumphant improbability can best be understood against the broader background of developments and assumptions and hopes which made the improbable possible.

In spite of the many consequences of Japan's attack on Pearl Harbor—7 December 1941—the British, from the Prime Minister downwards, were still optimistic about what could be achieved in Africa, and their mood was still aggressive. It was stimulated by the relative casualty figures for *Crusader*. Apart from his losses during the retreat to Agheila, Rommel had been forced to abandon his troops on the frontier. The last of these was captured on 17 January, and the total German–Italian deficit now stood at 38,300 (killed, wounded and missing)—of whom 13,800 had been captured on the frontier—while the equivalent British figure was 17,700. Three hundred aircraft had been lost by the British, and substantially more by the Axis. For tanks as for aircraft the figures are approximate: about 340 were lost by the Axis and certainly many more by the British—the exact difference being blurred by doubt as to how many breakdowns and casualties were ultimately recovered. In Whitehall and Cairo the results of *Crusader* therefore looked encouraging; Rommel had been driven back, and on balance it appeared that 8 Army had not paid too great a price for its victory—according to the statistics. The current mood of the British has been summarised by Sir Francis Tuker, commander of 4 Indian Division: 'Many a great captain has said that it is not so hard to win a battle but it is the mark of an accomplished commander to exploit one. We now had to exploit.'

As it happened, an exploitation westwards of 8 Army's local success in *Crusader* would fit into the larger strategical concepts which were being evolved by the Anglo-American High Command. Shortly after the Japanese attack Churchill visited Washington, and the Chiefs of Staff of the two countries reached rapid agreement about their first priority—the defeat of Germany. To this end, planning for an American landing in North Africa (*Super Gymnast*, a variant on *Gymnast*, the code word for a possible British landing in Tunisia) was started with a target date of May 1942. Into this plan the British project *Acrobat*—an advance through Tripolitania—would dovetail. *Acrobat* had already been studied as a possibility by Auchinleck before *Crusader* began: it now became his objective. 'I am convinced that we should press forward with *Acrobat* for many reasons', he wrote to Churchill on 12 January, and though Alanbrooke, the new C.I.G.S., had reservations he nevertheless signalled to Auchinleck about the project on 21 January, the very day that Rommel's new offensive was launched, 'I attach the greatest importance to it and all it entails.' But at this date *Acrobat* was impossible. The British, as will be seen, lacked the necessary strength and facilities. The preoccupation of Auchinleck and Ritchie with Tripolitania meant, however, that when Rommel struck he caught them mentally off balance—a vital advantage.

The first reason for the present weakness of the British in the Middle East was the sudden and unexpected collapse of their naval power in the Eastern Mediterranean. Whereas during the pre-*Crusader* period the Navy and the R.A.F. dominated the convoy routes, by the beginning of 1942 both were impotent. Everything seemed to happen at once. More German submarines had arrived, and *Fliegerkorps II*, following Hitler's plan, had been transferred to Sicily and under Kesselring started on an attempt to abolish Malta which would continue for months. On 13 November the carrier *Ark Royal*, on 25 November the battleship *Barham*, and on 14 December the cruiser *Galatea* were torpedoed and sunk. On 19 December the cruiser *Neptune* and the destroyer *Kandahar* were sunk and the cruiser *Aurora* seriously damaged in a minefield off Tripoli, and on the same day Italian frogmen in the harbour of Alexandria so damaged the battleships *Queen Elizabeth* and *Valiant* that they were temporarily useless. Meanwhile, on 10 December the *Prince of Wales* and the *Repulse* had been sunk by the Japanese off Malaya. Thus in one month the certainty was established that Rommel would be substantially and regularly reinforced, while the British would be unable to maintain from the sea an advance to Tripolitania.

The second reason was Japan. Although the principle was laid down in Whitehall, after the first shock of Pearl Harbor, that no units or equipment should be withdrawn from the Middle to strengthen the Far East, it could not be maintained by a Britain under-equipped for global war. Indents on Auchinleck soon began to flow. Apart from the diversion of 18 Infantry Division and artillery and R.A.F. units which were already in transit, 17 Indian Division (still in India but ear-marked for Iraq) was now withheld; anti-aircraft regiments started to go; six bomber squadrons and a Blenheim squadron were put under orders; a consignment of Hurricanes was whipped away; 7 Armoured Brigade with 110 Stuart tanks was generously offered by Auchinleck in response to a 'hard request' by Churchill; finally—and inevitably—he lost 6 and 7 Australian Divisions and nearly lost 9 Australian and 2 New Zealand. Some of these transfers were immediate, some were phased; but their significance was twofold. Auchinleck's strength was reduced, and in the foreseeable future he could have no confidence that the Middle East would continue to keep its customary priority in the allocation of troops and equipment. He was now a commander whose sea-power and supplies had been drastically curtailed: and 'on January 21 the improbable occurred'.

The part played by luck in a commander's career is difficult to assess, but no realist would disregard it. In the Second World War, for example, Montgomery was certainly lucky to arrive in Egypt at a time when the Allies were just beginning to obtain an overwhelming superiority in *matériel*, and Percival was certainly unlucky to arrive at Singapore when defeat was inevitable. For Rommel luck ran both ways. When he first reached Africa in 1941 he was fortunate to be faced by an army enfeebled because of the calls made on it by the Greek campaign; he was, arguably, unlucky when on 7 August 1942 a German fighter killed General Gott, the commander-designate of 8 Army, for it is improbable that the battle-weary Gott would have handled Rommel at El Alamein with the alert professional confidence displayed by Montgomery. In January 1942 luck was on Rommel's side: a combination of circumstances, for many of which he had no responsibility, produced a situation on his own front which allowed him to exercise his special genius. Given luck, the test of a commander is whether he can exploit it: Rommel used his opportunity ruthlessly.

This opportunity was created by British weakness at sea and consummated because of British weakness ashore. It was at sea that Rommel's fortunes first took a turn for the better. 'On 5 January,' according to Bayerlein, 'a convoy of ships carrying 55 tanks and 20 armoured cars, as well as anti-tank guns and supplies of all kinds, landed at Tripoli. This was as good as a victory in battle, and Rommel immediately began to think of taking the offensive again.' (Here, incidentally, is an example of an anomaly which can often be observed in the history of the desert war. A shipment of tanks arrives for the Germans—they are soon in action, and the German spirit revives. A convoy of tanks reaches the British—and soon signals pass between Cairo and Whitehall explaining why modifications are necessary, crews must be trained, and reinforcements which look so formidable in London cannot be hurled straight from the docks into battle. Why did this happen? Though the truth is complicated, there were two main reasons. By 1939 the Germans had settled on a basic tank design and their panzers in the desert were progressively advanced members of a single family*; whereas 8 Army's tanks—Matildas, Valentines, Crusaders, Stuarts—lacked a common parentage. Transit from dock to battle-field therefore took longer for these individual types, because each required, in relation to its German counterpart, a higher degree of specialised attention. The British also had the habit of reinforcing unit by unit, whereas the Germans tended to reinforce existing and experienced units by drafts. Thus Rommel always had a core of battle-hardened troops and tested equipment in his front line, while the British often exposed complete squadrons and regiments of raw troops and unreliable tanks to the searching test of action.)

The British weakness at Agheila was first diagnosed not by Rommel, but by his staff. In a conference at the *Panzergruppe* H.Q., on 12 January, von Mellenthin estimated that during the next fortnight Rommel would have superiority, but thereafter his opponents would gain in relative strength. These calculations were based on intelligence provided by the Wireless Interception Service, and supported by the eye-witness of Westphal who, flying over the enemy front, observed their vulnerable dispersion. Rommel was not immediately convinced, but when he had been won over he committed himself completely. On 21 January, the day he prescribed for the attack, he wrote to his wife 'the Army launches its counter-attack in two hours' time. After carefully weighing the pros and cons, I've decided to take the risk. I have complete faith that God is keeping a protective hand over us and that He will grant us victory.' But though he hinted to his wife, he had followed Wavell's policy in 1940 and revealed little to his superiors. On that same day he noted in his diary: 'I had maintained secrecy over the Panzer Group's forthcoming attack eastwards from Mersa el Brega and informed neither the Italian nor the German High Command. We knew from experience that Italian Headquarters cannot keep things to themselves and that everything they wireless to Rome gets round to British ears. However, I had arranged with the Quartermaster for the Panzer Group's order to be posted up in every *Cantoniera*' (Road Maintenance Depot) 'in Tripolitania on 21 January. . . .

---

* Illustrations 15–18 demonstrate this.

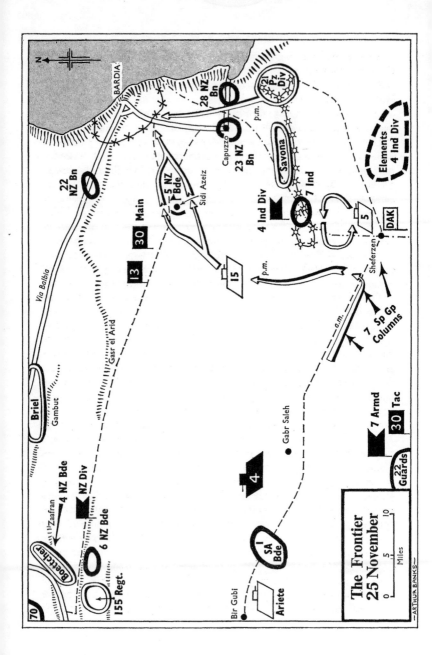

The Frontier 25 November

Excellency Bastico in Rome learnt of our intention through this, of course, and was furious that he had not been told before. He reported to this effect to Rome, and so I was not surprised when Cavallero turned up in person at Mersa el Brega a few days later.'

This was a bizarre way of maintaining security at the expense of allied solidarity. Kesselring comments, regretfully: 'It is unquestionable that the first condition of a successful surprise is absolute secrecy, and every means to obtain it was certainly justified. But it was equally sure that such behaviour would add to the difficulties of the coalition command.' He covers himself in his memoirs by saying 'the fact that in these discussions I played a conciliatory part does not imply, as I have read since the war, that I was against the operation'. But Rommel, the commander on the spot, had to disregard such diplomatic niceties in a situation where quick action was imperative. Nevertheless, his handling of the Italians in January 1942 illustrates his limitations as the integrator of an allied command. (Though Rommel did once, in a remark to his son Manfred, reveal an intuitive understanding of his allies. 'Certainly they are not good at war. But one must not judge everyone in the world only by his qualities as a soldier: otherwise we should have no civilisation.')

Rommel had been right to accept and act upon his staff's appreciation of the British defences. These can be summarised as a lamentable repetition of the faults in the disposition of their forward line which, a year ago, led to a lightning defeat. They can only be explained by preoccupation with *Acrobat*; by Auchinleck's conviction that Rommel lacked the power for an immediate riposte; by the unsophisticated optimism of Ritchie; and by a consequent feeling that the Germans could be bluffed with shadow forces. For the British front line was indeed no more than a shadow. 7 Armoured Division had been withdrawn to rest and refit. 1 Armoured Division, the replacement, was short of 22 Armoured Brigade (exhausted in *Crusader*): its training period in England had been dogged by misfortune and since its arrival in Egypt, during November 1941, it had had virtually no opportunity to become desertworthy. Lumsden, its commander, had been wounded and followed by a stranger to the division, Messervy. When Rommel attacked on the 21st 'the only troops within a hundred miles of the enemy', as the *Official History* states, 'were those of the incomplete 1 Armoured Division, the 22 (now renumbered 200) Guards Brigade, and part of Oasis Force, which was being broken up'. Moreover these weak units were widely dispersed, were suffering from the effect on their transport of the rough terrain, and were uncertain about their maintenance. This was because the capture of Benghazi had not meant the capture of a viable port. Its harbour was shattered, the *Luftwaffe* was mining its waters, winds were blowing fiercely from the worst quarter, there were wrecks below the surface and few tugs afloat. The maintenance of 8 Army's forward units therefore depended on wheeled transport moving over extended lines of communication, and daily replenishment was hardly enough to meet daily needs—still less to start stock-piling. The back-stop of 1 Armoured was 4 Indian: but, again because of administrative difficulties, the division's three brigades were scattered eastwards—one at Benghazi, one ıt Barce, and one at Tobruk. In view of the lessons of the spring of 1941 ıhese arrangements were optimistic, and Rommel took full advantage of them.

His devices to achieve surprise were as effective as those of the British which preceded *Crusader*. 'The regrouping of our forces', according to von Mellenthin, 'was carried out in short night marches; all reconnaissance—particularly by tanks—was forbidden and tanks behind the front were camouflaged as lorries. Movements of motor vehicles towards the front were forbidden in daylight.' The secret was withheld not only from the Italians and the German High Command but also from the Afrika Korps' commander: he was kept in ignorance until the 16th, and briefing of divisional commanders did not occur until the 19th. On the night of the 20th Mersa Brega village and a stranded ship in the harbour were set alight to suggest the burning of dumps before a withdrawal. These security devices were aided by the local inadequacy of the R.A.F. Sand-storms covered the deployment of the Afrika Korps, and heavy rain put the airfield at Antelat out of action, so that early on 21 January four fighter squadrons flew back to Msus, and one to Gazala, just when their presence was required over the front line. After the battle, on 4 February, Rommel wrote to his wife that 'it went like greased lightning'. Most of the preliminaries had turned in his favour, and it is a measure of his robust and resilient character that in spite of defeat and retreat he was now to exploit his advantage with such speed and assurance.

Two columns started the attack on the 21st. One, made up from elements of 90 Light and 21 Panzer, moved down the coastal road, the Via Balbia. In the normal German fashion it was given an *ad hoc* title, Group Marcks. The second column, consisting of the bulk of the Afrika Korps, advanced inland over the desert to the north of Wadi el Faregh. The surprise they achieved was not rewarded on this first day by spectacular results, for the bad going prevented the Germans from reaching forward more than some 12 miles. But the effect on 8 Army was disproportionate. Retreat began immediately. Stuka attacks disconcerted the inexperienced Support Group of 1 Armoured, and the bad going which hampered the Germans in their advance hampered still more the British in their retirement. Sixteen field guns and many transport vehicles were thus abandoned during the day.

In this battle Rommel found himself again. During *Crusader* he was un-certain—sometimes competent and confident, sometimes incompetent and indecisive. But now he functioned with the clarity and drive he had displayed a year ago. On the evening of the 21st, realising that the British were already surprised and shaken, he put himself at the head of Group Marcks, deter-mined to move on Agedabia before the British could recover from their shock. By 1100 hours on the 22nd he had arrived and was issuing orders to Crüwell for the next stage. These envisaged an encirclement of the British. A machine-gun battalion was to move on Antelat, the Group Marcks on Saunnu, and the main Afrika Korps with the Italian mobile troops would fill the gap between Agedabia and the Group Marcks. As the cordon closed, the various Axis units would turn to the south-east and together force the trapped British away from their communications.

'It was an ambitious plan', says von Mellenthin, 'and was only partially successful. Owing to a serious lapse in staff work at Afrika Korps Head-quarters, Saunnu was not occupied by 21 Panzer after the departure of Group Marcks, and the enemy took advantage of this gap to extricate the bulk of 1 Armoured Division.' But von Mellenthin misses the point. Rommel's operations on the 21st and 22nd, though they had not captured much ground, conquered his enemy's mind—in two ways. On the one hand the troops who had taken the shock of his advance surrendered their positions and started to surrender their morale: on the other Ritchie, who arrived back at the front from Cairo on the afternoon of the 23rd, completely misinter-preted the situation. He thought that he was dealing with a 'reconnaissance in force'; that the German armour was still to the west of Agedabia; and that there would soon be 'a God-sent opportunity to hit him really hard when he puts out his neck as it seems possible that he may be already doing'.

This was not the picture in the front line. 'The basic idea of each side on 23 January was simple enough: the British wanted to draw back 1 Armoured Division and the enemy wanted to catch as much as possible of it in their net. The result was a number of separate encounters during the day, spread over a wide area.' Thus the *Official History*: 'but on the 23rd Rommel had other preoccupations'. The day before, his command had been re-entitled *Panzerarmee*: he had now, with his new status, to deal with Cavallero, who arrived on the 23rd to complain again about Rommel's disregard for protocol and to protest about the way his operations were launched without consulta-tion or permission from his titular superiors. Rommel's diary for the 23rd records: 'General Cavallero brought directives from the Duce for future operations. Everything indicates that Rome is anything but pleased with the Panzer Army's counter-attack, and would like to put a stop to it as soon as possible by issuing orders. During the discussion Cavallero said: "Make it no more than a sortie and then come straight back." I was not standing for this and told him that I had made up my mind to keep at the enemy just as long as my troops and supplies would allow; the Panzer Army was getting under way and its first blows had struck home. We were first going to drive south and destroy the enemy south of Agedabia; then we would move east and later north-east. I could always fall back to the Mersa Brega line if things went wrong, but that was not what I was after; my aims were set much higher. Cavallero implored me not to go on with it. I told him that nobody but the Führer could change my decision, as it would be mainly German troops who would be engaged. Finally, after Kesselring had made some attempt to back him up, he went off growling.'

Kesselring's recollections of the 23rd illustrate the tensions which Rommel and he had to endure in their military relationship with the unmilitary Italians. 'I myself flew Cavallero to the conference on the 23rd in my *Storch*, as this was the only aircraft on the tarmac and Cavallero insisted on my accompanying him. The meeting was longer than expected, so that we had to take off on the return flight when the sun was already setting to land in the dark at El Agheila. So a German Field-Marshal flew the senior *Maresciallo d'Italia* over the desert in an aircraft unsuitable for night flying and safely delivered his very suspicious passenger into the arms of his numerous generals. The *abbraci* (embracings) and *bacci* (kisses) that followed our landing are no flight of my creative imagination.'

The fighting on the 23rd was confused and indeterminate, and on the 24th Rommel read the battle incorrectly. Possibly because of the distracting influence of Cavallero he failed to realise how the British had managed to extricate themselves from his cordon: as von Mellenthin says, 'much time was wasted in sweeping an empty battlefield'. Once again, however, the effect on his opponents had been greater than Rommel appreciated: for a study of this operation is ultimately a study of decline in British morale. Though his troops had disengaged on the 23rd, Godwin-Austen signalled to Ritchie early on the 24th that he could no longer resist an enemy whose strength had so far been little damaged, and advocated a general retirement to Mechili. Ritchie replied by recommending persistence in the defence of Benghazi, but allowed Godwin-Austen discretion as to a withdrawal.

This involved precautionary arrangements for the evacuation of the port, and the local naval liaison officer naturally reported to his own Commander-in-Chief. A copy of his signal reached first the Admiralty and then Churchill, whose infuriated response, 'Why should not the 4 (British) Indian Division hold out at Benghazi, like the Huns at Halfaya?', caused Auchinleck to rush

forward to 8 Army's H.Q. Thus once again a sequence of events and combination of personalities—Churchill's rage; Auchinleck's intrusion; Ritchie's
optimism; confused policies within 8 Army—united to provide both a perfect
setting for the kind of armoured stab which Rommel could organise with
absolute mastery, and a perfect contrast with the political and military
pressures, aimed at keeping him on a leash, with which he had constantly to
contend.

On the 25th Rommel was off the leash. The Afrika Korps moved north in
unison against 1 Armoured. 15 Panzer's diary noted that its tanks 'broke into
the enemy at a tearing speed and threw him into complete confusion'.
Though Crüwell halted at Msus, the British armour kept on withdrawing
and Godwin-Austen accepted defeat by ordering 4 Indian to pull out of
Benghazi and Messervy to move to Mechili. Auchinleck and Ritchie, however, intervened. Interpreting Rommel's moves as yet another 'reconnaissance in force', they cancelled the instructions for 13 Corps' withdrawal.
Ritchie's orders stated that 'the most offensive action is to be taken together
with the greatest risks'.

By these orders he had himself taken the greatest risks. They and Godwin-
Austen's protests had been exchanged over the wireless, and Rommel was
listening. He now decided on another unorthodox thrust. To exploit the
British indecision 90 Light would push along the coast road and the Italians
up through Soluch, while Rommel himself, with the Group Marcks and 3
and 33 Reconnaissance Units, would do the unpredictable by attacking Benghazi through the hard going of the hills and valleys to the south-east of the
port. This surprise was to occur on the 28th, and was to be aided by a feint towards Mechili by the Afrika Korps. It would be a genuine surprise, because
Ritchie's counter-moves had been planned to begin on the 29th.

The feint succeeded. While Rommel's other pre-dispositions were concealed from the air by bad weather, the fake move on Mechili was spotted
and interpreted by Ritchie as Rommel's spearhead. 1 Armoured was therefore ordered to attack the rear of this hypothetical force, while 4 Indian was
directed on the troops advancing athwart the coastal road, towards Benghazi.
Ritchie's appreciation of his army's state at this moment indicates how Rommel had misled him: 'the enemy has divided his forces and is weaker than we
are in both areas. The key word is offensive action everywhere.'

This, as Ritchie might have put it, was whistling to keep one's courage up;
for in fact 4 Indian, increasingly aware of the developing pressure on Benghazi, awaited from minute to minute an armoured relief from the south.
'When would 1 Armoured's move start to be felt?', Tuker asks in his memoirs. 'We rang Army—and learnt to our consternation that the whole of the

eastern flank had gone off on a wild goose chase after a phantom force of enemy armour falsely reported to be moving on Mechili. Dispersion, dispersion, and dispersion.' Tuker reported that Benghazi was indefensible without armoured support: Ritchie, unable to provide it, permitted him to evacuate. The bait had been swallowed: and in the meantime the out-flanking attack on Benghazi by Group Marcks was almost complete. Rommel was up at the front with them. In spite of the rugged terrain, the darkness and down-pours, they reached blocking positions to the south-east of Benghazi by the evening of the 28th. The retreating Indians were soon caught in their net. Though many of the division escaped, Tuker was now recommending a further withdrawal, while Messervy on 30 January reported that 1 Armoured could not meet more than 25 German medium tanks with a hope of defeating them. In the midst of this confusion and pessimism Rommel, at 1000 hours on the 29th, entered Benghazi.

The whole operation was characteristic of the qualities which he so often displayed in 1914-18, in France in 1940, and regularly in Africa—rapid appreciation of a tactical possibility, rapid organisation of his troops to exploit it, and personal leadership at the critical point. The pattern is recurrent. In this case it meant that the British had again to surrender the whole of western Cyrenaica and withdraw to positions south of Gazala; that Godwin-Austen asked to be relieved of his command (and was relieved) because he rightly felt that his appreciation of what was happening, overruled by Ritchie, was correct; and that Rommel was promoted to Colonel-General. On the day that he entered Benghazi he received a signal from Mussolini permitting him to do so! But Rommel translated this signal in the broadest sense. His success seemed to him, inevitably, to open up wider prospects. Mussolini (and Bastico) considered that the area south-west of Benghazi must now be considered as the point of consolidation for the Axis: Rommel wished to push further to the east—in spite of his shortage of fuel. The result was a compromise: in the circumstances, a realistic one. The defeated British were at Gazala: Rommel placed a thin skein of mobile troops in front of them, and held the main force of the *Panzerarmee* well back in the Jebel, and westwards around Antelat and Mersa Brega.

'This', says Bayerlein, 'concluded the winter fighting. Both sides now prepared for the approaching decisive battle of the summer.'

VIII

Gazala

The policy which the Axis should pursue in the Mediterranean and North Africa during the spring and summer of 1942 was constantly debated but never wholly resolved. For the German High Command Russia was still a magnet more powerfully attractive than the African provinces could be for Italy. In March Rommel flew to O.K.H. to discuss plans for the future, but he found Halder and his colleagues too engrossed in preparations for the summer offensive in Russia to be able to bend their minds to a 'colonial war'. At the end of April Mussolini, Cavallero and Kesselring also visited Hitler at Obersalzberg: the theme was the same—what to do, or what not to do, in Africa?

In his *Papers* (which from the spring of 1942 are again a translation of his own records) Rommel is bitter about the result of these discussions. 'The German High Command, to which I was subordinate, still failed to see the importance of the African theatre. They did not realise that with relatively small means we could have won victories in the Near East which, in their strategic and economic value, would have far surpassed the conquest of the Don Bend. Ahead of us lay territories containing an enormous wealth of raw materials; Africa, for example, and the Middle East—which could have freed us from all our anxieties about oil. . . . It was obvious that the High Command's opinion had not changed from that which they had expressed in 1941, namely, that Africa was a "lost cause".'

Within the emotional exaggeration is concealed a truth. A partial truth, for the passage of time had in fact moved Hitler closer to acceptance of a forward policy on Rommel's front. But the key question, during this spring, was not what should be done in Africa but how to tackle Malta. Rommel fully understood the island's value. 'The heavy Axis air raids against Malta, in particular, were instrumental in practically neutralising for a time the threat to our sea routes. It was this fact which made possible an increased flow of material to Tripoli, Benghazi and Derna—the reinforcement and refitting of the German-Italian forces thereupon proceeded with all speed.' Nevertheless, he gradually changed his mind and ended—as did Hitler—by believing that an advance into Egypt would be more important than a conquest of the island. Earlier he had wished to have 'this pleasant task entrusted to my own army', but von Mellenthin observes that 'he was anxious for the High Command to take Malta, but if this could not be done before June he preferred to launch his attack on the Gazala line without waiting for Malta to fall'. From this choice of priorities the end of the war in Africa partly derives. During the next few months Rommel would indeed drive 8 Army back to a point where retreat could no longer be accepted, but in so doing he would expose his supply line nakedly; his army in its turn would be left without energy to resist, and would be compelled to withdraw. 'This decision', Kesselring bitterly comments, 'sealed the fate of North Africa.'

The result of the Obersalzberg meeting in April was a directive endorsed by both Hitler and Mussolini which permitted Rommel to start another attack—with the reservation that after capturing Tobruk he was to revert to the defensive, while the main Axis effort was diverted to Malta. Kesselring had worked out comprehensive plans. Two parachute divisions were to be used, under the competent General Student who had been responsible for the conquest of Crete. The airfields south of Valetta were to be bombed, anti-aircraft positions and coastal batteries neutralised, and then the airborne forces were to fly in—a diversion was to be mounted simultaneously from the sea. But this was only a plan on paper for an invasion which never occurred. During the spring of 1942 the decisive fact was that while the Axis—and Rommel in particular—could not make up their minds about Malta, Churchill saw the defence and relief of the island as the main Mediterranean concern . . . a preoccupation which led the Desert Army into disaster.

This was because Auchinleck was under constant compulsion from Churchill (which in the end wore him down) to advance in Malta's aid long before, in his professional judgement, his army was ready. (The prolonged exchange of signals between them is set out in Chapter 17 of John Connell's biography of Auchinleck.) It reached its peak at the beginning of March, when Alan Brooke noted in his diary, on the evening of the 2nd, 'another bad Monday . . . found P.M. had drafted a bad wire for Auchinleck in which he poured abuse on him for not attacking sooner'. This draft was tactfully rephrased, but it still concluded 'we consider that an attempt to drive the

Germans out of Cyrenaica in the next few weeks is not only imperative for the safety of Malta on which so much depends, but holds out the only hope of fighting a battle while the enemy is still comparatively weak and short of resources of all kinds'.

For the encounters which ended with the fall of Tobruk these exchanges of view between the opposing commanders and their respective political superiors had great significance. Rommel, irritated and frustrated though he might be in regard to his larger strategical aims, was nevertheless not essentially distracted from his main tactical purpose, the capture of the port. Auchinleck, however, defeated in his dialogue with Churchill, found that all his efforts to win time for reinforcement and training of 8 Army culminated in

Prime Minister to General Auchinleck   *8 May 1942*

The Chiefs of Staff, the Defence Committee, and the War Cabinet have all earnestly considered your telegram in relation to the whole war situation, having particular regard to Malta, the loss of which would be a disaster of the first magnitude to the British Empire, and probably fatal in the long run to the defence of the Nile Valley.

2. We are agreed that in spite of the risks you mention you would be right to attack the enemy and fight a major battle, if possible during May, and the sooner the better. We are prepared to take full responsibility for these general directions, leaving you the necessary latitude for their execution. In this you will no doubt have regard to the fact that the enemy may himself be planning to attack you early June.

The effect of this *Diktat* and the preceding debate was that, because 8 Army's dispositions along the Gazala Line were made on the assumption that the British would attack before the Afrika Korps, they proved an unsatisfactory system of defence when Rommel and not Auchinleck moved first: unsatisfactory because, in the first place, 8 Army built up immense forward dumps of supplies. Ten thousand tons of stores were to be accumulated at Tobruk, 26,000 at Belhamed, and 1000 at Jarabub. When Rommel advanced, awareness of these huge stock-piles hampered 8 Army's freedom of manœuvre. They had to be protected . . . but in a mobile battle the need to protect fixed and vulnerable points can be fatal. Most of them had been filled when the battle began—at Belhamed alone there were one and a half million gallons of fuel—and the effect of a supreme effort by Auchinleck's base areas to feed his forward units was that the abundant supplies they received for their assault proved to be a reason for defeat when they themselves were assaulted.

The dead weight of the dumps, however, was less important than the tactical deficiencies of what was called the Gazala Line. Ritchie, on 16 May, declared his aggressive intention to be 'to destroy the enemy's armoured

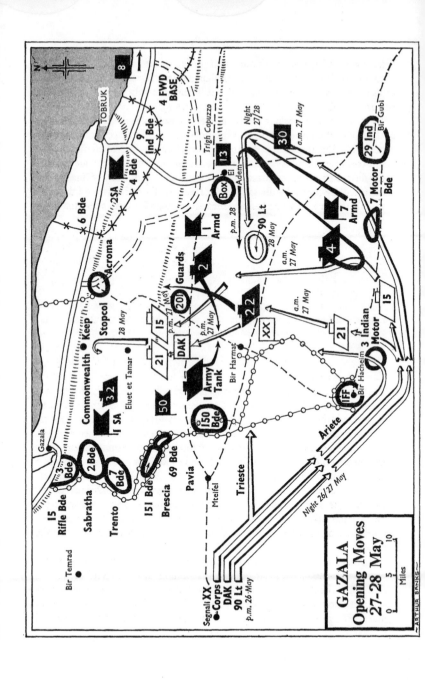

GAZALA
Opening Moves
27-28 May

Miles
0   5   10

~ARTHUR BANKS~

N

TOBRUK

8

4 FWD BASE

Trigh Capuzzo

9 Ind Bde

Ind Bde

2SA

4 Bde

6 Bde

Gazala

15 Rifle Bde

3 Bde

Sabratha

2 Bde

Trento

7 Bde

151 Bde

69 Bde

Brescia

Pavia

Mteifel

Commonwealth Keep

Acroma

Stopcol

Eluet et Tamar

1 SA

32

50

1 Army Tank

150 Bde

Bir Temrad

Guards

201

15

21

DAK

Bir Harmat

XX

1 Army Tank

1 Motor

IFF

Bir Hacheim

3 Indian Motor

Ariete

Trieste

Night 26/27 May

Segnali XX
Corps
DAK
90 Lt
p.m. 26 May

p.m. 27 May

p.m. 27 May

28 May

28 May

1 Armd

2

2 2

Box El Adem

90 Lt
p.m. 28

a.m. 27 May

28 May

a.m. 27 May

7 Armd

4

15

21

a.m. 27 May

Night 27/28

30

7 Motor Bde

29 Ind
Bir Gubi

a.m. 27 May

forces in the battle of the Gazala-Tobruk-Bir Hacheim position as the initial step in securing Cyrenaica': but as a defensive position, should such prove necessary, the 'Line' was inadequate. Running due south from Gazala, it consisted of a sequence of 'boxes'—infantry localities, wired and mined—with great gaps between them which could be neither blocked by artillery nor effectively plugged by tanks. On the left flank, especially (the most dangerous flank), this was the weakness. Furthest south, in their lonely fortress, lay the Free French at Bir Hacheim. Between them and the next box northwards, that of 150 Brigade, was a gap of some 13 miles. North of 150 Brigade's box stretched another six-mile gap to 69 Brigade. To call this a Line was a mistake: a grave mistake, because such words soon begin to stand for something real.

There were two courses open to Rommel. He could move his armour in a great curve to the south of Bir Hacheim, out-flanking the minefields, and then turn left, driving for Tobruk past the rear of the British defences: or he could attack further north on a narrow front and seek to penetrate the British positions by frontal assault. As it happened, Auchinleck sent to Ritchie on 20 May a long letter assessing the action Rommel would probably take and defining the moves necessary to counter it, and on the same day Rommel issued his orders for the attack. Auchinleck thought that Rommel would try to crack the central minefields and merely feint against Bir Hacheim. He urged Ritchie to keep his tanks *en masse*, astride the Trigh Capuzzo, and emphasised that they should be freed from commitments to the infantry. But Ritchie and his generals felt that *Crusader* had revealed the risks involved by leaving, in the desert, infantry formations unprotected by armour, and thus exposed to piecemeal destruction: moreover, Norrie thought that the main German attack would come in the north while Ritchie believed that a sweep south of Bir Hacheim was more probable. So 1 Armoured was kept behind the centre of the line, west and south-west of El Adem, while 7 Armoured was placed further to the south than Auchinleck had advocated. The divergence of opinion between Auchinleck, Ritchie, and their divisional commanders, which was to be so disastrous a feature of the coming battle, was already taking effect, and bore fruit in a dispersion of armour and elaboration of alternative plans which muddled 8 Army before and during the conflict.

Rommel, on the other hand, issued instructions to his army on the 20th which were simple, clear-cut, and as usual optimistic. He himself intended to move with the Afrika Korps (now under Nehring). His mobile forces, concentrated near Rotonda Segnali, were to advance to the east some 10 to 15 miles and then, after dark on the 26th, turn south-east, with Ariete and

Trieste following. The Italian divisions were to move on a centre-line north of Bir Hacheim while the Afrika Korps overran the French box. In the morning the Afrika Korps was to turn northwards and make for Acroma, while 90 Light, conforming to the east of them, harried El Adem and Belhamed. This whole flanking effort was to be aided by a diversion in the north, which was intended to suggest (as Norrie had anticipated) that the main thrust was coming between the sea and the Trigh Capuzzo. For this feint Crüwell, due back from leave on the 25th, was given overall command of 10 and 21 Italian Infantry Corps, some German infantry regiments, and most of the Axis artillery. Rommel's appreciation was that within four days he would have captured Tobruk (he thought that Bir Hacheim would be taken in an hour!) and the administrative support for his mobile wing was calculated on this basis.

But though Rommel's plan was bold and simple, it was marred by misapprehensions. The first was that the 'Gazala Line' was a defensive system efficiently designed. 'The entire line', he says in his *Papers*, 'was remarkable for the extraordinary degree of technical skill which had gone into its construction.' Arguing from this premiss, he concluded that the British had erred in forgetting that a 'Maginot Line' with an open flank is vulnerable—an assumption which led him to thrust through the open desert. Though this was certainly the right manoeuvre, he made it for the wrong reason and with a false picture of his enemy. Secondly, he thought that the British were 'completely motorised' and did not appreciate that the average infantry battalion had to be ferried from point to point by transport provided from a pool. Conscious of his own weakness in this respect—the Italians were particularly immobile—he had an exaggerated impression of his enemy's ability to move. Thirdly, he did not know that 8 Army now had 167 Grant tanks, with their powerful 75-mm. gun, and that 1 Armoured Brigade with 75 more Grants was on the way forward. Nor did he know that the 6-pounder anti-tank gun had now been supplied to his enemy in substantial numbers. Finally, he misread the situation at Bir Hacheim, believing that the minefields ended well to the north of the French, and not appreciating that what the *Official History* calls the 'mine marsh' embraced their box. This failure of intelligence was as important as his misinterpretation of the minefields at Alam Halfa.

Rommel also suffered at this time another defeat in the obscure but critical battle for information. Alan Moorehead notes in *The End in Africa* that the Germans 'leaned heavily on the machine and trusted it. They never tried out the odd exciting things we did—things like the Long Range Desert Group . . . they liked to do things *en masse*.' 8 Army drew on many sources for its irregulars, and it was certainly a non-member (in spirit) of the United

Kingdom, 'Popski' or Colonel Peniakoff, who founded his Private Army to do 'odd exciting things'. In principle, however, Moorehead's comment is accurate. But Rommel had his own 'Popski'—a strange Hungarian called Ladislaus Edouard de Almasy. 'He first appeared in the Libyan Desert', says Kennedy Shaw in his *Long Range Desert Group*, 'in 1929 accompanying the Prince of Lichtenstein on a journey from East Africa to Egypt by car. From then until the outbreak of the Nazi war Almasy was often travelling in Libya, usually at somebody else's expense. He had a real passion for the desert and much of it he knew extremely well.' Kennedy Shaw adds: 'I think all governments interested in the Libyan Desert—British, Egyptian, Italian—wondered if Almasy was a spy working for the other side.'

In the spring of 1942 it became clear that a *Sonderkommando Almasy* was operating in the bad lands of the Qattara Depression. The detection of its purpose is a curious story. Stuart Hood, an intelligence officer at G.H.Q. Cairo, had the task of keeping a card-index of the officers in the *Panzerarmee*. One day he was ordered to find out all he could about a man called Almasy. He knew Almasy had been around in Cairo and in the desert before 1939—had, indeed, been a member of the Turf Club. Hood talked to various people and then went to the library of Cairo University, found a book by Almasy, and hit on the answer. Almasy's pre-1939 ventures in the Qattara Depression derived from his reading in Herodotus that large quantities of Greek vases were exported to Egypt annually and that, once there, they disappeared. He worked out the reason: they were being planted by stages as dumps of water along a route which could cross the impassable Depression. Now, in 1942, Hood had a similar intuition. He realised that this was what Almasy himself was attempting with his *kommando*. The R.A.F. was alerted and reconnaissance flights photographed the tracks of his vehicles. But nothing more was heard of Almasy: in any case, the L.R.D.G. had observed his activity and mined his most probable routes. Yet this Hungarian equivalent of a Peniakoff on the British side is worth recording, for apart from his there were few Axis activities comparable with those of the L.R.D.G. Indeed, Rommel was never able to benefit from the kind of eye-witness of 8 Army's activities far behind their front which, from their observation posts on the coastal road, the Long Range Desert Group transmitted continuously to Cairo about Axis reinforcements.

Nevertheless . . .

26 May 1942

Dearest Lu,

By the time you get this letter you will have long ago heard from the Wehrmacht communiqués about events here. We're launching a decisive attack today.

During the first hours of Rommel's offensive both sides found themselves baffled: nothing went according to plan. At the last moment Rommel altered his orders, giving Ariete the task of taking Bir Hacheim instead of the Afrika Korps. (But the new orders never reached Trieste: and their adherence to their unaltered instructions would later have an important effect on the battle.) This change of plan allowed the Afrika Korps to move more freely to the south of Bir Hacheim. Their advance was spotted during the night of the 26–27th, but 7 Armoured and 30 Corps were sluggish in reacting. Consequently, while the British tanks occupied their pre-arranged battle positions in a leisurely fashion, the Germans overran 3 Indian Motor Brigade to the south-east of Bir Hacheim and then disrupted 4 Armoured Brigade, who fell back to El Adem. In the east 90 Light were simultaneously surprising 7 Motor Brigade. Rommel had thus caught off its guard and disintegrated 30 Corps—its left wing, certainly, and its Command, for Norrie and his H.Q. were compelled by 90 Light to withdraw into the El Adem box, and Messervy (who soon escaped) with several of the senior staff of 7 Armoured had been taken prisoner.

But though 22 as well as 4 Armoured Brigade had suffered severely, and though 7 Motor and 9 Indian Brigades as well as 3 Indian had been scattered during the day, at its end Rommel's verdict was: 'It was clear that our plan to overrun the British forces behind the Gazala Line had not succeeded.' Why? 'The principal cause', says Rommel, 'was our underestimate of the strength of the British armoured divisions. The advent of the new American tank had torn great holes in our ranks.' (The new American tank was, of course, the Grant: these, with their 75-mm. gun, as well as the 6-pounder anti-tank gun, were the technical surprises sprung by the British at Gazala.) But on this first evening neither side could claim a superiority based on either a tactical or a technical advantage. Norrie had had to withdraw, and Messervy had been captured; but that night, Rommel records, 'contact had been broken with my staff. Lieut.-Col. Westphal, my I.A., had pushed on with a number of signals lorries to the Afrika Korps, whereas I myself, with the rest of the army staff, was located at night-fall about two miles north-east of Bir El Harmat.' Ariete had failed to take Bir Hacheim, and had lost many tanks; Trieste was still stuck in the minefields; Crüwell's diversion in the north had made no real impression, and on the right of Rommel's line 90 Light was out of touch. 'The 90 Light Division under General Kleeman', Rommel remembered, 'had become separated from the Afrika Korps and was now in a very dangerous position. British motorised groups were streaming through the open gap and hunting down the transport columns which had lost touch with the main body. And on these columns the life of my army depended.'

A plan of action had to be evolved for the next day. Rommel confesses that he had been in a state of 'high tension' at the very beginning of his attack; but it had begun well, as von Mellenthin records. 'The move of this column of several thousand vehicles had been prepared in minute detail; compass bearings, distances and speeds had been carefully calculated; dim lights concealed in petrol tins indicated the line of march, and with the smoothness of a well-oiled machine the regiments of the Afrika Korps swept on to their refuelling point south of Bir Hacheim.' By midday Rommel had been confident. 'At this stage', von Mellenthin noted, 'Rommel thought that the battle was won.' And yet when night fell he found the two Panzer divisions curled up in hedgehog positions between the Rigel Ridge and Bir Lefa, with a third of their tanks out of action and, in 15 Panzer's case, with fuel and ammunition almost exhausted.

Nothing is more disconcerting for a commander than the knowledge that the first phase of his offensive has gone wrong. It is the testing moment when nerve can fail. During these hours of natural uncertainty Rommel was aware that 'our plan to overrun the British forces behind the Gazala line had not succeeded'; but, nevertheless, he stuck to his objective. Indeed he had already taken the measure of Ritchie. 'I looked forward that evening full of hope to what the battle might bring. For Ritchie had thrown his armour into the battle piecemeal and had thus given us the chance of engaging them on each separate occasion with just about enough of our own tanks. This dispersal of the British armoured brigades was incomprehensible.'

So Rommel decided to continue, on the 28th, his drive to the north. It was a daring decision, for his army was now strung out on a thin line between Bir Hacheim (still unconquered) and the escarpment. But this day's actions established the pattern for the whole battle. The British armour continued to attack in 'penny packets'—von Mellenthin noted that 'the operations on the 28th furnished a striking example of the breakdown of command on the British side'. And Trieste, following their original orders, had marched up to the minefields and started to clear a route through them—the practical fact which, exploited by Rommel's inspiration, led directly to the taking of Tobruk.

Sustained supply is essential for armour. Rommel's line now ran round Bir Hacheim and then due north to the escarpment, and it was continuously exposed to flank attacks. He was in fact operating round a right-angled bend, and fuel and ammunition were already running short. His answer was to produce one of those combinations of instant decision and personal leadership which few of his opponents could match. Patton, perhaps, was his peer: Patton ruthlessly swinging his tank divisions, within hours, from a drive east to a drive north when the news of the Ardennes offensive reached him, and once again redeeming by pure professional expertise all that his reputation had lost from many foolish acts. So now Rommel made a quick decision and ordered that the Afrika Korps must concentrate as soon as possible, while he himself, during the night of the 28–29th, led in person some invaluable supply columns (which had rounded Bir Hacheim) up the eastern edge of the mine-fields to the hungry 15 Panzer. He then placed his own H.Q. beside that of the Afrika Korps. He was where he always wanted to be, commanding the battle from a position near to its heart.

This system of instant command did not, however, impress Kesselring. Crüwell's *Storch* had landed behind the British lines early on the 29th, and he was captured, leaving Kesselring to fill the vacuum. 'I then learnt', he acidly observes in his memoirs, 'the difficulties of a commander whose hands are tied by subordination to a headquarters that issues no orders and cannot be reached. Moreover, the stimulating effect of Rommel's presence on the decisive flank was offset by his immediate exposure to all the fluctuations of battle. One must have heard eye-witness accounts to realise what went on among Rommel's staff on the first day of the tank battle.' An understandably subjective picture: but Kesselring had the grace to continue: 'the second day decided it: a glorious one for our panzers and their commander', and to add that when he was able to join Rommel at his headquarters 'it was a joy to watch Rommel's amazingly expert technique in directing a desert command'.

The fierce armoured engagements throughout the 28th, in the area of the Knightsbridge Box, between 2 and 22 Armoured Brigades and the Afrika Korps were indecisive—at the end of the day both sides were exhausted and both had suffered heavy losses—but Rommel had got what he wanted. 'In spite of considerable casualties in the panzer divisions', says von Mellenthin, 'the day ended in our favour, for 90 Light, Ariete, and the Afrika Korps were now in close contact. The British armour had suffered heavily—once again their command had failed to co-ordinate the tank brigades.' The pattern of the Gazala battle is in fact one of progressive failure by the British command to grasp what was happening and a steady imposition of his will by Rommel. The gathering together of his forces on the 29th, though it produced no immediate decision, was the start of a process which would push the British back from Tobruk. This day's actions had consumed more of his precious supplies of fuel and ammunition. But they had not only inspired him to begin to concentrate his scattered forces in the area between the Sidra and Aslagh Ridges—the region which was to be immortalised as *The Cauldron*—they had also misled Auchinleck and Ritchie. 'Quite rightly', says the *Official History*, 'the British commanders were thinking big.' Quite rightly? Auchinleck was

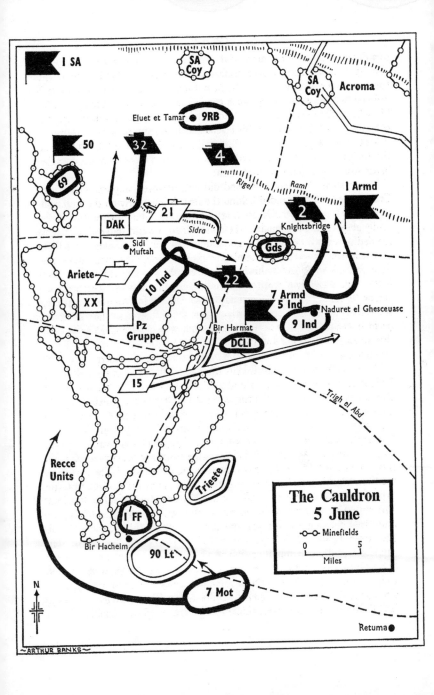

I SA

SA Coy

SA Coy   Acroma

Eluet et Tamar ● 9RB

50   32   4

69   Rigel   Raml   1 Armd

DAK   21   2

Sidra   Knightsbridge

● Sidi Muftah   Gds

Ariete   10 Ind   22

XX   7 Armd
5 Ind

Pz Gruppe   ● Bir Harmat   9 Ind   Naduret el Ghesceuasc

DCLI

15   Trigh el Abd

Recce Units

Trieste

I FF

Bir Hacheim ●   90 Lt

7 Mot

N

Retuma ●

**The Cauldron
5 June**

○—○— Minefields

0   5

Miles

~ARTHUR BANKS~

dreaming of an advance whose forward elements might reach Mechili and Benghazi; Ritchie thought the German armour could still be smashed. But these were day-dreams in the rear. Rommel in the front line had calculated exactly how his opposite numbers, facing him across the wire and the minefields, would behave. His orders on the evening of the 29th were for the completion of a gap through the central minefields, consolidation of a bridgehead round its exit, and then—'I intended to pinch out Bir Hacheim!'

'I made this plan on the certain assumption that, with strong German motorised forces standing south of the coast road, the British would not dare to use any major part of their armoured formations to attack the Italians in the Gazala Line, for a counter-attack by my panzer divisions would have put them between two fires. On the other hand, I hoped that the presence of the Italian infantry in the front of the 1 South African and the 50 British Divisions would continue to persuade the overcautious British command to leave those formations complete in the Gazala line. It seemed to me highly improbable that Ritchie would order these two infantry divisions to attack the Italian infantry corps without support from other formations, for such an operation would not have fulfilled the normal British demand for what they supposed to be 100% certainty. Thus I foresaw that the British mechanised brigades would continue to run their heads against our well-organised defensive front and use up their strength in the process.'

This was exactly what happened. Commenting on this decision in his notes on the *Rommel Papers* Liddell Hart observes that as a result of it Rommel 'was then enabled to profit by the tactical advantages of the defensive—when ably conducted—towards wearing down the British superiority of numbers. It was by his skilful "trapping" defence in the following days that he paved the way for another, and more decisive, stroke.'

The only unit in the area of the minefield gap which might have impeded Rommel, 150 Brigade, was eliminated during the next few days, while attempts by 13 Corps to relieve it were shattered. These were mainly infantry attacks, never assisted properly by the co-ordinated support of the armour. 150 Brigade fought to the end. 'The last sub-unit to go down was believed to be the platoon of the 5 Green Howards commanded by Captain Bert Dennis. Brigadier Haydon, who had commanded the brigade with conspicuous skill and gallantry both in France, and the desert, was killed.' The brigade's destruction was followed by another mismanaged effort to force Rommel out of the *Cauldron* position by infantry attack. During the night of 4 June, 30 Corps was to advance over the Aslagh Ridge while 13 Corps made a diversion in the area of the Sidra Ridge. Tank penetration was to follow. But the whole operation—*Aberdeen*—was a catastrophe. 'If all went

Field-Marshal Rommel, 1944.

Rommel with Hitler in Poland, 1939.

Blitzkrieg: France 1940

7th Panzer Division in the French countryside.

A knocked out German panzer Mk II in a French town.

The 7th Panzer Division crossing the La Bassée Canal on a pontoon bridge, 27 May 1940.

Rommel and his staff on the Libyan Front in North Africa. Von Mellenthin is second on the left.

Personal reconnaissance: Rommel flies to the front. Africa, 1941.

Rommel greeting General Gariboldi, 1941.

'The protagonists on both sides were fully motorised formations, for whose employment the flat and obstruction-free desert offered hitherto undreamed of possibilities.' – The Rommel Papers

German armoured car: 'reconnaissance reports must reach the commander in the shortest possible time.' – The Rommel Papers

Rommel's 'secret weapon': the 88mm gun.

Panzer III with short 50mm. gun

Panzer III with long 50mm. gun

Panzer IV with short and low velocity 75mm gun.

Panzer IV with long and high velocity 75mm gun.

Hitler presenting 'the oak leaves to the Knight's Cross of the Iron Cross' to Rommel.

German supply trucks kicking up the sand.

Frontier barbed wire entanglements.

Kesselring and Rommel.

Rommel before Tobruk.

Rommel's Advance Headquarters near Tobruk, photographed from his Fiesler Storch.

Matilda's outside the perimeter of Tobruk, November 1941.

'The Feldherr of the front line': Rommel (with binoculars) reconnoitres from the top of an Italian M13 tank.

British tank hospital in the Western Desert, December 1941. The patient is a Crusader.

Rommel inspecting uncompleted British defences in the Alamein Line, 1942.

The Western Desert, October 1942: British field artillery and anti-aircraft guns pass a 25 pdr gun position.

'The Western Wall': Rommel on a tour of inspection in the Pas de Calais before D-Day.

France, 1944: Rommel and SS commander Sepp Dietrich.

Rommel with von Rundstedt.

Rommel's own drawings of what he thought D-Day would be like. In a message to his troops 22 May, 1944, Rommel wrote: 'The main defence zone on the coast is strongly fortified and well manned; there are large tactical and operational reserves in our rear area.'

Following the failed bomb plot Hitler shows Mussolini the damaged conference room.

Following Rommel's forced suicide he is buried with 'full military honours'.

After the war veterans of the Afrika Korps set up this memorial to their former highly respected commander.

according to plan', General Carver comments, 'the whole area occupied by D.A.K. and Ariete would in this way be quartered with troops; but the broad arrows of the planners' maps would in fact represent a series of in-experienced battalions, weakly armed with anti-tank weapons, driving or walking over many miles of open desert to objectives which were several miles from each other. If ever an operation resembled sticking one's arm into a wasp's nest, this did; and, in its final version, it certainly did not produce the armour on the minefield gaps "in rear of the enemy".' In his despatch Auchinleck wrote of *Aberdeen*: 'the failure of Eighth Army's counter-attack on 5 June was probably the turning point of the battle.'

There followed the beginning of the end at Bir Hacheim. '*Rommel lance de plus en plus d'éléments blindés*,' wrote a French observer. By 10 June, under Rommel's personal supervision ('I frequently took over command of the assault forces myself', he recalled, 'and seldom in Africa was I given such a hard-fought struggle') the French garrison had been compelled to withdraw with the loss of 1000 prisoners, 24 guns and hundreds of vehicles. Rommel had now opened up his right wing and started to clear a supply route through the centre of his line. It was an extraordinary recovery from the first phase of his offensive, when his supplies were endangered and his flank was exposed. Of the *Cauldron* battle the *Official History* observes: 'General Rommel had judged to a nicety the strength necessary to hold it, and had hoped to see the British exhaust themselves—as indeed they did. With his quick eye for the run of a battle he soon saw that their plan had gone astray, and showed his quality by being ready to take advantage of it.' Rommel's own characteristic comment is 'now our forces were free ... on the afternoon of 11 June, I put the Bir Hacheim force on the move to the north in order to seek a final decision without delay'.

His objective was El Adem—that small strip of sand and stone which, as so often in the desert war (like a village, a Mametz Wood, a trench or a redoubt in the Somme or Passchendaele battles), acquired a significance which bore no relation to its relative insignificance ... though there was, of course, the airfield. 15 Panzer, 90 Light and Trieste advanced north-eastwards in its direction while 21 Panzer feinted due north from Sidra Ridge, with Ariete, to distract the British forces in the Knightsbridge area. It was a fan-shaped movement designed to by-pass and envelop the hard core of British resistance. Von Mellenthin criticises his commander for failing to concen-trate his reduced force into a single threat: but on the 11th and 12th Rommel succeeded in achieving a final superiority over the British armour and a definite ascendancy over Ritchie's mind.

By the evening of the 11th Rommel was up in the El Adem area. His troops were scattered all over and around the Gazala Line, but at this central and critical focus the British, as usual, were also divided in their purposes. On the morning of the 12th Norrie wanted to go one way and Messervy another: trying to find Norrie, to argue it out, Messervy was cut off and had to go into hiding. In his absence Norrie decided to pull his armoured brigades together under the command of 1 Armoured Division; but in the meantime Rommel had acted. He ordered 15 Panzer to attack 2 and 4 Armoured Brigades from the south, while 21 Panzer tackled their rear. 'These orders', says the *Official History*, 'were to have disastrous results for the British.' It was a typical Rommel pincer, nipping his enemy as they were redeploying. The dusty conditions allowed the German anti-tank gunners to work in the front line as they had been trained to do, and by the end of the day, though Lumsden at 1 Armoured H.Q. had striven to stabilise a front for his tanks and had just about done so, 'the afternoon's actions', says General Carver, 'saw the balance of tank strength pass finally and firmly to Rommel.'

Ritchie, that evening, was already fearing that his weakness in armour would allow Rommel to cut off his infantry divisions in the north—as indeed Rommel planned to do, for, as he recalls in his memoirs, 'the initiative was ours'. His account of his activities next day is most instructive. 'In the morning I set off with my *Kampfstaffel* to a ridge south-east of El Adem, where I observed the course of the battle between 90 Light Division and the Indians. Incessant British bomber attacks were giving 90 Light Division a bad time. Later I tried to get through to 15 Panzer Division, but our vehicles were heavily fired on from the north and south and pinned down in the open for several hours. It was afternoon before I reached the 15th, whom I then accompanied in their attack to the west. During the evening we were bombed by some of our own Stukas. They were being chased by British fighters and, lame ducks that they were, were forced to drop their bombs on their own troops for the sake of some extra speed. However, the three of us—Bayerlein, the driver and I—escaped without a scratch.' In the diaries and memoirs of the Great Commanders it is sometimes possible to hit upon a passage which conveys the tang of their personality and a sense of the way they behaved when the guns were firing. This quiet paragraph, like so many in Rommel's *Papers*, surely transmits the feel of what it was like to be a 'front-line General'.

13 June was the day which both effectively ended the Gazala battle and saw the beginning of the fall of Tobruk. The determining factor was the withdrawal of 201 Guards Brigade from its box at Knightsbridge. This had served as a pivot of manœuvre for the British armour throughout the battle without being directly attacked. Now, on the 13th, the Scots Guards were

forced off the Rigel Ridge and the whole brigade retired during the night of the 13–14th. 'This brigade', says Rommel, 'was almost a living embodiment of the virtues and faults of the British soldier—tremendous courage and tenacity combined with a rigid lack of mobility. The greater part of the armoured force attached to the Guards Brigade was destroyed, either during that day or on their retreat the following night.' This was true now in respect of the whole of the British armoured forces. By the evening of the 13th they had been reduced to some 50 cruiser and 20 infantry tanks. Rommel had achieved a superiority in armour of two to one, and as master of the battle-field he was also in a much better position to recover his own damaged tanks.

So there remained Tobruk, whose defence or abandonment was the subject of complicated and confusing communications between Ritchie and Auchin-leck, and Cairo and London. Auchinleck was determined that in the event of a retreat an invested force should not be left behind in Tobruk. Churchill, on the contrary, always 'presumed that there was no question of giving up Tobruk'. Ritchie, as the moment of decision crept closer, developed an am-bivalent policy whereby Tobruk might be temporarily cut off on the assump-tion that new Allied forces, assembled on the frontier, might achieve its relief. The wishful thinking of both the British military and political directors was ended by Rommel, who now proceeded to take the port.

IX

The Hard Summer

1942

The first task that now faced Rommel was to sweep away the remains of his enemy from the outskirts of the Tobruk *enceinte*, and to bind a firm ring around its defences from west to east.

On the 14th there was a criss-cross of communications between Ritchie and Auchinleck, each arguing from a different premiss. At 1130 Ritchie sent out an instruction declaring that he intended 'to withdraw to the frontier and occupy the frontier defences', adding that for as long as possible Rommel must be denied El Adem and the western approach to Tobruk. In the evening he signalled to Norrie: 'main contribution which 30 Corps can make is in conjunction with 13 Corps to prevent enemy closing eastern exits Tobruk . . . having regard to your resources a mobile policy will best achieve your object. . . .' In a signal to Auchinleck at 2310 he bluntly declared that in his view, if he could not stop the investment of Tobruk, he should accept it—temporarily. 'If this is a correct interpretation of your ideas', he added, 'I accept responsibility.' Auchinleck, however, was thinking on different lines. At 0750 he sent 8 Army a directive, which was not received until shortly before midnight. It ended:

7(a) The general line Acroma-El Adem-El Gubi is to be denied to the enemy.

(b) Our forces will not be invested in Tobruk, and your army is to remain a mobile field army.

(c) The enemy's forces are to be attacked and destroyed as soon as we have collected adequate forces for an offensive.

Auchinleck and Ritchie were communicating through a cloud of misunderstanding. The result was that the immediate dispositions of 8 Army could not have been arranged more suitably for Rommel, whose aggressive spirit on the 14th is indicated by this entry in his *Papers*: 'Full speed ahead was ordered, as British vehicles were now streaming east in their thousands. I rode with the tanks and constantly urged their commanders to keep the speed up. Suddenly we ran into a wide belt of mines. Ritchie had attempted to form a new defence front and had put in every tank he had. The advance halted and our vehicles were showered with British armour-piercing shells. I at once ordered the reconnaissance regiments to clear lanes through the minefields, a task which was made easier by the violent sandstorm which blew up towards midday. Meanwhile, I ordered our 170-mm. guns to open fire on the Via Balbia. The thunder of our guns mingled with the shock of demolitions. . . .' Once again, the Feldherr of the Front line speaks.

The westward bulge of Commonwealth divisions in the north was hastily deflated: during the night of the 14–15th 1 South African Division passed through Tobruk (their stores having been destroyed), while 50 Division broke out during the darkness, and by 16 June was re-organising on the frontier. On the 15th Rommel was able to write to his wife:

15 June 1942

Dearest Lu,

The battle has been won and the enemy is breaking up. We're now mopping up encircled remnants of their army. I needn't tell you how delighted I am. We've made a pretty clean sweep this time. . . .

This mopping up was mainly of individual units scattered around the perimeter of Tobruk: the hard core of 8 Army was now far to the east. It was an operation for which Rommel and his Afrika Korps had been given much practice by the British; destruction of detached posts had become all too familiar. First came a disappointment. Rommel hoped to force his armour during the night to a point where it could cut the coastal road east of Tobruk; his troops, however, were exhausted. They slept during the night and at dawn, as the South Africans retreated down Via Balbia, they were still asleep. At 0800, according to General Carver, 'Rommel had arrived to see von Bismarck and realised that the manœuvre on which his heart had been set since 26 May had failed'. His dream had evaporated: but Rommel was still master of the field.

The British, on the other hand, were uncertain about what was happening to their retreating divisions. 'Not until 17 June', says the *Official History* (about the arrival of 1 South African and 50 Division in the frontier area) 'was it known with any certainty what was their state of completeness.' Outside Tobruk, 29 Indian Infantry Brigade was left at El Adem, and during the

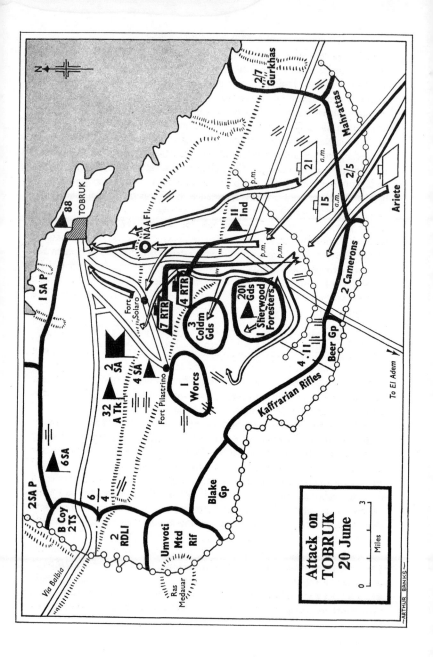

Attack on
TOBRUK
20 June

15th it repelled three attacks by 90 Light and one by 21 Panzer. In the evening the Panzers captured an outpost, B 650. During the 16th attacks on El Adem continued so effectively that the Indian Brigade was withdrawn during the night, 90 Light noting in its diary that this 'removed the southern corner-stone from the advanced defence line of Tobruk'. Rommel immediately ordered his Afrika Korps, with Ariete, to push on to Gambut and its airfield. 'We wanted to divert British attention from Tobruk, and at the same time gain the necessary freedom of movement in our rear for the Tobruk attack. Primarily, however, this advance was directed against the R.A.F. . . . '

It had three consequences. Tobruk was robbed of close fighter support; it smashed the last hope of immediate relief: and it cut the coastal road to the east of the port, completing its isolation. This was a direct result of the defeat, on 17 July, of 4 Armoured Brigade, all that Messervy could now muster to deal with Rommel's tanks. The Brigade no longer consisted of true units: it was a combination of relics. Its 90 runners came mainly from four regiments whose survivors had been thrown together to form the 1/6 and 3/5 R.T.R. Weary men and tired equipment, inevitably ill-organised, met Rommel's equally weary but triumphant 15 and 21 Panzers during the afternoon of the 17th, and by the evening were in full retreat.

The Afrika Korps immediately turned to the north, capturing *en passant* 4 Armoured Brigade H.Q. and a number of units of the retreating 20 Indian Brigade. Rommel, with his *Kampfstaffel*, arrived at Gambut with the leading troops at about 2200. The British fighters had been ordered to evacuate the airfield during the day, and as their next base to the eastwards, Sidi Azeiz, seemed open to attack by the German armour they retreated to Sidi Barrani on the 19th. By his ruthless exploitation of the victory at Gazala Rommel had thus created a situation in which the conquest of Tobruk was only a matter of time. The citadel was uncovered in the air: the only possible relieving force had been repelled: and all the weaknesses of its garrison, its defensive organisation and its command would soon be exposed. By the 19th Rommel had also worked the Afrika Korps into positions south-east of Tobruk and pushed 90 Light further east towards Bardia. Many supplies—especially ammunition—were picked up in the process. Ariete, Pavia and Littorio were moving up to screen the southern and south-western rim of the fortress. And so, after the hectic improvisations of the last few weeks, Rommel must now have felt a calm sense of what Montgomery called 'balance'. Yet even on the 19th fantasy ruled in Cairo. The Commanders-in-Chief were engaged in preparing an appreciation which was forwarded to London during the 20th, declaring that 'we hope therefore that Tobruk should be able to hold out until operations for relief are successfully completed after resumption of our offensive'. At 0520 that day the bombing which preceded Rommel's final assault began, and by 0745 the anti-tank ditch on Tobruk's frontier had been bridged and the German armour had started to advance.

Beyond its own defences Tobruk was naked. Within them there was no more reason for hope, and though at dawn on the 20th Rommel clearly sensed that his enemy had been defeated even before he attacked, he could not have been aware of how, from Klopper's headquarters down in the Pilastrino caves all the way forward to the minefields Rommel's pioneers were breaching, everything was radically different from the situation he had tried to tackle 12 months ago—an alert, agressive and self-confident resistance by an Australian garrison determined to do or die.

The indecision at the heart of Tobruk's collapse in 1942 stemmed partly from the record of its commander. Brigadier Klopper took over the two brigades of 2 South African Division on 14 May. He and his staff had had virtually no operational experience: nor, for that matter, had his brigades. In January they had captured Bardia and Sollum; but this was no training for stopping an imperious assault by a buoyant Rommel. Klopper's inexperience was not aided by the unwarranted confidence of Gott, who inspected Tobruk's defences on the 16th and declared that they were 'a nice tidy show'—a conclusion which strongly supports the view that had Gott instead of Montgomery commanded 8 Army at Alamein the result would have been different! Gott, like Ritchie, was willing to accept an investment. His attitude must have added to the floundering Klopper's confusion, faced as the latter was by instructions forwarded from Auchinleck that an investment was not to be permitted.

There were various comings and goings: Ritchie flying into Tobruk to talk to Klopper, Auchinleck flying up on the 18th. But though next day Auchinleck, back in Cairo, signalled to Smuts (who had a special concern about the South Africans), 'have no intention of giving up Tobruk, which I hope is only temporarily isolated', the truth was that Klopper was now on his own, and that next morning he would have to deal with a *Blitzkrieg* which neither he nor his superiors had predicted. Churchill had certainly not done so: he believed with that passionate self-conviction of which only he was capable that Tobruk was a rock, like Gibraltar or Malta. For him the unthinkable was impossible; and the loss of Tobruk was unthinkable. Klopper had therefore to cope with a political as well as a military dilemma.

Put very crudely, it might be said that in the command structure the Commonwealth divisions were to 8 Army as the Italians were to Rommel; they had a divided allegiance. So, faced with an operation which must put his irreplaceable men in hazard, Klopper felt a need to communicate with his own people just as, in a similar situation, Freyberg felt he must talk to the New Zealand government. But at Tobruk on 20 July telegrams were not enough.

Reassurance from outside was useless because the internal defences of the fortress, with an assault already imminent, were either obsolete, missing, or unidentified. Yet it was with these blunted tools that the unfortunate Klopper had to carry out the job: in effect, he was asked to do too much. Apart from his South Africans, the only fighting troops (there were many base troops in the area) were three brigades—32 Army Tank Brigade, commanded by Willison, a veteran of the previous siege whose advice Klopper disregarded; 201 Guards Brigade (in which there was only one Guards battalion) whose Brigadier only assumed command on 17 June; and 11 Indian Brigade, which contained a high proportion of raw reinforcements. In anti-tank and anti-aircraft equipment the shortages were grave—there were only 55 2- and 6-pounders, and eight Bofors in an anti-tank role: and 18 3·7 A.A. guns with a light regiment, 2 South African L.A.A. The field artillery consisted of three regiments plus a few attached batteries and a couple of medium regiments. Here again there was a lack of organisation and foresight. Inter-communication between the gun-groups was so poor that there was no possibility of concerting massed fire on a threatened sector of the perimeter: and though down by the harbour there were 130,000 rounds of 25-pounder shells, 18,000 medium, 115,000 2-pounder and 23,000 6-pounder, the forward gun positions had not been sufficiently stocked to enable them to sustain a sudden attack, while no proper plans had been laid to service them. Klopper appears to have intended to co-ordinate his artillery under his C.R.A.; but there is no evidence that this occurred, and from what subsequently happened it appears that the guns were never effectively linked. Yet it is one of the oldest lessons of siege warfare that the surrounded force must endeavour to concentrate its available fire-power on the threatened point: many a siege has been thwarted by such arrangements.

Had he done so, however, Klopper must still have succumbed. He was faced by other, irremediable weaknesses. The scale and siting of the minefields around and inside the perimeter were a mystery; it was not fully appreciated that, because of the previously prevailing doctrine that Tobruk should not endure another siege, many of the mines laid a year ago had been lifted for use at Gazala. And the fragments of armour available, like the fragments of artillery, were not, and perhaps never could have been, co-ordinated: nor was there any air cover.

In this recipe for disaster the absence of air support was a most potent element, for Rommel had obtained from Kesselring 'the willing consent to use the *Luftwaffe* at its greatest possible strength to deliver a nightly concentrated attack on the front to be assaulted'. The formula used so effectively in France in 1940 was repeated. All the bombers in North Africa and some from Greece and Crete were employed. For close support the landing grounds at Gazala and El Adem made a shuttle-service possible, and on the day of the assault 580 German and 177 Italian bomber sorties were flown. The withdrawn Desert Air Force could not hope to counter so powerful an offensive. And Klopper, in Tobruk, failed to organise his ground patrols with sufficient aggressiveness for him to be able to appreciate that Rommel intended to move swiftly. The latter was right in his impression, on the eve of the 20th, that 'our movements had only been partially and inaccurately observed by the enemy, and there was therefore every chance that our attack would achieve complete surprise'.

At 0500 on the 20th Rommel stood beside von Mellenthin on the escarpment to the north-east of El Adem, ready to scan the Tobruk perimeter at dawn. The concerted attack by the *Luftwaffe* and the Afrika Korps started at 0520 and to Rommel it must have seemed the pinnacle of his military career—as indeed it was. For so long the capture of Tobruk had been an ideal: now it was inevitable.

The plan of assault was simple. Fierce air and artillery bombardments descended at zero hour on a narrow front held by 11 Indian Brigade—part of the south-eastern perimeter where Wavell had broken through in 1940 and Rommel intended to penetrate in 1941. All observers of the onslaught from the air remember its violence: 'a great cloud of dust and smoke rose from the sector under attack', says von Mellenthin, 'and while our bombs crashed down on to the defences, the entire German and Italian Army Artillery joined in, with a tremendous and well-co-ordinated fire.'

This was a tactical blitz behind which lurked a strategic deception. Rommel had intentionally held the Afrika Korps to the east of Tobruk, around Gambut, implying that it lay there to deal with British armoured thrusts from Egypt and possibly to advance to the east. Now, conforming to the pre-ordained plan, it turned back to the west, and began to force its way through the gaps in the minefields and over the anti-tank ditches which Rommel's engineers were breaching and bridging. Klopper, down in Tobruk (without proper communications, or a co-ordinated defence, or a policy he could understand), was unable to deal with such sophisticated simplicity, whose sources were professional certainty and physical strength. At Tobruk Rommel was clear in mind and sure of his power, while Klopper was bemused and weak. Not surprisingly, therefore, Rommel's tanks entered the town of Tobruk during the evening of the 20th, at the moment when the harbour was being demolished.

The story of Tobruk's collapse need not be told in detail. The Afrika Korps pushed on from point to point, and Rommel recorded that 'at 0500 hours on 21 June I drove into the town of Tobruk . . . at about 0940 hours on the Via Balbia, about four miles west of the town, I met General Klopper, G.O.C. 2 South African Infantry Division, and Garrison Commander of Tobruk. He announced the capitulation of the fortress of Tobruk'. Within 24 hours Rommel (in his 49th year) was appointed a Field-Marshal by Hitler; true to his style, he forgot to put his new badge of rank on his shoulder until he reached Alamein, and after he received his baton from Hitler in September he said to his wife 'I would rather he had given me one more division'.

To Churchill he gave a shock comparable only with the moment when the Prime Minister received the news of the sinking of the *Prince of Wales* and the *Repulse* by the Japanese off Malaya. It was traumatic. But the context within which the news arrived was important: Churchill was in Washington with Roosevelt. And thus—as so often happened—a victory in the field which brought Rommel short-term results robbed him of its long-term consequences: the telegram Roosevelt passed without comment to Churchill at Washington, 'Tobruk has surrendered with 25,000 men taken prisoner', released the Sherman tanks which were agents of victory at Alamein. 'The whirligig of time brings in its revenges.'

Following one Shakespearean quotation with another, it was now a matter for Rommel of 'letting slip the dogs of war'—his armour. The frontier, Cairo and Alexandria, the Canal and the oilfields in the Persian Gulf seemed glittering and attainable prizes. 'It was a great moment', the *Official History* observes, 'and no Fate whispered that he would never experience a greater.'

For a cavalry commander the emotional pressure as he feels that he has his enemy on the run is difficult to control: Patton in France and Germany is a perfect example. After the fall of Tobruk Rommel was obsessed: 'I was determined at all costs to avoid giving the British any opportunity of creating a new front and occupying it with fresh formations from the Near East.' He therefore decided that he must disregard Malta and press the defeated British to the limit of his and their strength. In his *Papers* he frankly admits that 'it was a plan with a chance of success—a try on'. The chance was unfortunately diminished by his inability to look over 'the other side of the hill'. As the year wore on he came to appreciate more and more the advantages for the Allies in the Middle East of America's entry into the war; but at Tobruk his vision was blurred. Should he have anticipated in the consummation of his victory that he had sown the seeds of his ultimate defeat?

In the moment of triumph he had no reason to expect that Auchinleck, who had taken over Cunningham's command during *Crusader*, would now replace Ritchie. But the Prime Minister's pressure and the C.-in-C.'s instinct produced . . .

General Auchinleck to C.I.G.S.   *25 June 0905 hours*

Am taking over command 8 Army from Ritchie this afternoon. Propose send him on leave temporarily to Palestine but consider he should go home soon as possible and be given command of a corps or a General Staff appointment. . . .

Ritchie's experience raises an interesting question about Rommel to which I return in my last chapter: what is a commander's ceiling? Ritchie's was clearly that of the commander of a corps, and not of an army: directing a corps he did well in north-west Europe. Auchinleck misjudged Ritchie's capacity in pushing him into control of 8 Army during *Crusader*, and thereafter retaining him in spite of his ineptitude at Gazala and what can only be described as a misinterpretation of his orders at Tobruk.

Rommel (and Montgomery) possessed the strength which every Great Captain needs—a ruthless ability to sack. At last—and too late—Auchinleck appreciated that as a commander in the field he might be Ritchie's, as he was Cunningham's, superior, and once again he took over responsibility for facing in the field a victorious Rommel. This switch, from the intellectual problem of administering the vast area of the Middle East to the practical requirements of commanding an army in action, does not seem to have troubled Auchinleck. When I put the point to him he made light of it. Still, it *ought* to have caused a tremendous strain, for whereas Rommel was now at his peak, having been continuously in action since his arrival in Africa and having steadily extended his professional expertise, Auchinleck had been distracted by affairs of state: but it was Auchinleck who was to be the victor in the engagements between Tobruk and Alamein. The ease with which he made the transition may well be explained by the simple fact that a natural fighting soldier was happy to return to the battlefront: like Rommel, Auchinleck was most at home within sound of the guns.

Rommel began the next phase with an error. The issue was Malta. From his own *Papers* and from the reminiscences of Kesselring and von Mellenthin one can reconstruct the debate which followed the fall of Tobruk. It is clear that the Field-Marshal was determined, after his victory (and in spite of his earlier protestations about the need to capture the island) that the decision to halt his army while Malta was invaded should be jettisoned. He acted both directly and deviously. While he was normally the incarnation of the politically detached 'front-line general', this is a period of his career whose diplomacy reminds one of Haig—Haig's use of a private line to the King in his dispute with his Prime Minister about strategy on the Western front. Rommel exploited his private relationship with Hitler. His direct route was a message on 22 June to von Rintelen in Rome, for transmission to O.K.W. and Mussolini, stating that 'the first objective of the *Panzerarmee*—to defeat the enemy's army in the field and capture Tobruk—had been achieved', and that the logical consequence of his shattering of the British morale was instant pursuit into Egypt. He asked the Duce to lift the existing restrictions on his freedom of movement. At the same time he acted indirectly by sending a liaison officer to put his case to Hitler. He thus sought to by-pass the objections of his superiors in Africa, for during consultations on the 21st Kesselring, and on the 22nd Bastico, had opposed his ideas. The temperature of the discussions ran high, and Rommel was so far excited that he invited Bastico to dine with him in Cairo!

Both the dictators—mistakenly—accepted Rommel's arguments. They did so willingly: but their decision cost them Africa. The survival of Malta was fatal to their cause. Hitler, remembering Crete, had never been happy about the proposed airborne assault, and in spite of pressure from his navy he was persuaded that Rommel's success must be reinforced. He therefore told Mussolini that 'it is only once in a lifetime that the goddess of victory smiles'. Mussolini, for his part, was enchanted at the thought of both avoiding an assault on Malta (about which he had always been dubious) and, at the same time, committing his army to a conquest of Egypt which seemed assured. During the night of 23–24 June von Rintelen signalled to Rommel: 'Duce approves intention of Panzer Army to pursue enemy into Egypt. . . .' On 27 June the Duce issued an order that Suez should be seized and the Canal closed, and on the 29th he appeared at Derna (pilot of his own plane), to be available for a Roman entry into Alexandria astride a white horse.

These aberrations of the Axis dictators illustrate the frail base of judgement on which their commanders in Africa could rely. Rommel used their weakness to support his strength: he offered them success, and they succumbed. On the British side political pressures of a different kind also affected the conduct of affairs in the desert. Churchill was in a dilemma. On 25 June he told Auchinleck that 'whatever views I may have had about how the battle was fought or whether it should have been fought a good deal earlier, you have my entire confidence and I share your responsibilities to the full'. But on that same day he heard in Washington that a motion had been tabled in the House of Commons registering a lack of confidence in 'the central direction of the war'.

The difference between dictatorship and democracy is that, whereas it is convenient for a dictator to produce results, a Prime Minister who needs to maintain a majority vote *must* produce them: and Churchill now sought results. He desperately required from the Middle East something encouraging to pass on to Parliament and the public, after his empty-handed return from his visit to Roosevelt and the knowledge that the House of Commons was simmering with rebellion. So, as Rommel and Auchinleck clashed again during the summer of 1942, there were pressures working behind each of them which were militarily unsound: military history, however, is a by-product of political history. Mussolini had ordered his horse and Churchill had to face Parliament: Rommel and Auchinleck were the residuary legatees.

Auchinleck's first problem on assuming command was to cope with the situation at Matruh—a minor version of Tobruk. Rommel advanced rapidly along the African shore and by 26 June threatened the small harbour, its defences, and the line of Commonwealth troops hastily emplaced due south from the fortress. His intelligence was wildly at fault. He thought that behind the minefields encircling Matruh there were four divisions of infantry—50 and 2 New Zealand, 5 and 10 Indian—and that 1 Armoured lay to the south on 8 Army's left and exposed flank. In fact 10 Indian was the main fighting unit in Matruh; the two brigades of 50 Division were further back along the coast, south of Gerawla; and 2 New Zealand Division (Kippenberger in *Infantry Brigadier* gives a vivid account of their experiences) was still further to the south on the escarpment at Minqar Quaim—one of their battalions, 21, was planted even further to the flank and even more exposed, at Bir Khalda. 5 Indian had been split up into scattered groups. The effect of these arrangements, which were in train before Auchinleck replaced Ritchie and which he was unable to modify before Rommel attacked, was that his front was relatively strong on the flanks but feeble in its centre. Auchinleck determined, nevertheless, to keep the battle fluid.

The fight outside Matruh took its character from these dispositions, Rommel's misunderstanding of them, and the perennial lack of co-ordination between the British infantry and armour. Rommel's attack on the 26th (interesting in that Rommel was attacking the centre of what he assumed to be the line, whereas normally he operated round a flank) swept over two weak columns in the yawning gap between the wings—Leathercol and Gleecol—while 21 Panzer began to encircle the New Zealanders on Minqar Quaim from the north and north-east, not realising that they were tackling part of a corps position rather than a flanking force. Rommel did not comprehend that he had put himself between the jaws of 8 Army: 8 Army was unable to close them.

Rommel still thought that the New Zealand Division was locked in Matruh, while the British were too disorganised to take advantage of his impetuosity. But the old pattern was repeated. By the evening of the 27th 90 Light severed the coast road to the east of Matruh: though their extended salient placed the Germans in great danger, the eyes of the British were now on the rear. Auchinleck's instructions implied retreat. They certainly weighed with his subordinates—especially Gott—and predisposed them to the further withdrawal which, to a greater or lesser degree, his divisions successfully achieved. During the night of 27–28 June 13 Corps broke out eastwards (though 10 Corps in Matruh, by a confusion of communications, did not learn that this was happening until the morning. In consequence the Matruh garrison lost heavily in their attempt to escape.) At Minqar Quaim the New Zealanders made a spectacular break-out by night through the German ring. 'Rommel may have been lucky,' as von Mellenthin observes: but it is also true that, as he puts it, 'Mersa Matruh was certainly a brilliant German victory.' Auchinleck's intention was to keep 8 Army as an entity: it disintegrated at Matruh. To his everlasting credit he was able in the next few weeks to produce a form of order out of chaos, and to exploit the flaws in the Axis situation created by Rommel's headlong advance—a situation which can only be described as brilliant but disastrous.

During July 1942 Rommel came to a dead end. What has been called 'the hard summer' was a period in which he ceased to make his enemy dance to his tune. For an armoured commander to lose the initiative is fatal, and during July 1942 Rommel lost it irrecoverably. The engagement in which he was decisively defeated at the beginning of the month—an attempt to rush the Alamein box on 1 July—was his climacteric: afterwards he mainly conformed to his enemy's will. In his earlier operations in the desert Rommel planned and his opponent reacted, but after this month it would be the other way round; if Kasserine is cited as an example of Rommel moving with freedom, the answer must be that it was his inevitable response to *Torch*. Auchinleck, during July, and Alexander and Montgomery from August onwards, were pipers calling the tune: Rommel never recovered a position from which he could effectively impose his will. His genius was to be inspiring and creative in the attack, and it was unfortunate that, from July 1942 onwards, he had to use his talents in defence.

His defeat in the many actions which made up what is sometimes called First Alamein stemmed from three sources. In these July battles he had to face a pugnacious opponent; for, from the moment that Auchinleck took over, his declared principle was 'these damn British have been taught far too long to be good losers. I've never been a good loser, I am going to win.' Secondly, Rommel's supply lines were at their extremity. And thirdly, the Desert Air Force was now keyed up to its highest pitch: German documents during July regularly record day and night raids on their lines and communications which disrupted morale and efficiency. Figures speak for themselves: between 1 and 27 July the R.A.F. flew some 15,400 sorties. The coming of the Spitfire greatly helped the fighters over the front line, and whereas British bombers were constantly active over the German rearward communications, (right back to their supply ports) Alexandria, Suez, Port Said and Haifa were strangely unaffected by the *Luftwaffe*. These were omens; but for Rommel the most ominous fact was that during July, in spite of errors and uncertainties, the Commonwealth divisions up and down the Alamein Line gradually asserted themselves to a point at which he had to start establishing *defensive* positions—the point at which von Mellenthin noted that 'we had just failed'.

Looking back, Rommel searched for reasons for his failure. The ones he found were, not unnaturally, self-justifying. Taking the realistic line that 'in modern warfare supplies decide the battle', he indicted what he called the Quartermasters—all those responsible for feeding him through Germany and Italy and across the sea. He also indicted the Italian navy for its ineffective protection of his convoys, and cited the corruption of the Fascist authorities. But he was not sufficiently self-critical to be able to observe that his present deficiencies were precisely those the Italian command had predicted if he pressed on from Tobruk. How rarely, in the literature of the Second World War—or any war—does one find a senior commander prepared to admit his defects! Slim's *Defeat Into Victory* is an outstanding case of a man who, having exercised the highest authority, is prepared to paint himself 'warts and all'.

1 July was the testing day. Rommel was determined to maintain momentum, and to this end sacrificed the profit of adequate reconnaissance—as he had often, successfully, done before. When his army moved forward during the early hours of the 1st it had scanty and inaccurate information about the British dispositions; the maxim of the Royal Artillery that 'time spent in reconnaissance is seldom wasted' was again proved true. Rommel's plan entailed an initial drive by 90 Light and the Afrika Korps south of the ring round Alamein and north of Deir el Abyad: after this penetration 90 Light was to swing north, rush for the coast, and so cut off the El Alamein box from the east. Afrika Korps was to swerve to the right, making a 22-mile march through the darkness, and cut off 13 Corps by cleaving its way as far south as Alam Nayil. Italian infantry was to follow in the tracks of 90 Light, and the Italian 20 Corps was to support the Afrika Korps.

In theory this was a sound scheme—if somewhat repetitive of the final assault on Tobruk. It was typical of Rommel's thinking: clear-cut, ambitious, dramatic. But it ignored the facts. It took, for example, no account of the presence of 1 South African Division, with its brigades laid out just in the area where 90 Light would have to make a left turn to outflank the Alamein box and reach the sea. And so, in the early afternoon of the 1st, when 90 Light was hit by the concentrated fire of the African artillery, 'something', according to the *Official History*, 'like panic occurred'. 'Finally our troops were pinned down in terrific artillery fire', says Rommel. 'An SOS came in from 90 Light Division, as the divisional artillery was no longer battleworthy. I at once sent in Kampfstaffel Kiehl south of the division and drove up myself in an armoured car to get a view of the situation and make my decisions. However, heavy British artillery fire soon forced us to turn back.'

The impetus of advance on Rommel's left was thus blocked by unexpected opposition. On his right, earlier in the day, he had witnessed a similar check. To the east of Deir el Abyad lay Deir el Shein, occupied by a new brigade, 18 Indian. Neither Rommel nor Nehring knew it was there. Two of its three battalions had not seen action; it had only had time to scratch out of the rocks some sort of defensive position; it lacked ammunition, and its artillery and armoured support was what was called a 'lash-up'. Nevertheless, it fought to the death. During the day it was overrun, and by the evening was finished: but its resistance gained precious hours for the British defence. (Rommel thought a whole division was involved.)

Both wings of the German advance were thus brought to a halt. Oscillating between them, Rommel experienced the full rigour of the battle. Late in the afternoon, up with Kampfstaffel Kiehl in support of 90 Light, he and Bayerlein had another narrow escape. 'British shells came screaming in from three directions, north, east and south; anti-aircraft tracer streaked through our force. Under this tremendous weight of fire, our attack came to a standstill. Hastily we scattered our vehicles and took cover, as shell after shell crashed into the area we were holding. For two hours Bayerlein and I had to lie out in the open.' The South Africans were taking their revenge on the conqueror of Tobruk.

During the next two days fighting continued intensively along the Alamein Line: an infinity of tactical moves by both sides. Then Rommel decided: 'I would call the offensive off for the moment after the next day's battle', and formed the opinion that 'General Auchinleck ... was handling his forces with very considerable skill and tactically better than Ritchie had done. He seemed to view the situation with decided coolness, for he was not allowing himself to be rushed into accepting a "second best" solution by any moves we made.' In what he has so far published Montgomery, victor at Second Alamein, has not presented the victor at First Alamein in the best light: but Rommel, speaking for himself about the man who blunted his spearhead in the early days of July, makes it clear that this was the beginning of his end in Africa. It is a measure of Rommel that he could recognise with generosity the achievement of a worthy opponent; and of some flaw in Montgomery's humanity that he could not allow the glow of his own achievement to be shadowed by his predecessor's success.

The *Official History* puts the practical point obliquely, by observing that Rommel expected 'to have to remain on the defensive for at least a fortnight'. An armoured commander who makes such an admission while operating at the end of an uncertain supply line has already conceded defeat: for the essence of mobile operations is motion, and the most difficult problem is to get on the move again after a decisive halt. This is the crux at the heart of the idea of mobility; one especially difficult to resolve when supplies are short— another form of the dilemma which baffled commanders on the Western front in 1914–18, and one which taxed every desert general. Rommel usually kept moving by taking calculated risks about his supplies: Montgomery by contrast, when his time came, hesitated to advance because of an excessive preoccupation with his supply-train. The moment was now approaching when Auchinleck convinced Rommel that no more risks should be taken.

Throughout 2 July Rommel and Auchinleck were like two gladiators in the Colosseum—fencing and feeling for the other's weak spot. As 90 Light was making no progress Rommel switched the Afrika Korps to the north, in support of a further drive to cut the coastal road behind Alamein: while Auchinleck reckoned that the enemy's initiative might be checked by an attack westwards and northwards from the Ruweisat Ridge. Both operations were abortive. 8 Army's present policy of separating out into 'battle-groups' —variants on the 'Jock Column'—dissipated its undoubted strength in these July engagements; the Army was trying to improvise a form of deployment for which it was not properly trained and was psychologically ill-equipped. The basic German battle drill, elaborated by Rommel, made possible an instant cohesion of small units of tanks, artillery, infantry and armoured cars. 8 Army was still hag-ridden by jealousy and distrust—between armour and infantry; cavalry regiments and the Royal Tank Regiment; the Indian Army, the other units from the Commonwealth, and troops from the British Isles—and the 'mobile artillery groups' which Auchinleck was now demanding as a temporary expedient could never have been more than that and were probably not even expedient. He himself realised that they lacked a punch sufficient to 'drive home an attack against anything but very weak resistance'. As 8 Army struggled back to its last defences, forces *en masse* were required, and Auchinleck was much more effective as he drew his army—particularly his artillery—into concentration.

Indeed the operations during 3 July, the day when the scales began to tilt finally against Rommel, suggested the way things might and would go. Nine hundred sorties by the R.A.F. were about four times more than those of the *Luftwaffe*. But more significant was the fact that the British armour, ordered by Auchinleck to push north-west of Deir El Shein and get into the rear of the enemy, stood firm in positions south of Ruweisat and drew the Germans on to their line—the technique of the Afrika Korps.

'After an initial success', says Rommel, 'the attack finally became pinned down in concentric defensive fire.' Further south, the New Zealanders overran a sector of *Ariete*, taking 350 prisoners and capturing 44 guns—another indication of what was to come, for during the rest of the July battle Auchinleck intentionally and effectively picked on parts of the line held by the Italians and progressively weakened their will to resist, to a point where it virtually disappeared.* For Rommel this collapse of *Ariete* was a warning and a shock: the division had fought well in *Crusader* and at Gazala, 'but now the Italians were no longer equal to the very great demands being made of them'. These demands continued, for Rommel decided to pull out his mobile units from the front line and to bring up Italian infantry in a *roulement*. Indeed, the replacement of 21 Panzer by Italians on 4 July suggested to the British that a general withdrawal was imminent. But 8 Army's probing armoured cars, a New Zealand raid, and various independent columns established that the enemy was still there: Rommel was in fact re-grouping.

The *patois* of the military historian is dangerous. Standard words like 'regrouping', applied as they are in a general way to the movement of armies, corps, divisions and sub-units, can suggest, when only small forces are involved, that these are huge. It should therefore be remembered that Rommel's Afrika Korps had only 26 tanks available for action on 3 July (when the combined strength of 4 and 22 Armoured Brigades was well over 100), and that at the end of the day he signalled to O.K.H. that his divisions were reduced to 1200–1500 men. Not surprisingly, therefore, he concluded that 'he expected to have to remain on the defensive for at least a fortnight'. Until the end in Africa Rommel was now committed to improvisation in both tactics and logistics: previously he had had to improvise from time to time, but henceforth this would be a continuing need which started on 3 July. . . . 'Artillery Command reported that all batteries had exhausted their ammunition. Luckily, one effective battery was found with the Zech Group, and this succeeded in bringing the British advance to a halt with its last few rounds. I immediately gave orders for the extensive use of decoys, including dummy

* A vivid first-hand account of the Italians' experience during this phase of selective destruction may be found in *Alamein 1933–1962*, by Paolo Caccia-Dominioni.

tanks and 88-mm. A.A. guns, to take away the British taste for further attacks. Then we set about stocking up a few batteries with ammunition in the captured British strong-point Deir el Shein, which at least enabled us to keep a few batteries of 25-pounders (captured British guns) in action. The Italians still had stocks, and so were were able to regard the crisis as over for the moment.'

The desert now presented the spectacle of two commanders each passionately determined to destroy the other: each, however, driving forward tired and disorganised troops. Existence in the desert was at all times difficult—water was short, rations were short, there was little or no entertainment or leave, and letters seldom arrived. But accounts by the contingents of all the nationalities involved in First Alamein emphasise especially the conditions under which they then fought. *Crusader* was a winter battle—merciless, indeed, in its demands on the stamina of the troops on both sides: but at First Alamein the survivors of *Crusader* and their reinforcements faced the full rigour of an Egyptian summer. The 'dust devils' marched across the desert; the sun beat down relentlessly; flies were omnipresent; and a man was lucky if he had half a gallon of water a day to satisfy his every need. Afrika Korps and 8 Army shared equitably the discomforts of their Armageddon. In the end the Afrika Korps suffered the greater hardship, as it became progressively plain that their efforts were abortive. The golden joys of Alexandria and Cairo proved to be beyond their reach.

This was because, as Auchinleck gradually asserted his will, the pattern of the battle changed. It had once been the Commonwealth troops who rushed helter-skelter from one point in the desert to another, stopping a minefield gap, bringing aid to a 'box', succouring unsupported infantry units. During July 1942 the run of the fight altered. It was Rommel who was forced, step by step, to make these impromptu and desperate decisions. 'I was compelled', he says, 'to order every last German soldier out of his tent or rest camp up to the front, for, in face of the virtual default of a large proportion of our Italian fighting power, the situation was beginning to take on crisis proportions.' Occasionally mercurial in temperament—as the great cavalry leaders have usually been—Rommel had never so far felt such despair about his prospects in Africa. But now—and this comment summarises his attitude during July— 'we finally had to give up all idea of fighting it out with the British in the Alamein line ... the front had now grown static, and the British command was in its element.' Rommel of course recovered his aggressive instincts; but how did Auchinleck achieve this remarkable *bouleversement*?

His troops were exhausted, and some of his senior commanders had lost their zest. (Norrie, for example, who had led 30 Corps since November 1941, was replaced on 5 July by Ramsden.) But the more useless elements were sieved off to the rear; the *Panzerarmee* was kept on an alert which strained their taut nerves further by attacks up and down the line; Rommel's introduction of Italian infantry into his forward defences (to release his Afrika Korps into reserve) was matched by successful destructive probes into the new Italian positions; and by 9 July Auchinleck had manœuvred Rommel into spreading his thin force right across the 'Alamein line' from the Mediterranean down to Qattara, while the Commonwealth divisions achieved a superior concentration on their right flank. 'Next morning, 10 July, we were awakened at about 0500 hours by the dull thud of artillery from the north. I at once had an inkling that it boded no good. . . . I at once drove north with the Kampstaffel and a combat group of the 15 Panzer Division and directed them on to the battlefield.'

The sound Rommel heard was the *Trommelfeuer* which reminded veterans of the First World War of gunfire along an earlier Western front. Italian positions on the Tell el Eisa ridge were being attacked by 9 Australian Division, which had just joined 30 Corps. Their strike went well for them, and only just missed *Panzerarmee*'s H.Q. where von Mellenthin, as he graphically describes, found himself early on the morning of the 10th a witness of an Italian retreat 'in panic and rout'. Sabratha was shattered. But von Mellenthin took the sort of decision with which isolated British commanders in a similar position were faced during the German breakthrough after 21 March 1918: he improvised with what was available—the staff and soldiers of his H.Q., in his case, and elements of 382 Regiment of 164 Division which was now being flown in by stages. Rommel rushed north with his hastily assembled Panzer Group, and somehow during the 10th the situation was stabilised—temporarily, since air and artillery support for the Commonwealth troops was overwhelming, and further attacks on the 11th both completed the destruction of Sabratha and effectively maimed Trieste.

Tell el Eisa was soon captured. Counter-attacks during the next few days paid no dividends, and by 14 July Rommel decided to let the northern front rest. 'We were forced to the conclusion that the Italians were no longer capable of holding their line.' In his depression the Field-Marshal was sustained by news that the German offensives which were intended to capture Stalingrad and the eastern oilfields were making progress; but between 14 and 17 July his line was again seriously stretched by attacks Auchinleck launched on the positions held by Pavia and Brescia in its centre, around the Ruweisat ridge. At Second Alamein Montgomery's Chief of Intelligence, E. T. Williams, diagnosed the method whereby Rommel had interleaved German with Italian units—'corseting'—a diagnosis which much impressed Montgomery and radically affected his re-planning during the battle. But Auchinleck had anticipated Montgomery: at First Alamein he cut out the cloth between the stays of the corset! His assaults on Tell el Eisa and Ruweisat were part of this process, which had been strongly advocated by Dorman-Smith.

The Ruweisat attack was the first of three further attempts by Auchinleck to throw Rommel off balance, using the method of tapping in hard on his Italian divisions and compelling him, by a switch of front, to rush his German units up and down the line to provide stop-gaps. The method was exhausting for the Germans, nerve-racking for Rommel, and murderous for the Italians —although in each of the three attacks the performance of the Commonwealth troops, characterised as so often by individual acts of great bravery, was, taken as a whole, a sad display of inept planning and incompetent techniques. During these days there was a wide breach between Auchinleck's own will for battle and his troops' determination to soldier on . . . a breach left open by an inability on the part of his senior and middle-range commanders to foresee, to co-ordinate, to control. Things were *not* right with 8 Army. Had it in latter July—remembering its many comparative advantages—been conducted with the instinctive and ruthless tactical skills Rommel had imposed on the Afrika Korps the result might have been different. Yet the actual result was enough: the many sacrifices of 8 Army during these battles was justified by the outcome—concession of defeat by Rommel, something unthinkable at the time of the taking of Tobruk.

The attack on the Ruweisat ridge by 2 New Zealand Division began at 0430 on 15 July. Both its brigades made good progress, but each left pockets of resistance in their rear which prevented the essential pre-dawn reinforcement by anti-tank guns. In the early light, one group of German tanks got among 5 New Zealand Brigade and took 350 prisoners. On the front of 4 Brigade Rommel rapidly assembled reinforcements which attacked during the afternoon. Again the infantry was overrun with heavy loss, and the Brigade H.Q. was captured. 1 Armoured Division had been given the task of protecting the New Zealanders, but the latter's casualty list of 1405 was certainly not compensated for by a feeling that they had been effectively supported.

Auchinleck now shifted his weight to the Deir el Shein front, still impressed by the diminishing capacities of the Italians and the sense that the Germans were regularly being caught on the wrong foot. 5 Indian Division was to aim at the Deir during the evening of 21 July while the New Zealanders thrust into El Mreir. The weakness of the plan was that during the first phase the raw 161 Indian Motor Brigade was to attack and in the second 23

Armoured Brigade, which had only landed earlier in the month, was to exploit. The British habit of moving inexperienced units into the line as complete units was now to be revealed at its worst. Everything, moreover, was rushed: and the plan failed to take account of the fact that the increasing use of anti-tank mines at Alamein was steadily extending the time needed to ensure armoured reinforcement. So all went wrong again. 6 New Zealand Brigade reached its objectives as usual, Nehring drove panzers in on them in the early hours of the 19th, 700 casualties were sustained, and during the following morning 23 Armoured Brigade drove into disaster. The gaps for their advance were narrow and not properly cleared: they stuck, the Germans counter-attacked, and 23 Armoured lost 87 tanks. 2 Armoured Brigade tried to break through to help them and the New Zealanders, but they too were repulsed with a loss of 21 tanks. (In the north there was a parallel venture on the 22nd. The Australians attacked with great gallantry about Tell el Eisa but the Valentine tanks supposed to support them never connected with them properly, and had to withdraw with the loss of 23.)

At the end of the month Auchinleck made another effort in the north. This time South Africans and Australians attempted to make a hole in the minefields around Mitireiya. Again there was muddle and confusion, and a failure to link armour and infantry: the result was 400 casualties for 24 Australian Brigade and 600 for the British 69 Brigade.

These are the hard facts about a success within which there was a failure: 8 Army ought to have done better. But Liddell Hart puts the basic situation plainly; 'the difference in the total loss on either side was not large—and Rommel was not able to afford the loss. His account makes clear how perilously close he was to defeat in July. Moreover, his frustration in itself was fatal.' During these months it was (strategically) essential for Auchinleck not so much to win—though this would have been agreeable—as not to lose. He prevented the defeat of his army when this would have been critical: but in the process he sustained a personal defeat, for he failed to retain the confidence of Churchill. At the end of July the difference was that the performance of his forces in Africa was not vital for Hitler, whereas for Churchill 8 Army was temporarily the instrument of his supreme ambition. The Prime Minister therefore called for the Cairo Conference, which effected the final conquest by Rommel of British commanders who had confronted him: in one way or another he was responsible for the disappearance from the desert of Wavell, Cunningham, then Ritchie, and now, very soon, of Auchinleck. This was, as Churchill himself once put it, 'a fair cop'.

One of Winston's most endearing qualities was his capacity to look himself in the eye and discern the truth. 'During this month of July,' he wrote, 'when

I was politically at my weakest and without a gleam of military success, I had to procure from the United States the decision which, for good or ill, dominated the next two years of the war.' He got it: *Torch* in late 1942 and the invasion of north-west Europe deferred. Whether the decision was right or wrong is not to be argued here: the relevant point is that once it had been taken the Prime Minister's immediate preoccupation was naturally with the Middle East; here his armies were in action, here was where something dramatic could be achieved—instantly. On 31 July Stalin invited him to Moscow, and thus everything fell into place. He would proceed *via* Cairo. Here he would gather together the men he trusted, and confer about an army which seemed to be in the doldrums (and which, like himself, was having a bad press). With them he should be able to make such rearrangements as might produce victories he could report to Parliament, to Roosevelt, to Stalin, to the world. This is no caricature of Churchill's mood in July 1942: concern about his personal status was permanently and naturally intermingled with a dedication to the Commonwealth's military success—and never more than during this month. So into Cairo flew Alan Brooke from England, Wavell from India, and his old comrade Smuts from South Africa.

A fascinating trend to be observed in the records is how Rommel dominated the minds of the statesmen and servicemen at the conference—just in the way that Auchinleck, by his summer promulgation (see p. 245), had ordered his troops not to think. The Chiefs of Staff Committee had already advised the Middle East Defence Committee earlier in the month that 'much will depend on whether you are able to defeat Rommel . . . we realise that whole Middle East position mainly depends on success against Rommel or continued resistance of Russia'. Throughout the Cairo Conference, in fact, the name of the Field-Marshal was a *leitmotiv*.

Russia's continued resistance was critical. Until the possibility became impossible, Rommel and the British Chiefs of Staff were at one in their appreciation of what might flow from a German break through the Caucasus and into Persia. This development was always envisaged by Rommel and was, indeed, the basis of his strategy. It was examined at the Cairo Conference at the highest level as something that might soon happen, and contingency plans were reviewed. Between Rommel, O.K.W. and O.K.H. there was never a real meeting of minds about what the Axis might ultimately achieve in the Middle East—and of course it can be argued that Rommel was always too optimistic, and in his thinking ignored the dangers of the vast open flank which a German penetration southwards, such as he visualised, would lay bare to the Russians. Nevertheless, here is an occasion when it is possible to look, from his point of view, at 'the other side of the hill'. In Cairo the representatives of the Chiefs of Staff; Auchinleck, speaking for the Middle East Command; and Wavell, speaking for India, all registered their concern about the northern flank of the Commonwealth Armies. What Rommel hoped for the British feared.

The *Official History* puts the issue tersely: if 'the Germans completely defeated the Russians and were determined to drive the British from the Middle East, a grave situation might arise during the spring of 1943'. In this strategic picture Churchill, as well as his military advisers, placed Rommel as the key figure. Sir Ian Jacob, who went out to Cairo as part of the Cabinet Office staff and who shrewdly assessed 8 Army's situation, noted in his diary for 8 August (having just returned from a desert visit which must have provided him with the most painful moment in his life—the handing over to Auchinleck of the order of dismissal: 'I felt', he says, 'as if I were just going to murder an unsuspecting friend . . .') that when he reported to Churchill on his return he found 'his mind is entirely fixed on the defeat of Rommel, and on getting General Alexander into complete charge of the operations in the Western Desert. He does not understand how a man can remain in Cairo while great events are occurring in the Desert, and leave the conduct of them to someone else. He strode up and down declaiming on this point, and he means to have his way. " Rommel, Rommel, Rommel, Rommel," he cried, "what else matters but beating him?" '

Churchill had his way: and history will have *its* way about his misunderstanding and mishandling of Auchinleck. But from the point of view of a military study of a German Field-Marshal the intimate details of the Cairo Conference are irrelevant—they belong to British military and political history. For Rommel what mattered was the conclusion. It might well have gone *his* way: Churchill's initial decision was to move Alexander from command in the imminent *Torch* to a general command in the Near East, Montgomery from England to replace Alexander, and Gott to take over 8 Army. All informed opinion suggests that the very thing Churchill was demanding—a fresh approach—could not conceivably have been provided by a veteran. The Germans supplied an answer. A fighter of the *Luftwaffe* shot up the transport plane bringing Gott back to Cairo, and he was killed.

Gott's unexpected death caused a swift reappraisal, as a result of which Alexander was retained as Generalissimo in the Middle East while Montgomery was switched from *Torch* to command of 8 Army. A new phase now began in the desert, in which Rommel's prospects were obscure. The Commonwealth Army was invigorated by a new set of leaders and an increasing flow of equipment. Rommel could expect neither. On 2 August he wrote to his wife: 'I'm thankful for every day's respite we get. A lot of sickness.

Unfortunately many of the older officers are going down now. Even I am feeling very tired and limp. . . . Holding on to our Alamein position has given us the severest fighting we've yet seen in Africa. We've all got heat diarrhoea now, but it's bearable. A year ago I had jaundice and that was much worse.'

Hindsight must always be resisted: but it is interesting to reflect on the course the Cairo Conference might have taken had Churchill been able to read this letter. Auchinleck's accolade, it reveals the straits to which he had reduced the army of the Axis.

X

Alam Halfa: The Turning Point

1942

The violent battles of the last few weeks were now followed by a lull, for both armies were exhausted. On the British side there were two other reasons for inactivity. Auchinleck had reported to the Chiefs of Staff that his policy was temporarily defensive because of lack of resources and the enemy's consolidation of his positions, and the attention of the High Command in the Middle East was diverted from the front by the Cairo Conference—diverted to those investigations and discussions which ended with the appointment of Alexander and Montgomery.

But there could be no lull for Rommel, who had no illusions about his situation. In his memoirs he observes that though the Allied losses in July had been greater than those of the Axis, nevertheless Auchinleck had not paid too great a price: 'the one thing that had mattered to him was to halt our advance, and that, unfortunately, he had done.' At the beginning of August, in fact, Rommel had to try to resolve the classic dilemma of the desert campaigns—that of the general who, having pushed forward to the limit of his supply lines, could no longer maintain the impetus of his thrust. The British had been faced by the same problem after Beda Fomm, and again after *Crusader*.

Rommel's solution was characteristic. In theory there were three courses open to him. He could retreat to a point where he might hope for adequate logistic support; he could stand in his present positions, fortifying them as powerfully as possible and only engaging in defensive action; or he could launch yet another major assault. General Wolfe once remarked that war is an option of difficulties. Rommel selected the most difficult of his options by deciding to attack the southern section of the Allied line with the aim of penetrating to Cairo and the Canal. His decision has been much criticised, and it is important (before considering the course of the battle he provoked) to review the factors that influenced him. From time to time Rommel acted so impulsively that he appeared to be driven by instinct rather than reason. But he thought hard before embarking on what his troops afterwards called 'The Six Day Race' (the name of a popular German cycling event) and his decision was neither casual nor irresponsible.

To retreat was impossible. Rommel was temperamentally aggressive, but he was ready to retire when there was a genuine need; he had demonstrated this readiness earlier in the campaign, and would do so again during the final phase of Alamein and also during the withdrawal to Tunisia, when more than once he fell back while his German and Italian superiors were insisting on standing fast. But though the desert is often described as the perfect battle-ground—a terrain on which the operations of war were conducted in a 'pure' state—this is not correct. Not one of the desert commanders—not Wavell, not Auchinleck and certainly not Rommel—was allowed to concentrate on the purely military requirement: they could never forget their political masters. Rommel always had to remember Hitler.

In his memoirs Rommel devotes much space to the considerations which led him to risk the battle of Alam Halfa, but none to the arguments in favour of a policy of retreat. He had his own reasons for rejecting such a policy, but he knew that even had he advocated it Hitler would have opposed it with all the ruthlessness he revealed when Rommel later wished to withdraw from Alamein. Hopes had run high during the summer offensive. Mussolini's white charger had been prepared for 'a Roman entry into Cairo and Alexandria'. The Duce had arrived in Africa 'accoutred with the Sword of Islam'. An Italian had been nominated as the civil administrator of Egypt, and Hitler had agreed that Egypt would belong to the Italian sphere of influence.* Rommel had therefore to assume that Hitler and Mussolini would react violently against a proposal to retreat.

He had also to bear in mind a strategic possibility. Ever since Admiral Raeder had interested Hitler in the Grand Design—the notion that German Armies moving south-eastwards from Russia through the Caucasus might achieve with the Afrika Korps a pincer movement whose jaws would close on Suez—Rommel's *Panzerarmee* could no longer be thought of in terms of a detached force. The connection between the two fronts is well illustrated by a letter to Mussolini from Hitler sent on 4 August: 'However long it takes to consolidate our position, I have, like you, given orders to

* 'It will suffice if a suitable person is accredited to the Italian Resident in Egypt as the representative of Rommel, as operational Commander-in-Chief.' *Hitler's Table Talk*, p. 573.

throw into North Africa everything of value in the way of support, reinforcements, and replacements. . . . It will be difficult and complicated for us to do this. The formation and maintenance of such a strong group of air transport for Africa at the moment of our big offensive in the Caucasus means slowing up the advance of our armoured divisions out there.'

In August the northern half of the German pincer was still in motion. On 9 August 1 Panzer Army entered the Maikop oilfields and Piatigorsk fell the next day. On 22 August the swastika was raised over Mount Elbruz, on the 25th Mosdok was taken, and it was not until 6 September that the last Soviet naval base on the Black Sea, Novorossisk, was in German hands. These victories brought the spearheads of Hitler's armies into alignment along the northern ridges of the Caucasus and presented a grave threat to the whole allied position in the Middle East—especially to the oilfields. The threat had already been appreciated by the British. On 9 July a meeting of the Chiefs of Staff had been impressed by a report from the Oil Control Board that if Abadan and Bahrein were lost, some $13\frac{1}{2}$ million tons of oil would have to be replaced from other sources, and the extra transport involved would mean building 270 more tankers—which was impossible. Their recommendation to the Middle East Defence Committee was therefore that 'you should strain every effort towards defeating Rommel'.

The threat still remained in August, and in such a context it is difficult to imagine Hitler (or Rommel) agreeing to a retreat from Alamein: on both strategical and political grounds, this was an option that Rommel was bound to reject. General Bayerlein has confirmed that he was vividly aware of the relationship of his own operations to those of the German armies in Russia. On the first morning of Alam Halfa, Bayerlein recalls, Rommel left his truck with a troubled face and said to his medical adviser, Forster: 'Professor, the decision I have taken to attack today is the hardest I have ever taken. Either the army in Russia succeeds in getting through to Grozny and we in Africa manage to reach the Suez Canal, or. . . .' Rommel then made a gesture of defeat.

To stand fast was also unacceptable. After the capture of Tobruk Rommel had pressed forward into Egypt for the specific purpose of preventing a stabilisation of the front. He sought to avoid what he called mechanised static warfare because 'this was just what the British officers and men had been trained for. The good points of the British soldier, his tenacity, for instance, would have the maximum effect and the bad points, such as his immobility and rigidity, none at all.' But in August, he appreciated, precisely this was happening. The northern and central sectors of the Allied front were being converted into a series of inter-connected 'boxes', new minefields were being laid in the south, and on the far left of his enemy's line the Qattara Depression prevented him from manœuvring round an open flank. He therefore decided that he must attempt one final attack through the southern part of the Allied defences before they became impenetrable and robbed him for ever of the opportunity for those fluid, mobile operations in which he believed the Afrika Korps to be superior. Moreover, as he rightly observed: 'in static warfare, victory goes to the side which can fire the more ammunition.' He knew that in such a *Materialenschlacht* he must lose, and it was his concern about supplies which, above all, persuaded him to attack.

Because he displayed the attractive qualities of a cavalier, Rommel's popular image is that of the 'front soldier', the man who finds his supreme expression in action. But Liddell Hart has pointed out that there are two forms of military genius—the conceptive and the executive—and that in Rommel's case they were combined. In other words, while Rommel was a brilliant operational commander he was also capable of brooding about the war and seeing it as a whole. The executive commander is distinguished by his practical conduct on the battlefield: the conceptive by his ability to understand new tactical or strategic ideas and also to penetrate to the heart of those broader issues—political or economic—which may ultimately affect him in the field. During the summer of 1942, Rommel detached his mind sufficiently from the daily problems of the battle to comprehend one of these issues: he became convinced that the entry of the United States into the war was crucial. His realism and his imagination told him that America's industrial power would swing the technological balance in favour of the Allies—and that this was an irreversible process. His thoughts about the way the war must be conducted were guided by this intuition until the day of his death.

It influenced his planning before Alam Halfa, for he was aware that 'several large convoys had arrived in Suez during July and air reconnaissance had reported the arrival of several hundred thousand tons of shipping', and he estimated that another 100,000-ton convoy would arrive in September. (It actually arrived on 3 September, delivering the 300 Sherman tanks and 100 self-propelled guns which Roosevelt had transferred from the American Army after he and Churchill had received the news of the fall of Tobruk.) His purpose in attacking, therefore, was to move before Britain, fed by America, could defeat him by sheer weight of *matériel*. The period of the full moon at the end of August seemed to be his last chance, because the front line was now so close to the ports and bases of the Allies that their massive reinforcements of men and equipment could be rapidly brought into action, whereas his own replenishment must necessarily be slow.

Rommel had not misjudged the Americans. On 21 June Roosevelt made his transfer to the British of the tanks and artillery just issued to his own armoured divisions: when a ship carrying the tanks' engines was sunk (off Bermuda) another fast ship was filled with engines and immediately despatched to join the convoy.* On 30 June he addressed a six-point questionnaire to General Marshall 'on the assumption that the Delta will be evacuated within ten days and the Canal blocked'. Though Marshall believed that nothing could be done to affect the situation immediately, steps were then taken whose consequences were now significant for Rommel. In spite of protests from Chiang Kai-shek, heavy bombers of the American Tenth Air Force were diverted from China to the Middle East, and at the beginning of July, in response to a request from Churchill, Roosevelt cabled Stalin to ask him to agree that 40 A-20 bombers, intended for Russia, should also go to Egypt. He made the point that the situation in the desert directly affected the supply route to Russia through the Middle East.

Stalin agreed. And thus, in various ways, the increasing tide of American aid which Rommel had anticipated was now beginning to flow. The Bostons and Baltimores and Tomahawks in the air, the Honeys and Grants and Shermans on the ground, the Priest self-propelled gun, the White scout-car and the invaluable jeep, all of which were or were soon to become familiar sights in the desert, were only a part of the immense American contribution to Rommel's final defeat.

His own shortages were grave. He estimated that his German divisions alone were 16,000 under strength. Most of his transport—about 85%—consisted of captured British or American vehicles for which the stocks of spares were limited, and it had proved impossible to use the railway from Tobruk to El Daba to ease the pressure on the coastal road. Between 1 August and 20 August his *Panzerarmee* consumed almost twice as many supplies as were ferried across the Mediterranean. He was short of 210 tanks, 175 troop-carriers and armoured cars, and at least 1500 other vehicles, while the rations for his men were 'miserable and so monotonous that we were sick of the sight of them'. Because of his lack of ammunition, an embargo had often to be placed on all forms of harassing fire, whereas the British 'hammered away with their artillery for hours on end at our troops'. The Italians favoured their own formations, but half of the 220 tanks in 20 Motorised Corps were now liable to break down because of mechanical defects. And yet, Rommel calculated, there were standing ready in Italy (in some cases for many months) at least 2000 lorries and 100 guns earmarked for his army, while in Germany a further 1000 vehicles and 120 tanks were held on call.

The swift and copious reinforcement of the Axis command at the other

* So Churchill in *The Second World War, Vol. IV*. Presumably these were spare engines.

end of the Mediterranean, after the *Torch* landings, shows that the supply line through Italy to Africa could function efficiently when someone was determined to make it work. Nevertheless, in August Rommel was desperately short of supplies. The reasons for this are complicated, but the first is undoubtedly a strategic error on the part of Hitler and Rommel: the decision to abandon *Operation Herkules*, the capture of Malta.

Hitler's support of Rommel against those pleading for an assault on the island is properly described by Kesselring as 'a mortal blow'. It had immediate consequences for the *Panzerarmee*. By 22 August, 32,000 tons of cargo reached the island from the five ships which survived the *Pedestal* convoy. Twenty-nine Spitfires were flown in on 17 August from the carrier *Furious*, and three submarines, the *Otus*, the *Rorqual* and the *Clyde*, arrived with ammunition, torpedoes, and fuel for the fighters. Hitler had not matched the British determination symbolised in Churchill's message to the Admiralty that he must be able to say that 'the Navy would never abandon Malta'. The result for Rommel was that in the air, and on and under the sea, the British forces in Malta were now able to harass his supply routes from Italy with increasing effect. Kesselring was right. Moreover the *Luftwaffe* in the Mediterranean had now been weakened not only by the survival of Malta but also by the diversion of squadrons to the Russian front.

A second reason for Rommel's difficulties was the command structure within which he had to work. As a German Field-Marshal he had to pay attention to Kesselring, but as an Axis commander whose army was composed of both German and Italian units his direct responsibility was to Bastico, and the arrangements for his supplies lay in Italian hands. *Comando Supremo* in Rome governed the movement of men and stores in Africa. Rommel had long been critical of the system whereby the German Military Attaché in Rome, General von Rintelen, dealt with *Comando Supremo* on his behalf about these all-important logistics: he believed that this task should have been given to Kesselring, and that von Rintelen lacked both the necessary drive and the necessary status to promote the interests of the Afrika Korps. At last, on 16 August, Bastico was by-passed and Rommel's army was made formally responsible to *Comando Supremo*; a liaison group was to be set up in Africa under General Barbasetti di Prun to co-ordinate the administrative traffic. But this re-organisation was slow to take effect, and it produced no results before Alam Halfa.

A consequence of this Italian grip on his supply lines was that even the reinforcements which did reach Rommel, whether of men or material, were unsatisfactory. In early August 164 German Light Division and the Italian *Folgore* Parachute Division (both of which had been earmarked for the capture of Malta) began to arrive, but neither had any transport, and a heavier strain was thus placed on the already over-burdened lines of communication. Yet at the same time the Italian *Pistoia* Division (at least two-thirds of its complement, with between 300 and 400 of its vehicles) was sent across the Mediterranean although it was not intended for immediate use at the front. There was also a lack of proportion in the rate of refitting Italian and German units actually in the line. The Italians received a steady flow of new vehicles, but though Italian and German cargoes were supposed to be loaded in the ratio of one to one, the Afrika Korps was not, in practice, treated as an equal partner.

Another factor was the aggressiveness of the R.A.F. Apart from the interference with Rommel's sea-communications which was mounted from Malta, the Desert Air Force throughout August maintained a continuous attack on the African ports and the coastal road through and along which Rommel's supplies were forwarded to the front. An average of 50 bombers was out every night during this month to raid Tobruk and the smaller harbours: in all, 1646 sorties were flown. Reconnaissance was also continuous—along the coast as far as Derna and inland to Jarabub and Siwa. The German reaction was weak; in the first half of the month the fighters of *Fliegerführer Afrika* were short of fuel, and counter-bombing on Port Said and Alexandria was slight and unsuccessful.

Nevertheless, in spite of his shortages and because of them Rommel concluded that to attack was essential. In justice to him, one further point must be underlined. With the advantages of hindsight it has become evident that Alam Halfa, like Medenine, was a typical 'Montgomery defensive battle': neatly and simply organised, tightly controlled, following exactly a premeditated plan. But in these early weeks of August Rommel had not yet gained the impression of Montgomery which he formed during the action—that of 'a very cautious man, who was not prepared to take any risk'. He did not know beforehand what he decided afterwards, that Montgomery's handling of the battle would be 'absolutely right and suited to the occasion'. In planning his armoured thrust in the south he could only be guided by what he had learned about the capacity of his opponents in the fighting of the last few months.

Auchinleck had stopped Rommel, but at Gazala and in the bitter actions along the Alamein Line the British had continued to display many tactical weaknesses, particularly in their use of armour and the co-ordination of tanks and infantry. General Kippenberger, the official New Zealand historian, commanded 5 New Zealand Brigade in the abortive attack on the Ruweisat Ridge of 14–15 July, when the failure of their supporting armour to arrive at dawn caused the New Zealanders to be overrun, after a counter-attack by German tanks, with the loss of four battalion commanders out of six and 1400 casualties. He sums up this disaster with the comment that 'the fundamental fault was the failure to co-ordinate infantry and armour. That is impossible without a common doctrine, a sound system of inter-communication, and training together.' This was only one of many instances: no common doctrine existed, and there was still no training together. One of the reasons for Auchinleck's decision to avoid further offensive actions at the end of July had been his knowledge that 8 Army required this training, and before the battle of Alam Halfa Rommel was justified in believing that a sudden *Blitzkrieg* assault by his panzers might throw the British into confusion. He was proved wrong; but on the evidence available to him at the time it was a fair assumption.

His plan of attack was ambitious and predictable: a repetition of his sweep round the south of Bir Hacheim on 27 May. He intended to hold in the north, feint against the Ruweisat Ridge in the centre, and press hard on his right with 15 and 21 Panzer Divisions of Nehring's Afrika Korps. The main striking force was to concentrate between Bab el Qattara and the El Taqa plateau and to advance eastwards at 2300 on 30 August. After penetrating the British minefields, it was to wheel to the left, pause, and prepare for the main action. Rommel calculated that his line of battle would now be formed by Reconnaissance Units 3 and 33 on his eastern flank; next the Afrika Korps; then 20 Italian Corps and 90 Light Division, while a mixed group under 10 Corps would provide a pivot of manœuvre on the left. Next morning at 0600 his army would drive to the north and encircle the enemy. 'Things,' he said, 'were then to move fast. The decisive battle was on no account to become static.' He relied particularly on a slow reaction, for experience had shown that it always took the British command some time before decisions were reached and put into effect. Speed and surprise would achieve success.

The plan required the Afrika Korps to advance 30 miles in seven hours. 'Seeing that this distance had to be covered at night,' the *Official History* observes, 'over almost unreconnoitred ground, known to be mined, but to an unknown extent, it is evident that the timing was, to say the least, wildly optimistic.' Rommel's final objective implied an even greater optimism, for he aimed at capturing a number of the Nile bridges by a *coup de main*. He also hoped to start a revolt by the Egyptian Army. The map in his *Papers* (p. 259) indicates his aim. While his infantry pinned the British to the Alamein line von Bismarck's 21 Panzers were to outflank Alexandria and von Vaerst with his 15 Panzers and 90 Light was to drive on to Cairo. Here 20

Italian Corps would relieve them: and thereafter von Vaerst was to capture Suez while the Italians secured the Nile Valley. Rommel had been warned that there was not a single pontoon bridge in Africa, but he thought that his sudden offensive would throw the British into such disarray that no demolitions would be attempted.

This plan has often been condemned as 'a gambler's last throw'. But it must be seen in perspective. Rommel had possibly been mistaken in rushing so far to the east after Gazala, and was certainly mistaken in proposing that the capture of Malta should be shelved. There were nevertheless sound reasons, granted his present situation at Alamein, for seeking to recover the initiative. His fault lay in attacking with a tactical scheme which it was impossible to implement, and for strategic objectives which were too grandiose. The state of his health perhaps accounts for the failure of his judgement. During August he was depressed and frustrated—as is evident in his memoirs and his letters to his wife. His manner in his dealings with the Italians became so brusque that relations were more than usually strained. But he was also physically weak. His medical adviser, Forster, and General Gause, his Chief of Staff, signalled to O.K.W. that he had chronic stomach trouble, nasal diphtheria, and a poor circulation, and that he was unfit for command. Great Commanders, as well as commoners, are subject to psychosomatic disorders. It is an odd coincidence—and I do not know how much weight should be placed on it—that Rommel was not only plagued by gastric disturbances in the desert, but also during the early weeks of the German offensive in 1914. Too little attention is paid, in military studies, to the health of the commander. In Rommel's case, his health certainly affected his capacity to command. He considered that Guderian was the only man suitable to replace him, but O.K.W. rejected the proposal, and Rommel therefore remained at his post. It is not surprising, therefore, that at Alam Halfa his faculties were not at their most acute.

Sound tactics, moreover, require reliable information.* Rommel's hope that he could burst through the British minefields was based on inaccurate reconnaissance. He later confessed that he had planned on the assumption that the front was only thinly mined; and though the strength of the *Luftwaffe* increased towards the end of August, it was unable to give him a full picture of the British defences or the efforts being made to improve the protection of the Delta—'a series of extreme measures for the defence of Cairo and the water-lines running northwards to the sea', in Churchill's words.

The crux was the character of his opponent. Auchinleck and his staff had foreseen a German move in the direction of Alam Halfa, and on 27 July the

* See, however, Appendix Two.

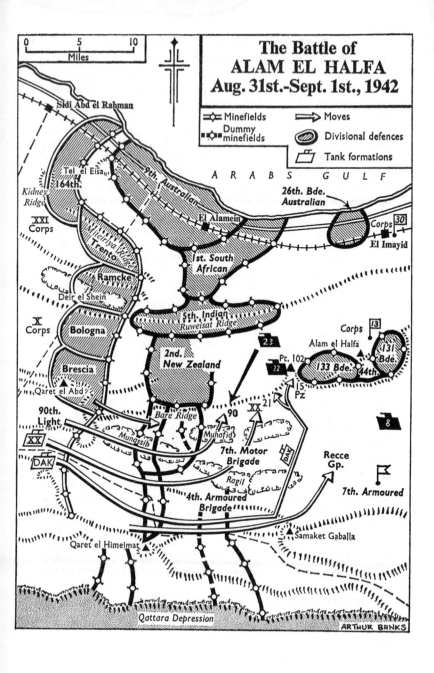

Deputy Chief of Staff, Dorman-Smith, had submitted an appreciation in which he predicted that 8 Army would have to undertake a defensive battle in the Alam Halfa area, and suggested that the troops who would have to fight in it would need training and exercise on the ground. He also forecast a later battle in the north—a British break through the enemy positions about El Alamein. It was a prophetic document. (Montgomery denies absolutely that when he assumed command these plans were placed in his hands.) Montgomery's contribution was to make a similar appreciation and then to convert it into an effective scheme of defence, and to control the course of the battle with an iron hand, so that Rommel was unable to profit from those tactical deficiencies which the British had previously displayed. The difference between the two commanders was that Rommel was now tired and ill, whereas Montgomery was fresh and self-confident. In his autobiography, the latter is frank about his aim: 'What I now needed was a battle which would be fought in accordance with my ideas and not those of former desert commanders; furthermore, it must be a resounding victory. . . .'

Montgomery saw the position at Alam Halfa as a right angle. Its northern side began with the refused flank of the New Zealand box (see map on p. 154), to the east of which lay the Alam Halfa ridge itself. On this he placed two brigades of 44 (Home Counties) Division: the third, 132, was sent to support the New Zealanders on their western front. (44 Division had only recently disembarked, and it had hurried forward as a result of Montgomery's personal intervention.) Between these two strong points, at the western edge of the ridge, 22 Armoured Brigade was ordered to dig in its tanks. North of the line 23 Armoured Brigade was held back as a mobile reserve, and 8 Armoured Brigade was put into positions which would form the eastern side of the angle.

South of this trap 7 Armoured Division, which at present consisted of light formations, was to harry Rommel's flank and rear and to attack his transport columns. Montgomery had been definite in his instructions to Horrocks, the Commander of 13 Corps, who had just flown out from England, that in no circumstances was he to allow his armour to become involved in close fighting: he wanted Horrocks' tanks to become part of a *corps de chasse* at Alamein. In his recollections Montgomery describes how he dealt tersely with Renton, the commander of 7 Armoured, as the latter began to ask him when the tanks could be 'let loose'. There was little hope, in fact, that even had Rommel's thrust proceeded according to plan, he would have been able to exploit those wild and unco-ordinated charges by British tanks which had so often occurred in the past.

Montgomery's dispositions imposed his will on his opponent before the the battle started. Rommel could not move east beyond the Alam Halfa ridge without attempting to clear it and protect his left flank: if he attempted to do so he would be drawn on 22 Armoured Brigade, and by insisting on their occupying hull-down positions Montgomery and Horrocks had applied the defensive principle which Wellington so frequently used in his campaigns—that of achieving surprise by installing troops on a reverse slope. Moreover, in making his unavoidable attack on the ridge Rommel would be forced to push his armour through a series of depressions—Alinda, Munassib, Muhafid and Ragil—which would hamper his mobility and expose him to bombing by the R.A.F.: and Montgomery had already established that firm liaison with the Desert Air Force which was to pay so many dividends in the close, tactical support of his army.

These arrangements by Montgomery have often been praised—in some cases by uncritical admirers. But the hard-bitten Kippenberger of the New Zealand Division, who had fought in Greece, in Crete and in the earlier desert battles as a battalion commander who became more wary with every week of experience, a man frequently critical of his superiors, says that 'the whole plan for the battle was thoroughly explained to us and I liked it more than that for any action I had taken part in. More pleasing even than the plan was the ready, balanced feeling that we all had.' At the time I was a raw regimental officer in the artillery of 44 Division, whose field gun positions were on the Alam Halfa ridge, and I can affirm that this was a feeling which somehow managed to filter down even to us, green reinforcements. While it is easy, therefore, to dismiss Rommel's attack as that of a desperate gambler, it should be remembered that something had happened in 8 Army of which he could have hardly been aware until he had been taught by experience.

He was apprehensive about his supplies—especially petrol and ammunition—right up to the eve of the battle. On the 22nd he sent von Rintelen his minimum requirements. On the 27th—when the moon was already full—Kesselring flew to meet him and promised that in an emergency 500 tons of petrol a day would be despatched by air. Cavallero told him that tankers under heavy escort would be arriving in a matter of hours. None of these promises were fulfilled. But in spite of his doubts Rommel came to a final decision, which was influenced by his knowledge that if he let this period of the full moon pass 'our last chance of an offensive would be gone for ever'. An order was issued for the attack to begin on the night of 30 August. He wrote to his wife with a mixture of confidence and concern.

The R.A.F. was in action even before the Afrika Korps began to breach the minefields. German concentrations had already been observed, for though the reconnaissance planes of the Desert Air Force had been more vigorously attacked by the *Luftwaffe* towards the end of August, a watch had been maintained—particularly by the Tomahawks and Hurricanes of No. 208 Squadron. As dusk fell on the evening of 30 August, Albacores dropped flares and Wellingtons bombed the Axis tanks. This was ominous: and when the Germans probed the minefields they found them to be deeper and more elaborate than had been foreseen, and were harassed in the moonlight by the motorised infantry of 7 Armoured Division, with their 6-pounders. The field artillery of 7 Armoured in the south and the New Zealanders in their northern box combined to delay the engineers as they tried to lift the mines.

Rommel was on the telephone at his H.Q. throughout the night. Desmond Young, in his biography, suggests that this was a flaw in Rommel's control at Alam Halfa because his instinctive place was at the head of his troops: a fit Rommel would have led from the front. But he could have achieved little in the confusion of the minefield gaps—though the Rifle Brigade defending them thought that the Afrika Korps was attacking without its usual verve. The first gap was not completed until 0430: more were gradually established, but at 0800 Rommel was informed, in his command post at Gebel Kalakh, that progress was very slow, that Nehring had been wounded in an air attack, and that von Bismarck had been blown up on a mine. The battle had been lost in the first few hours: neither speed nor surprise could now be attained. But after consulting Bayerlein, who as Chief of Staff of the Afrika Korps had temporarily taken over command, Rommel decided to continue his attack.

This was indefensible; there are times when it is as important for a commander to disengage as it is for him to attack, and here was one. Rommel should have realised that the British were now aware of the direction and scope of his attempted penetration and that there was no point in pursuing it. He should have appreciated that their counter-measures must inevitably reduce his speed, and he knew that he had not enough petrol for extensive manœuvre. The mental and physical lassitude produced by the intestinal disorders of the desert war could be overpowering; this may account for his second wrong decision. Having made it, he also modified his plan: he ordered the Afrika Korps (which von Vaerst took over during the day) to switch its attack to the north immediately, instead of pressing further eastwards before making a turn. Thus it was directed straight at the dug-in tanks of 22 Armoured Brigade and the anti-tank guns of their supporting infantry. Horrocks had held an exercise before the battle to rehearse the action to be taken if this happened, and the panzers would now have to advance past aiming-posts which had already been set out in front of the British to provide their tanks and guns with an exact range. In earlier descriptions of the battle it was sometimes suggested that this move was due to the planting by British intelligence of a false 'going map', which persuaded the Germans that their best route would lie through areas of soft sand. But though there is evidence that such a map reached *Panzerarmee* H.Q. (from General von Thoma, for example, after his capture at Alamein), there is none to suggest that it was a factor in Rommel's change of plan, which was dictated by his new tactical situation.

The change of direction of the Afrika Korps produced what was, from the British point of view, the only critical episode in the battle. From about 1130 a prolonged dust storm compelled the R.A.F. to stop its attacks, and under its cover the Afrika Korps was able to re-organise: at 1530 tanks started to roll to the north. 22 Armoured Brigade, placed in a semi-circle round Point 102, had light squadrons some miles forward to observe and decoy; these gradually became engaged, but as they withdrew it appeared that the Germans were moving still further to the east. So Roberts, the brigadier commanding 22 Armoured, ordered his tanks to leave their dug-in positions, show themselves, and if necessary be prepared to attack the German flank. The ruse worked. About 1800 the Germans became aware of them, halted, re-formed their front to face the north, and moved straight for the 22nd's line.

'Dug-in positions' sound impressive, but it was difficult to exploit them with Grants. These had a high silhouette, and their main armament was carried in a sponson low down in the body. To engage, therefore, the commander had to expose most of his tank. The strength of 22 Armoured lay in its Grants, and they did not know that although Rommel had been starved of supplies he had received not only some 70 of the Mark III Specials (which had first appeared at Gazala) but also 27 Mark IV Specials: these had improved armour, and a long 75-mm. gun which could penetrate at a range of 3000 yards.

The centre of Roberts' line was held by the County of London Yeomanry. As they exposed themselves to engage, the powerful guns of the Specials began to pick them off one by one, and soon all 12 tanks of 'A' Squadron were out of action. There was a wide gap in the centre of the line, yet Roberts did not dare to move his flanking regiments to fill it because there were so many German tanks along his front that he would have risked encirclement. He therefore summoned forward his reserve, the Royal Scots Greys, and he has described his intense anxiety as he waited, watching the German advance and calling on his wireless, 'Come on the Greys, get out your whips.' Heavy artillery concentrations were directed on to the Afrika Korps, but it was difficult to stop a tank attack with explosive 25-pounder shells. The Germans were beginning to get among the Rifle Brigade, whose 6-pounders, holding their fire until the enemy was 300 yards away, had some effect—one sergeant claimed five 'kills'. Then, just as light was fading, the Greys poured into the gap and the crisis was over. It was more dramatic than real, for as soon as the presence of both panzer divisions had been identified 23 Armoured Brigade with its 100 Valentines had moved forward on to the right flank of 22, and even had the Afrika Korps achieved a penetration, this would have been sealed off. During the day the Germans lost 22 tanks in action and more for other reasons, and von Vaerst now withdrew for the night. His abortive operations, including the grind through the Ragil depression, had consumed much petrol for no result.

Rommel's situation was steadily deteriorating, for the fuel promised by Kesselring and Cavallero had not arrived and would not arrive. 5000 tons were due to reach him by 3 September: by the 2nd 2600 tons had been sunk and 1500 were still in Italy. Supplies flown over by the *Luftwaffe* were consumed in the course of transporting them to the front. On the night of 31 August–1 September his replenishment was already failing: and, in addition, the dust of the day's storms had settled, so that the R.A.F. was able to circle above his leaguers, dropping more flares and bombing his soft transport. From the Alam Halfa box the artillery of 44 Division continued their shelling. As the *Official History* observes, the fighting capacity of the D.A.K. was 'considerably reduced by the enforced dispersal, lack of sleep and the strain of waiting for the next bomb'.

The next morning Rommel made his third mistake, by ordering 15 Panzer to advance unsupported in the direction of the Halfa ridge. It is difficult to explain why he should have made so fruitless a decision unless it was because he felt, wearily, that as he had gone so far he should make yet another effort. In his *Papers* he says that he used 15 Panzer on its own because of lack of petrol: but for an attack on so obviously powerful a position by what was now so weak a force this is an implausible explanation. It may be that he had not realised that the Alam Halfa ridge was occupied in strength. Stukas had certainly bombed it with precision the previous day: but whereas 8 Army now had a close liaison with its airmen, and enjoyed more rapid intelligence and more rapid support, there was still a dangerous gap between the *Panzerarmee* and the *Luftwaffe* in Africa. In any event, the last hours of Rommel's offensive at Alam Halfa were an anti-climax.

15 Panzer made no progress. By throwing out an anti-tank screen on their right they prevented 8 Armoured Brigade from moving westwards along the edge of the Alam Halfa minefields to reinforce Roberts, and after the Sherwood Rangers had lost seven tanks the brigade commander pulled back, following his instructions to avoid becoming too deeply committed. But on this day the dust did not inhibit the R.A.F.; pattern bombing, by what the

Germans now called the 'party rallies', continued. Seven officers were killed at the H.Q. of the Afrika Korps, and Rommel, now up at the front, was lucky to avoid death when a bomb splinter pierced a spade lying beside his slit trench. 'The red-hot metal fragment', he remembered, 'fell beside me.' During the afternoon he moved his command post, but the bombing and shelling of his formations intensified. By the evening there was only one petrol issue left for the *Panzerarmee*, the equivalent of a run per vehicle of 100 kilometres over good going. Rommel was already contemplating retreat, and after his command post had again been bombed during the night he decided to thin out and then withdraw.

The retreat began on 3 September, and was completed on the morning of the 6th. On the evening of the 2nd Rommel had a conference with Kesselring, at which he described what he called the 'bomb carpets' of the R.A.F. and requested stronger assistance in the air. Kesselring promised reinforcements: but Rommel had no need to be concerned about his immediate future, for Montgomery did not intend to make any major effort to cut him off. During the battle he had prepared to exploit success, by pulling units into reserve from 30 Corps in the north and nominating General Lumsden to be ready to take command of a force which was to thrust for Daba if the opportunity arose. But after a visit to Horrocks on the afternoon of the 2nd he decided to let Rommel go, and to preserve his army intact for the decisive battle at Alamein with which he was already preoccupied. He gave Horrocks explicit instructions, in spite of the latter's protests, to allow Rommel to retain the heights of Himeimat because he envisaged that it would be necessary, for his Alamein plan, to persuade the Germans that the main point of the attack would be in the south: he wished Rommel's troops to be able to observe the false tanks and installations which he proposed to spread around the left of his line.

The only important attempt to hinder Rommel was made on 3 September, when 5 New Zealand Brigade and 132 Brigade from 44 Division made a night attack into the Munassib depression with the object of closing the gap between Himeimat and the north. This was a disastrous failure. On the left the New Zealanders made some progress, though the Maoris got out of hand and lost direction. 50 R.T.R., confused by German flares, ran on to a minefield and lost 12 tanks and their squadron commander. On the right 132 Brigade, in its first operation in the desert, fell into complete confusion. Its soft transport had been brought forward too soon and was hit by the enemy's defensive fire, so that the infantry was silhouetted against the flames of burning trucks. The ground was rocky, and digging difficult. As a result, the brigade suffered 700 casualties—a large proportion of 8 Army's total losses in the whole of the battle. It is strange that in their autobiographies both Montgomery and Horrocks should ascribe Rommel's retreat to the influence of this action, for the *Rommel Papers* show that it made no impression on him, while the definite decision to retire had already been reached.

Montgomery has been severely criticised for failing to cut Rommel off and destroy the Afrika Korps. But even had he 'let the armour loose' during the battle—as some of the old desert hands desired—it is doubtful whether the Germans would have been more decisively repulsed, and the Munassib fiasco powerfully supports his argument that more training was necessary before he could deliver a final blow. From Rommel's point of view the relief was welcome. He was now able to fall back on the line of the western British minefields and establish defensive positions among them: his armour moved even further to the west, and went into reserve. At 0700 on 7 September Montgomery halted all further efforts to push him back.

Rommel's total casualties (German and Italian) were 2910 men, 49 tanks, 55 field and anti-tank guns and 395 vehicles: General Alexander, in his despatch after the battle, reported that the British had lost 1640 men killed, wounded and missing, 68 tanks and 18 anti-tank guns. Rommel estimated that 1300 tons of bombs had fallen on his army—far more than in any previous action. Two thousand five hundred sorties were flown by the Desert Air Force and 180 by the U.S. Army Air Force.

These figures are small, by later standards. But as von Mellenthin observes in his *Panzer Battles*, Alam Halfa was 'the turning point of the desert war, and the first of a long series of defeats on every front which foreshadowed the defeat of Germany'. 'A turning point', de Guingand recalls, was the phrase applied to the battle by Wendell Willkie, who visited the Western Desert at this time. Its significance is disproportionate to its scope and duration, and does not lie simply, as is often suggested, in its effect on British morale: it also advanced new modes of war. The use of 22 Armoured Brigade was no more than a British variant of a technique Rommel had already evolved—the luring of the enemy's armour on to a concealed line of guns. But the continual pattern bombing by the Desert Air Force was an original development in that *tactical* employment of aircraft which was to be further elaborated in Africa (at El Hamma, for example, and in the final break-through in Tunisia at Medjez el Bab) and would lead directly to the massive assaults by heavy bombers in Normandy which preceded the attack on Caen, the operation by British armoured divisions called *Goodwood*, and the American penetration at St. Lo. The co-ordinated use of divisional artillery to fire concentrations from large numbers of guns on to a single target was also an advance in a process which led (through the opening barrage of 23 October at Alamein) to a steadily increasing technical superiority in this arm which reached its climax in north-west Europe: though it should be noted that better co-ordination of the British artillery had started during July 1942. Students of the First World War may recall the outstanding expertise of Colonel Bruch-müller in the organisation of vast artillery programmes, and may wonder why, between 1939 and 1945, the Germans, on their western fronts, never attained a comparable skill.

For Rommel, Alam Halfa was a revelation. It was the first time that he tried to fight an armoured battle with an absolute inferiority in the air. He realised that this lack was decisive, and that in the future it would be a per-manent weakness for Germany. In his *Papers* there is a long passage which sets out his thoughts on this aspect of his defeat and ends, pessimistically, with the remark that 'anyone who has to fight, even with the most modern wea-pons, against an enemy in complete control of the air fights like a savage against modern European troops, under the same handicaps and with the same chances of success'. He now saw that, apart from reducing the possibility of reconnaissance and counter-attack, to be overwhelmed in the air meant that a commander could neither deploy armour according to a strict plan nor rely on a timed programme. Assembly areas and the line of march must inevitably be disrupted. The deeper significance of the battle emerged during those months in Normandy when Rommel was responsible for planning the de-fences of the Atlantic Wall: his arguments with von Rundstedt about the proper counter-attack role of the panzer divisions in France were a direct consequence of what he discovered during his defeat among the sandy de-pressions between Himeimat and Alam Halfa.

XI

Second Alamein

1942

From one angle, a chessboard can appear to be mainly black squares: from another, the squares will seem predominantly white. So it was at Alamein. The many British accounts—however critical—present the battle as a conclusive victory confidently achieved; but for Rommel it was a disaster. There was nothing he could hope for during the preceding weeks, no possibility of success during the conflict, and the result was fatal both to the army and to himself: for here began the collapse of his Afrika Korps which was consummated in Tunisia, and the decline in his relations with Hitler which ended with his murder.

A commander's health, and a staff on which he can rely, are two factors of profound importance on the eve of a great engagement. When the battle begins, commanders are human beings who need to be sure both of themselves and of those around them who will have to carry out their orders. Before and during Alamein Rommel lacked these certainties.

He had not recovered from the gastric weakness from which he had been suffering since Alam Halfa, and because of this he was *hors de combat* in the last critical weeks before 23 October. On 23 September he flew back to Germany (under his doctor's orders) having handed over his command to a man inexperienced in the desert, General Stumme. 'He was rather put out when he heard that I proposed to cut short my cure and return to North Africa if the British opened a major offensive.' When he made this note in his *Papers* Rommel did not intend to be unfair to Stumme: his point was that he had anticipated an offensive, and felt that someone with special knowledge of fighting in the desert should be in charge of the defences—knowledge which, he well knew, was incommunicable. It could only flow from actual experience; and Stumme was a tyro while Rommel was a veteran. Uneasiness about Stumme was increased by his awareness that other veterans of his African army were withdrawing. Already, on 9 September, he had written to his wife 'now Gause is unfit for tropical service and has to go away for six months. Things are not looking too good with Westphal, he's got liver trouble. Lieut.-Col. von Mellenthin is leaving today with amoebic dysentery, so that every divisional commander and the Corps Commander have been changed inside ten days.' Both Napoleon and his Marshals, in effect, were removed on the eve of this desert Waterloo. Von Thoma took over the Afrika Korps, von Randow 21 Panzer, and Graf von Sponeck 90 Light. It is true that in 8 Army also, as Montgomery probed and assessed, officers were going and coming. The difference was that Montgomery was shaping his army to his will by retaining or introducing commanders in whom he had confidence: Rommel was losing men on whom he had learned to rely.

His reinforcement of generals was sufficient: in other respects, the story of his supplies before and during the battle is one of broken promises, German indifference and Italian *dolce far niente*; furthermore, the failure to take Malta now produced its most deadly consequences. Rommel made his position clear. Soon after Alam Halfa he reported to Hitler and *Comando Supremo* that 'the German troops of the Panzer Army Africa, who are bearing the brunt of the war in Africa against the finest troops of the British Empire, must be provided with an uninterrupted flow of the supplies essential for life and battle, and every available ship and transport aircraft should be employed for that purpose'. (Whatever the truth in the aspersions cast on Rommel about his readiness, in earlier years, to take risks administratively, there can be no doubt that in the autumn of 1942 his mind was dominated by the need to ensure his supplies.) He was concerned not only about *matériel*, but also about the simple necessity for food; far too high a proportion of both the old hands and the unacclimatised newcomers were now appearing on sick parade as a result of bad rations. Rommel submitted the figures of his requirements: 30,000 tons to arrive during September and 35,000 during October. These were based on his estimate of the minimum scale of stocks necessary to fight a battle—eight daily issues of ammunition, 2000 miles per vehicle of fuel, and 30 days issue of rations. 'I stated categorically that it would only be possible to guarantee a successful defence if these requirements were met.' In fact, by 19 October there was fuel for eleven and ammunition for some nine days' fighting: rations were still poor—especially vegetables—and spare parts as always were short. This situation continued. When Rommel stopped at Rome on the morning of 25 October, on his return to Africa, he was told by von Rintelen that only three issues of petrol remained in the African theatre. 'This', Rommel observed, 'was sheer disaster . . . the petrol situation made any major movement impossible.'

Other promises proved vain. For example, 22 Air Landing Division, a motorised infantry unit withdrawn from Russia, was supposed to be transferred to Africa but never arrived. On 23 September, *en route* to Germany, Rommel got the Italians to agree to provide 3000 men for road construction behind the front (to reduce wastage of petrol owing to driving in the sand); about 100 materialised. Seven thousand tons of rails and their sleepers were to be shipped to improve the railway; none came, and the only improvements were effected by 90 Light. The Italians said they would capture Kufra* to stifle the annoying operations of the L.R.D.G.; they didn't. When Rommel reached Hitler's H.Q. a few days later and reported on the weaknesses in Africa, the Führer and his staff gave assurance that during the next few weeks many flat-decked ferries with a shallow draught (*Siebelfähren*) would be added to the cross-Mediterranean transport fleet; a *Nebelwerfer* brigade of rocket batteries would shortly arrive; 40 Tiger tanks and self-propelled guns would also be dispatched. These were empty words. For Rommel the frustration and disappointment were enhanced by his sharp sense (described in the previous chapter) of rapidly growing Allied superiority, the convoys docking at Suez, and the remorseless output of America's industrial strength.

Malta's survival most directly affected his supplies of fuel: it impaired, in a telling fashion, both his capacity to manœuvre in front of Montgomery's attack and to withdraw when the attack succeeded. The statistics speak for themselves. Of shipping under German control 44,430 tons were sunk in the Mediterranean between August and December while the Italians lost nearly 276,000 tons in the Mediterranean and elsewhere. A high proportion of these losses occurred on Rommel's pipe-line. But it was not simply the scale of loss which mattered; the timing was also important. Rommel was now reduced to working on such tight margins that the destruction or arrival, on a particular day, of even a *single* tanker could have a grave or exhilarating effect on his plans.

So it was a sick, lonely and frustrated man who, in the short period between the withdrawal from Alam Halfa and his own departure from Africa, had to devise a means of meeting the coming offensive. The means were of his own devising. Some writers have declared or implied that apparent weaknesses in

* From Kufra the L.R.D.G., supporting other units like the S.A.S., led into position a number of raiding groups whose attacks on Tobruk, Barce, etc., paid small dividends on the eve of Alamein. They worried Rommel, who took especial precautions for the future defence of Tobruk. But he need not have worried. The operations were amateur.

the German defence system at Alamein were due to Stumme—for example, the separation of the Axis armour in two *blocs* behind the north and south of their line. This is not so. Bayerlein has defined the situation authoritatively by one of his footnotes in the *Rommel Papers*: 'it must be clearly stated that Rommel issued orders for the construction of the defences before his departure from Africa, and that Stumme merely executed them.' Stumme was soon to die; *requiescat in pace*, in so far as the defeat at Alamein was certainly not his fault.

For Rommel the prime question was, what strategy to adopt? To undertake a 'Hindenburg Line' type of retreat, leaving his opponent's massive preparations in the air, would have been an elegant solution which certain of his critics think he should have chosen. But Rommel was a realist, and this would not have been a realistic answer to the problem. He did not have enough fuel to enable him to withdraw to his partially prepared rearward position and, even if he got back safely to this reserve line, to avoid being pinned to the ground. Moreover he had to deal, as usual, with Hitler and Mussolini— both, as the record of the retreat from Alamein reveals, myopic about withdrawal: indeed when Rommel visited the Duce on 24 September he found that 'he still did not realise the full gravity of the situation', and when he reported to the Führer a few days later the atmosphere at Hitler's H.Q. was 'extremely optimistic'. For these reasons alone, Rommel before Alamein may be compared with Macbeth before Birnam Wood.

> *They have tied me to a stake; I cannot fly,*
> *But bear-like I must fight the course.*

Rommel had his own reasons for refusing to fly. It is often claimed by Montgomery's critics that at Alamein he planned 'a '14–'18 slogging match': but by his defensive arrangements Rommel made this kind of assault inevitable. He took advantage of the fact that for the first time in the desert there was no free southern flank, and, in effect, used the Qattara Depression to impose on Montgomery a battle-plan which (in view of his comparative weakness in tanks and all other equipment, and particularly in men) was for Rommel the most favourable.

The method he used was to plant more minefields before his front than either side laid in any position on the African shore before or after Alamein. In constructing a defence system to which (consciously or subconsciously) Montgomery reacted in terms of the First World War, Rommel used tactical concepts which the French had evolved at Verdun and the British and Germans developed during the spring and summer of 1918. 'The defences', he

166

says in his *Papers*, 'were so laid out that the minefields adjoining no-man's-land were held by light outposts only, with the main defence line, which was 2000–3000 yards in depth, located one to 2000 yards west of the first mine-belt. The panzer divisions were positioned behind the main defence line so that their guns could fire into the area in front of the line and increase the defensive fire-power of their sector. . . .' Rommel feared that Montgomery would 'chop a hole' somewhere along his front and push through it a mass of armour he was no longer able to match. This is one of the reasons why he put a German and Italian armoured division down in the south and a similar combination up in the north. He knew that if he brought his armour together, at a point too distant from a break-through, his small stocks of fuel might prevent him—if a hole was chopped—from immediately sealing off a penetration. At Alamein, as in Normandy, this fear caused Rommel to favour spreading rather than grouping his tanks: he aimed at quick and stunning local counter-attacks rather than a delayed but carefully organised *riposte* by concentrated divisions.

The minefields stretched from the coast to the Depression. In the south he was helped by *January* and *February*, the two British fields into which he retired after Alam Halfa; but over the whole of his front, by extraordinary efforts, a double belt of mines, and in some areas rather more, was planted. To cover them an economic scheme was devised. Inter-connected strips of mines led to 'boxes' which contained 'battle-outposts' (small detachments, widely dispersed); these outposts were disposed in depth amid the minefields. Behind them extended 'The Devil's Garden', a region filled with every kind of underground explosive—for example, Rommel remembered that 'vast numbers of captured British bombs and shells were built into the defence, arranged in some cases for electrical detonation'. This screen, more elaborate than any so far established in the desert, had a minimum width of two and a half miles and sometimes expanded to four and a half miles. Dogs were provided as an early-warning system: but their bark on 23 October, in the middle of the fiercest British barrage since 1918, must have been inaudible!

Rommel was aware that 'most of the mines available in Africa were un-fortunately of the anti-tank type, which infantry could walk over without danger'. This was indeed true; his Chief Engineer reported, just before Second Alamein began, that of the 445,000 mines on the front of the *Panzer-armee* only 3%—about 14,000—were anti-personnel. But these 'S mines', which were discharged by being trodden on or by catching a trip-wire, could destroy a whole platoon when their steel pellets were broadcast by an ex-plosion in mid-air. And at this stage in the campaign anti-tank mines could also be anti-infantry: for the idea of putting sand-bags on the floor of jeeps, trucks and Bren-gun carriers, which was later to save many lives, had not yet become a doctrine. Moreover, the great depth of Rommel's layout helped his army. British patrols could only examine the edge of the Axis minefields; a plan for clearing them could therefore be based on no more than frail information and much guesswork.

Nevertheless, it was a misfortune for Rommel that the most successful part of the elaborate training programme his opponent imposed on his army between Alam Halfa and Alamein was that which dealt with the clearing of minefields. Rommel was not the only Desert Fox. Montgomery had appreciated that the defences he planned to shatter were being constructed in a manner unprecedented in Africa, and that unprecedented means of grappling with them were called for. 8 Army's way of dealing with mines had so far been simple: men, usually in daylight, pushed bayonets into the sand in the hope of touching some 'foreign object', or examined the surface to discover where it had been disturbed by a minelayer. These aboriginal methods (which, because they were often carried out in the light, usually indicated to the enemy where a gap was about to be made) were now replaced by a more sophisticated technique.

The Chief Engineer of 8 Army, Brigadier Kisch, selected a remarkable character, Major Moore, 'one of the few men who have fought with a revolver at arm's length and personally wrestled with an armed enemy', and gave him the job of inventing such a technique and rapidly training 8 Army to apply it. Kisch collected the recommendations of his senior engineers about minefield clearance and handed them over to Moore with the challenging instruction: 'I am sure that there should be a drill for this, just as there is a drill for loading and firing field guns. Go away and come back in a week's time with your recommendations. When you have worked out a drill and I have approved it, you will form the Eighth Army School of Mine Clearance.'

Moore set up his school. Since Montgomery intended a battle by night, the first lesson Moore had to compose and teach was how to clear a lane in the dark, having reconnoitred it surreptitiously in the light; and if the lesson was to be effective it must include the drill which Kisch had requested. This was devised, and the lessons were taught: by 23 October most of the attacking divisions had their own Minefield Task Force. The Force's doctrine varied from division to division, and some of these specialised groups were helped by 'flail' tanks, converted Matildas which, with an extra engine, could whirl chains on a rotating shaft and thus beat the ground as they moved forward (exploding, it was hoped, mines in their passage). Neither the flails nor the Task Forces were wholly effective either on the night of 23 October or thereafter, but this enterprise was a sign that Rommel would have to deal with not only the superior force he had anticipated but also a foresight and an imagination he had not so far encountered.

The mines gave him cover: behind the cover must be a strategic plan, and Rommel's was founded on two principles:

'(a)   Our position had to be held at all costs.

(b)   Any penetration would have to be cleaned up by immediate counter-attack to prevent it being extended to a break-through, for it was my opinion that, if a break-through occurred, the British would throw their whole striking power into the breach.'

It was for these reasons that he tried the dubious scheme of sandwiching Italians between Germans all along his line—dubious because of the tensions involved. But doubt of the Italians' courage and tenacity, bred by experience in two wars, suggested to him—concerned as he was about a break-through on a narrow front—that he could not afford to leave any sector incapable of swift German reinforcement. Layering Italian units between Germans seemed the answer. Behind the front line in the south, therefore, 21 Panzer was married with Ariete, and 15 Panzer and Littorio were similarly joined in the north: their troops in each case were combined in three mixed battle-groups, while their divisional headquarters were placed side by side. (The infantry in the line were similarly sandwiched from north to south of the front.) This was a desperate remedy: perhaps a cooler judgement might have appreciated that Montgomery's *Schwerpunkt* must arrive in the north, and decided that the chief strength of the *Panzerarmee*, the German divisions, should therefore be concentrated on the left flank. But Rommel—ill and harassed—was short of time and obsessed by the growing strength of his opponent.

In weighing the strategy and tactics of Montgomery's successful plan for defeating Rommel at El Alamein one has to ask whether 8 Army's commander, so evidently confident at the time and so self-assured in his memoirs, has presented a true picture of his own mood and purpose. One thing is certain: the reading of the battle which post-war accounts have made possible suggests that Montgomery's mind was preoccupied by Rommel to a far greater degree than Montgomery was then or later prepared to admit. The course the battle was to take and the moves he made during it imply, when examined by hindsight, a concern on his part about Rommel which impaired his opera-tional judgement. The famous confrontation between Montgomery and the portrait of Rommel which he hung in his caravan had Freudian under-tones: Montgomery thought that in studying Rommel's face he was 'understanding his enemy'; but was he not trying to interpret, in his day-by-day contemplation, a man by whom he was hag-ridden?

Montgomery made not one but two plans for Alamein. The first, which like the second was for an operation whose code-name was *Lightfoot*, was issued to his senior commanders on 14 September; its object was an armoured victory. The attack was to be made in the north by 30 Corps, whose infantry was to clear passages in the minefields through which the tanks of 10 Corps would advance, so that this Corps could place itself 'on ground of its own choosing astride the enemy supply routes'. Tactically, this meant that when the infantry of 30 Corps had opened their gaps the armour of 10 Corps would pass through and swing to the left, using the Mitireiya Ridge as a fulcrum: then it would destroy the armoured counter-attacks which, Montgomery assumed, Rommel would insist on launching. He had not misread his adversary's mind.

But in this abandoned first plan, as in the second, there was an anomaly; the declared intention would not have been achieved. Montgomery made much of his re-grouping of 8 Army to enable him to pull back some of his armour to form a *corps de chasse*. For this purpose he extricated 1, 10 and 8 Armoured Divisions and assembled and trained them as 10 Corps under Lieut.-Gen. Lumsden. But in spite of his victory, there was no chase! Since Montgomery's second plan failed to produce an effective pursuit it seems unlikely that his first would have done so: in changing his mind he could not change the mentality which wrought a victory but prevented him from grasping its richest fruits.

On 6 October, dissatisfied by the state of training of his armour, he gave out new orders which laid the burden of the battle to an increased degree on his infantry. His own explanation, in *El Alamein to the River Sangro*, is: 'It had been generally accepted that the plan in a modern battle should aim first at destroying the enemy's armour, and that once this had been accomplished, the unarmoured portion of his army would be dealt with readily. I decided to reverse this concept and to destroy first the unarmoured formations. While doing this I would hold off the armoured divisions, which would be tackled subsequently.' This was the plan which governed the conflict at Alamein. It meant that 30 Corps must destroy Rommel's infantry *in their positions* while 10 Corps, having passed through 30, fended off Rommel's tanks: thereafter a great armoured battle was intended to follow which would be the end of the Afrika Korps.

The operation was to develop in three stages: first the 'break-in'; then what Montgomery called the 'crumbling' phase, and Haig would have recognised as 'attrition'; exploitation was to be the next step, when the rule would be 'improvise'. At the time Montgomery was strongly and sometimes bitterly criticised by his subordinates—especially the commanders of his armour—and he has not lacked subsequent critics. But war is a pragmatic affair. In the autumn of 1942 the Commonwealth craved for a success; and though Montgomery's conduct of Alamein can be faulted in detail, he provided Churchill and his country, India, Australia, New Zealand and South Africa with the success which seemed to reward their many sacrifices, and gave Roosevelt what at the time appeared a dramatic justification for pouring American aid into the Middle East. The Prime Minister and his Cabinet had their moments of doubt as the battle developed; but, in the end, Montgomery turned Rommel out of Egypt for the last time. This was enough: the details were irrelevant. When Lincoln sent Grant down to the Army of the Potomac in the final clinch of the American Civil War he did so because he thought that Grant was the man who would produce results: it was results that the 'free world' required from Montgomery in October 1942. Like Lincoln, the Allies needed a general who would 'deliver'.

Montgomery had a preponderance of power—some 195,000 troops opposed to about 50,000 Germans (the core of the *Panzerarmee*) and 54,000 Italians. In Rommel's force there were less than 500 tanks, in Montgomery's over 1000 at the front. The disproportion in artillery was similar—nearly 1000 field and medium guns on the British side set against about 500 German and Italian weapons, while in their supply of anti-tank guns the British also had a superiority of two to one (except that the Germans had 24 of their 88s). Generally speaking, therefore, Montgomery surpassed Rommel in strength on the ground by 100% both in men and material: in the air his advantage was even greater. Sorties for every purpose could be flown by the Desert Air Force with little fear of interference—for short- and long-range bombing, for tactical reconnaissance, for fighter cover over the front line. (Lord Tedder's memoirs, *With Prejudice*, describe this victory in the air from the standpoint of its architect.) All that Rommel had learned at Alam Halfa about the disabilities of a commander who, in modern war, lacks air superiority was once again proved to be true.

When Alamein began the two orders of battle were:

1. *The Axis*

From the sea to the railway, Bersaglieri and two battalions of German parachutists; then 164 Division, reaching to Kidney Ridge; opposite Mitireiya and stretching as far south as Ruweisat, the Italian Trento Division supported by one German parachute battalion and Bologna flanked by two battalions of German parachutists. Next came Brescia, also paired with two German battalions; and from Munassib to Himeimat the front was covered by Folgore (who in the next few days would show how the despised Italians could fight). The end of the line was filled in by Pavia and, in the no-man's-land south of Himeimat and east of the Qattara Depression, 33 Recce and the Kiehl Group. (The latter, far detached though they were from the main force, were to do good business. At dawn on 24 October, the Kiehl Group's eight captured Stuart tanks intercepted two battalions of the French Foreign Legion, killed their commander, and destroyed all their vehicles. This action summarily concluded any attempt by 8 Army to infiltrate south of Rommel's right flank.)

2. *The Allies*

In 30 Corps, from the sea to Ruweisat, the order ran from right to left . . . 9 Australian, 51 Highland, 2 New Zealand, 1 South African, 4 Indian (30 might indeed have well been named the Commonwealth Corps). From Ruweisat to Himeimat 13 Corps had 50 Division on its right, 44 in the centre and 7 Armoured on the left. 10 Corps, now consisting of 1 and 10 Armoured Divisions (8 was not brought up to strength; its H.Q. and ancillary units were used in the deception plan), deployed behind 30, though the move of the two divisions forward from their training areas was so organised as to suggest that 1 Armoured had not stirred, and that 10 Armoured had shifted to the south.

It is difficult to be sure about the feeling of the men in the Axis divisions that evening. Rommel's leadership had been personal: and he was now on the other side of the Mediterranean. His army—or at least its German elements— was by now so professional that it functioned automatically, whoever led: still, Rommel's absence must have counted. The Italians lived under a cloud of pessimism (relieved by the courage of some of the crews in their feeble and worn-out tanks, some of their gunners, and the parachute units in divisions like Folgore)—a despair which is well expressed in a conversation recorded by one of their more competent officers, the engineer Colonel Dominioni, in his *Alamein 1933–1962*. In this book he summarises the outlook of the older Italian commanders in the desert. 'We are going into this because we are under orders . . . and because we are still the same as when we were second lieutenants and we lined up our platoons to explain why it was necessary to take Trento and Trieste. And we had plenty of good reasons to give them. But what on earth can a second lieutenant tell his men today?'

As for 8 Army, I remember rejoining my Field Battery during 22 October, having been wounded at Alam Halfa, sent back to Cairo, and then clawed my way back, driven by that instinct to return to one's own people which only the 'regimental soldier' can understand. All was strange and confusing: I knew nothing of the Alamein plan. But nevertheless, returning to a battery which would fire all through the night of the 23rd, I was impressed by its confidence and exhilaration. The men knew what they had to do and looked forward to the doing: since Alam Halfa their gain in assurance struck me as enormous, and they took victory for granted. This spirit permeated the Army. Old hands and new shared a sense of elation: it was as though 8 Army believed in itself again. Of all the stories which were later told about that night, one of the most significant is related by Kippenberger. After everything that the New Zealanders had endured, their panache was unquenched. 'Somewhere about three o'clock' (on the morning of the 24th) 'Angus Ross, now Adjutant of the Twenty-third, appeared. He was dusty and dishevelled and brought a remarkable story. The first objective had been taken without nearly enough fighting to satisfy the battalion in its exalted mood. The men were surging forward. . . . They went through the standing bombardment and fought their way without artillery assistance to the foot of Mitireiya Ridge, about another 1500 yards.' (As Napier wrote about the Fusiliers at Albuera, 'nothing could stop that astonishing infantry'.) Throughout Alamein this note of enthusiasm and dedication is struck again and again . . . by 51 Highland Division, by the Rifle Brigade's anti-tank gunners at Kidney Ridge, by John Currie's 9 Armoured Brigade accepting an instruction to get across the Rahman track even at the cost of 100% casualties, by the Australians at Thompson's Post. Not since Wavell's first offensive, and not again till D-Day, was an Allied Army to attack with its morale at so high a pitch.

In his notes for the inspiring talk which Montgomery gave to his senior officers shortly before Alamein he jotted down: 'Organise ahead for a "dog-fight" of a week. Whole affair about 12 days' (12 days, interestingly, an amendment for 10 days). At 2140 on 23 October his prediction was put to the test: the counter-battery fire, a prelude to his attack, began. His intention was to use his superiority in artillery to blanket the Axis guns swiftly and unexpectedly before the zero hour for the main assault, 2200 hours. This bombardment, and the jamming of their enemy's signal system by specially equipped Wellingtons, accompanied by normal bombing, threw the Axis artillery into a state of disarray, so that several hours passed before it started to react in strength—at about 0400 on 24 October; a considerable benefit for 8 Army, as its columns moved forward in the darkness to implement Montgomery's revised plan.

This gave as an objective for 30 Corps in the north a line called 'Oxalic' (see map facing p. 163), whose capture involved an advance through mine-fields varying from three to five miles on the front of the four divisions concerned. In the early stages these divisions moved with relative ease through the mines and the outposts, but as night wore on the defence stiffened, and progress slowed. Down in the south 13 Corps had to control a 13-mile approach march by 7 Armoured through three of their own minefields, make gaps in the enemy's, and then establish a bridge-head, knowing that Montgomery had ordered that 7 Armoured must not be weakened because he would require them later. Put shortly: these attacks in the south by 7 and 44 Divisions did not distract the Axis command, failed to achieve a break-through, and were soon checked: the decisive actions at Alamein were fought in the north. This is where Montgomery's 'dog-fight' occurred and where Rommel, recalled by Hitler from his convalescence in Austria, realised (when he took over command on the evening of the 25th) that the critical area lay.

Rommel's return was due to Stumme's death. A new man in Africa, he had been understandably indecisive when the barrage began. Knowing that ammunition was short he restrained his artillery until enough information had filtered through his shattered communications to enable him to form a picture of what was happening. By dawn on the 24th he was still in doubt, and decided to see for himself. He drove up to the front unescorted, his vehicle was fired on, he somehow jumped out and clung to its side, and as his driver accelerated to escape it seems that Stumme had a heart attack and fell off his car without the driver noticing. His body was later recovered: but it was the news that he was missing which caused Hitler to telephone Rommel at his Austrian retreat and request his return. Rommel responded immediately, although 'I knew there were no more laurels to be earned in Africa'.

The situation with which he had to cope on his arrival was serious indeed—but it was less serious than Montgomery had intended it to be on the evening of the second day of his attack. During the night of the 23–24th 9 Australian had reached 'Oxalic' with one brigade and fallen short with the other; 51 Division had only touched the objective; the New Zealand Division had been mainly successful and some of the South Africans had carried out the plan. But along the whole front the instruction that the armour following the infantry should be 'used as necessary in order to ensure the capture of the bridge-head at all costs' was ineffective both in respect of the armoured brigades in close support of the infantry divisions, to whom it especially applied, and also of the *corps de chasse* pressing in their tracks. This was because the gapping of the minefields proved too difficult in the confusion of the battle, and also because the administrative arrangements for handling the armour's advance broke down. The two divisions of 10 Corps were responsible for clearing their own lanes. In spite of preliminary training their gapping parties were delayed by scattered mines, and their advance was also held up by the failure of the infantry of 30 Corps to reach their objectives. So at dawn on the 24th the British tanks had to deploy as best they could—cramped among mines, tactically in bad positions, and unable to manœuvre. Three divisional commanders of 30 Corps, Freyberg, Morshead and Pienaar, had registered before the battle their view that the tanks would fail to break through; and some of the armoured commanders had spoken even more forcefully. At dawn on the 24th it seemed that they had been right in their forecast. If they were, it was partly because the spirit Rommel had injected into the Afrika Korps persisted in his absence. On this night, when Rommel was still in Austria, his army fought doggedly an enemy who was using more men, more guns, more tanks, and more aircraft. One of the supreme tests of a Great Commander, it might be argued, is how his army performs without him: a test which the *Panzerarmee* (and Rommel) certainly passed during the first two days of Alamein.

In this phase of the battle the inability of commanders to look over 'the other side of the hill' is particularly relevant. Rommel wrote, 'feeling that we would fight this battle with but small hope of success, I crossed the Mediterranean in my *Storch* and reached headquarters at dusk (25 October)'. On his arrival he was given more information about Stumme's death, and in his *Papers* he remarks of Stumme that 'in view of the enormous British strength and the disastrous supply situation, he felt far from certain that he would be able to fight the battle to a successful conclusion. I, for my part, did not feel any more optimistic.'

But on the British side there was also pessimism. During the daytime hours of the 24th attempts were made to clear the two main gaps in the minefields so that 10 Armoured could advance. Securing the northern gap depended on an attack by 51 Highland Division, but they and their supporting armour disagreed about their geography—understandably, for the minefield stretched through and over sand and ridges which provided few points from which a precise orientation might be calculated. By the evening the Scots and their tanks had made some but not sufficient progress, even though during the day the Desert Air Force flew about 1000 sorties in support of 8 Army.

The struggle for the southern gap produced a different drama. 10 Armoured Division had been ordered to get over the Mitireiya Ridge during the night of the 24–25th. Mines were to be cleared by their engineers and 133 Infantry Brigade was to provide a pivot of manœuvre. A huge artillery programme was arranged, and the usual support in the air. But once again the *Panzerarmee* and the *Luftwaffe* managed to blunt the spearhead: as the British tanks formed up before zero hour, German bombers hit 8 Armoured Brigade, its vehicles (crammed in the minefield gaps) went up in flames, and the conflagration attracted even more bombs and shells. Confusion spread along the line, and impeded the columns attempting to move through the other gaps which had been cleared. Montgomery's staff now faced a difficult decision—should they wake him? His strength was his ability to dismiss all problems from his mind and retire to sleep with a detective story and no *Angst*: and he was adamant about not being disturbed. Rommel, on the contrary, sought the front line by day, but at night, and especially in the early hours of the morning, he lay awake thinking.

Montgomery was now asleep. At about 0230 on the morning of the 25th de Guingand had to decide, as Chief of Staff, what he should do. The night's moves by 10 Armoured Division had produced little progress and many casualties, partly from mines and partly from bombing. Gatehouse informed Lumsden, who put de Guingand in the picture. De Guingand acted: Lumsden and Leese were ordered to report to Montgomery at 0300. In the discussion which followed it was proposed that the night's operations should be abandoned, but, as General Carver puts it, 'Montgomery quietly made it perfectly clear that there was no question of this and that the original plan must be carried out, an order which he passed to Gatehouse on the telephone. When the meeting broke up Montgomery kept Lumsden behind, warning him that, if he and his divisional commanders were not determined to break out, others would be found who were.'

This was a turning point in the battle of Alamein and for the British Army during the Second World War. For better or worse, the 'cavalry concept' died that night: the 'old desert hands' had to swallow their resentment and their anguish because their tanks would no longer have a free role but would, thereafter, usually be units in organised actions involving all arms. Montgomery started a process which the Germans had long ago brought into being: the armour began to become part of the army. Alamein would be fought Montgomery's way—and Rommel would have approved: he too believed that a commander must command.

At 1130 next morning Montgomery met first Alexander and then his two corps commanders, and with them reviewed the night's results. These were that neither 8 nor 9 Armoured Brigade had made decisive advances: there was no promise of an armoured break-through, and Montgomery therefore gave up his scheme for an exploitation southwards by 2 New Zealand Division and switched his effort to the north, ordering the Australians to 'crumble'. During the night of the 25-26th they and 51 Highland on their left made more attacks, but by dawn the situation along the whole front (for 7 and 44 Divisions in the far south had failed to break through) was inconclusive. Montgomery spent most of the daytime of the 26th in contemplation.

Such were the main developments during the 24 hours before Rommel's return. His first preoccupation was petrol: and rightly . . . on 26 October the *Proserpina* was sunk with some 3000 tons of fuel and the *Tergestea* with 1000 tons of fuel and 1000 tons of ammunition also went down. (This illustrates the point made previously, that the timing of the arrival of individual tankers had now become more important to Rommel than mass delivery.) And his first report to Hitler's H.Q. on the evening of the 25th offered no hope; Trento halved, 164 Light already short of two battalions, his tanks already surrendering to his guns the containing of the British armour.

At 0500 hours on the 26th he learned (an exaggeration) that what he calls Hill 28 and his opponents knew as Kidney Ridge had been captured, and he seems to have been obsessed, during the day, with the attacks and counter-attacks in this area. He moved 90 Light and his *Kampfstaffel* (the group supposed to protect his own H.Q., whose tanks had already suffered from attacks by cannon-firing Hurricanes) in support. But here is another example of how things can seem from 'the other side of the hill'. Rommel's notion that the British were pushing through a *Schwerpunkt* in this area was not borne out in fact; there was heavy fighting, but no especial plan for a break-through. Rommel's later description of what went on is excessive: 'rivers of blood were poured out over miserable strips of land which, in normal times, not even the poorest Arab would have bothered his head about!' It was during the 26th that he made, too late, the significant move which was an attempt to concentrate his armour: 21 Panzer with part of Ariete was told to side-step north. 'I fully realised', Rommel says of 21 Panzer, 'that the petrol shortage would not allow it to return.'

The result of Montgomery's reflections that day was a change of plan. His attack was losing its dynamism, but his superiority was still great—he had some 900 tanks available through reinforcement despite his heavy losses. So he chose the classic stratagem—difficult to execute in the middle of a complicated battle, but always easier for the commander of a superior force—of regrouping 8 Army to produce a reserve which could deliver a final blow. His purpose was to extricate 2 New Zealand and 10 Armoured Division: he had his eye also on 7 Armoured in the south, but this presented no problem. It was the divisions in the north, locked in the battle, whose disengagement seemed difficult. The deadline for completing the manœuvre was dawn on the 28th.

Lumsden's immediate responsibility, at 10 Corps, was to 'make progress' west and north-west of Kidney Ridge, a curious feature which was as much a hollow as a ridge and whose location was, at this time, uncertain. What was known was that there were two other defended areas beyond it, one to the north named *Woodcock* and one to the south named *Snipe*. Hurried orders were issued to 1 Armoured Division on the afternoon of the 26th to capture these localities. Their execution coincided with a decision by Rommel to concentrate his forces on the same sector of the front; 15 and 21 Panzer, 90 Light, Littorio and various other elements converged.

On the British side there was confusion. The 2nd/60th were to take *Woodcock* and 2 Rifle Brigade *Snipe*. Discussion between their two colonels and the Highland Division on the left revealed a staggering discrepancy of 1000 yards in the fixing of the enemy positions by the Scots and the armour. (As it turned out, the veterans were wrong and 51 Division was right.) But time was short and argument was impossible: there was an agreement to disagree, and the 60th and the Rifle Brigade launched their attack without proper preparation or confidence about their objectives. In the north the attack on *Woodcock* failed.

The *Snipe* operation produced one of Alamein's most memorable encounters. Colonel Turner had spent weary days and nights in charge of a Minefield Task Force. Now, at 2200 on the 26th, he took forward a mixed force to grab *Snipe* and hold it until 24 Armoured Brigade reinforced at first light. 19 anti-tank guns, six from 76 Anti-tank Regiment and the rest the Rifle Brigade's own, were established in the position after many difficulties: and their gunner F.O.O. went astray—a serious shortage.

Rommel's attack hit this small and isolated British pocket at 0345 on the 27th, and from then until 2315, when the position was evacuated (one 6-pounder proudly towed out), the 19 guns in steadily diminishing numbers were constantly in action against blocks of Axis tanks. It was rather like the Battle of Britain in that the confusion of the dog-fights led to exaggerated claims: 76 German tanks or self-propelled guns were first thought to have been knocked out. Subsequent assessment settled for 32—an astonishing figure—and Colonel Turner was properly awarded the V.C. Elsewhere along the line Rommel's thrust met with no success; but it was at this point that the decisive resistance occurred. And though battalions of the Royal Sussex, also aimed at *Woodcock* and *Snipe*, suffered heavy casualties, while more British tanks were lost in discursive engagements up and down the line, Rommel's first major attempt to restore the situation failed. He was held, rebuffed and weakened, whereas the re-organisation of 8 Army proceeded according to plan; and Montgomery, after a period of self-examination, now conducted and finished the battle with a freedom only enjoyed by commanders sure of themselves and their troops. At Alamein this was the differential: Montgomery steadily achieved his aim with an abundance of troops he trusted, whereas Rommel had to manipulate an army whose Italian element he suspected and whose strength was inadequate. Rommel was compelled to conform, and could never originate: Montgomery, confident in his superior power, was free to remould the shape of the battle as he wished.

In this remoulding he misled Rommel—by changing his mind. His first plan for the final assault was to use 2 New Zealand Division in a drive along the coast which would exploit the Australians' success. During the nights of the 28–29th and 30–31st 9 Australian Division vigorously attacked the Axis salient on the extreme left of their line—the positions held by 164 Light and the Bersaglieri around the protuberance called Thompson's Post, a valuable point of observation. The fighting was savage. It was not a matter of infantry advancing in line behind a barrage in the classic fashion; there were several centre lines and the artillery plan (which even for Alamein was exceptional in strength) was unusually complicated. All, indeed, that Montgomery implied when he spoke of a 'dog-fight' occurred around Thompson's Post. The Australians slowly wound their way past the rear of this exposed pocket: and the effect of their endeavour was to convince Rommel that Montgomery's next move would be an all-out thrust down the coastal road. 'We assumed that the British were about to launch what they intended to be their decisive break-through and accordingly prepared ourselves, so far as our diminished strength allowed, to meet the attack. . . . I again informed all commanders that this was a battle for life or death and that every officer and man had to give of his best.'

Rommel was correct in his assumption. He adjusted his dispositions to meet the threat, and sensibly ordered a reconnaissance of a reserve line in the Fuka area. But unfortunately for Rommel Montgomery learned, after the attack on the 28th, that 90 Light had been moved into the coastal section. His attack on the 30th was therefore designed merely to convince Rommel that his thrust would occur in the far north: but in fact he had already changed his mind,* and his intention now was, instead of sending the New Zealanders down the coastal road, to put them into an attack on positions south of those which the Australians had been engaging. He hoped that the Germans had diverted their principal strength and that these positions would be mainly held by Italians. 2 New Zealand Division, reinforced by a brigade, 151, from 50 Division, and another, 152, from the Highland Division, was ordered to attack on a 4000 yard front and to clear a way for the supporting armour which was to crash through the defences along the Rahman Track. Through this hole 10 Armoured Corps was to advance and write off the German tanks

---

* This switch was accelerated by his Chief of Staff, de Guingand, and his Chief Intelligence Officer, E. T. Williams, who demonstrated to him the facts about Rommel's shift to the north and advocated a penetration further to the south than Montgomery had intended.

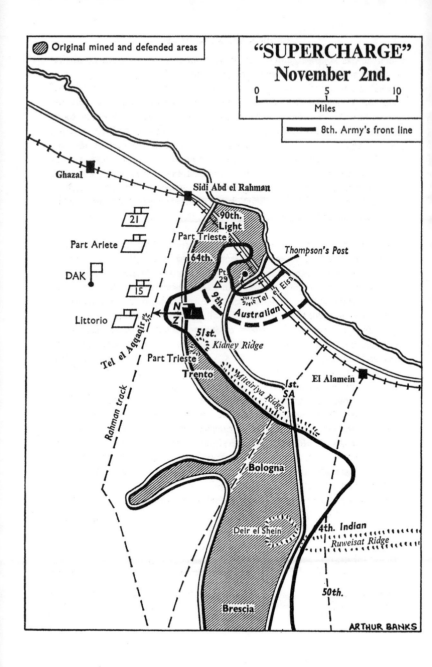

"SUPERCHARGE"
November 2nd.

Original mined and defended areas

0   5   10
Miles

8th. Army's front line

Ghazal

Sidi Abd el Rahman

21

Part Ariete

90th.
Light

Part Trieste

164th.

DAK

Pt.
29

Thompson's Post

15

Tel el Eisa

9th.

N
Z

Littorio

Australian

51st.

Kidney Ridge

Tel el Aqqaqir

Part Trieste

Trento

Miteiriya Ridge

1st.
SA

El Alamein

Rahman track

Bologna

Deir el Shein

4th. Indian

Ruweisat Ridge

50th.

Brescia

ARTHUR BANKS

which, it was supposed, must inevitably counter-attack. The name of this operation was *Supercharge*: zero hour was 0615, 2 November.

Both the attached infantry brigades (each supported by a quantity of Valentines) reached their objective. But 9 Armoured Brigade, the force intended to make the hole through which 1 Armoured Division might pour, was less successful. Its task was to take the Tel Aqaqir Ridge. At the briefing before the attack Freyberg, who was the responsible commander, said: 'We all realise that for armour to attack a wall of guns sounds like another Balaclava; it is properly an infantry job. But there are no more infantry available, so our armour must do it.' When John Currie, the brigadier of 9 Armoured, observed that this might entail 50% losses Freyberg replied: 'It may well be more than that. The army commander has said that he is prepared to accept 100%.'

This was very nearly the percentage of loss. 9 Armoured faced an approach march of 11 miles. Many of their replacement tanks had inefficient equipment. Their move through the minefield lanes was impeded by dust, shelling, and the disappearance of the lights which should have marked the gaps. The anti-tank guns which should have gone forward with them were delayed or destroyed. One unit took the wrong track, and had to turn round and start again. Still, at 0615 on 2 November the brigade advanced in an attack on the Rahman Track where Rommel's anti-tank guns were solidly emplaced, supported by dug-in tanks. Its spirit is indicated by this record of a squadron leader of the Wiltshire Yeomanry: 'Major Gibbs began his attack with 11 tanks all in unsound condition. His was the only compass in the whole squadron that worked. His Besa machine-gun was unserviceable, his 2-pounder very nearly so and his radio in very bad shape. At the start he had gone out on foot to give his troop leaders verbal orders.' Some officers of the brigade, it is said, charged into action waving swords. But though 9 Armoured got into the enemy's gun line,* and though 70 of its 94 tanks were put out of action (the remainder rallied, and continued to fight) the gun line on the Rahman Track was not breached.

Rommel's view at this time is presented dramatically in a letter to his wife.

Sunday 1 November 1942

Dearest Lu,

It's a week since I left home. A week of very, very hard fighting. It was often doubtful whether we'd be able to hold out. Yet we did manage it each time, although with sad losses. I'm on the move a lot in order to step in wherever we're

---

* A subsequent inspection revealed that 35 guns, lying within 100 yards of the dead tanks of 9 Armoured, had been destroyed. The brigade's sacrifices paid large dividends in the latter stages of the battle.

in trouble. Things were very bad in the north yesterday morning, although it was all more or less cleared up by evening. The struggle makes very heavy demands on one's nervous energy, though physically I'm quite well. Some supplies are supposed to be on their way. But it's a tragedy that this sort of support only arrives when things are almost hopeless.

As usual, Rommel was now continually concerned about his fuel. Promises had been given: Barbasetti had guaranteed a service of road tankers working from Tripoli to Benghazi, and Kesselring had offered a daily delivery by air of 300–400 tons. These promises were not fulfilled; in addition, more ships were sunk—on the 29th Rommel heard that the tanker *Luisiano* had gone, and on 1 November the *Tripolino* and *Ostia* were destroyed by British aircraft. Moreover Maleme airfield on Crete, from which supplies were being flown, was heavily bombed.

During the morning of 2 November Rommel sensed instinctively that the time had come to withdraw, and his most experienced opponent, Freyberg, also began to feel that this was so: Kippenberger notes that 'in the evening the General told Brigadiers that the enemy were cracking and warned us to have our transport ready for the break-through'. Rommel's decision was based partly on his knowledge that his fuel supplies were low, and partly on the report which von Thoma, the Afrika Korps' commander, submitted that morning: 'the front was holding, but only just.' His figure of tanks available for fighting was about 35: Montgomery could still call on hundreds. *Supercharge* is best summed up from the Axis side in Rommel's own words: 'It was now extremely difficult to obtain any clear picture of the situation, as all our communications had been shot to pieces and most of our wireless channels were being jammed by the enemy. Complete chaos existed at many points on the front.' He decided that the moment had come to make for the Fuka Line. It was now or never, if he was to have any hope of saving the unmechanised Italian infantry in the centre and south: and his decision was fortified by his unflattering reflection on the British conduct of the battle . . . 'seeing that the British had so far been following up hesitantly and that their operations had always been marked by an extreme, often incomprehensible, caution, I hoped to be able to salvage at least part of the infantry'. During the night of the 2–3rd he contrived some limited withdrawals; but at 1330 next day the thunderbolt descended.

To Field-Marshal Rommel

It is with trusting confidence in your leadership and the courage of the German-Italian troops under your command that the German people and I are following the heroic struggle in Egypt. In the situation in which you find yourself there can be no other thought but to stand fast, yield not a yard of room and throw every gun and every man into the battle. Considerable air force reinforcements are being sent to C.-in-C. South. The Duce and the Comando Supremo are also making the utmost efforts to send you the means to continue the fight. Your enemy, despite his superiority, must also be at the end of his strength. It would not be the first time in history that a strong will has triumphed over the bigger battalions. As to your troops, you can show them no other road than that to victory or death.

Adolf Hitler

This was the beginning of the end for Rommel. Previously he had, somehow, sustained a belief in his cause and in Hitler. Between 3 November 1942 and his death the pattern is one of steady decline in confidence: he now began, and continued, to see the Nazi régime more and more clearly for what it was, and to feel revulsion from what he saw. On this day, he recalled, 'a kind of apathy took hold of us as we issued orders for all existing positions to be held on instructions from the highest authority'. Since he first went into action as a young officer in France in 1914, there had been few occasions in his career characterised by 'a kind of apathy': but the despair was to grow. (Manfred Rommel points out that it was these outspoken comments which made his father, in 1944, decide to destroy the section in his *Papers* on Alamein: a decision his murder anticipated.)

In the evening he sent his A.D.C., Lieut. Berndt, to plead with Hitler. The pressure on his line had continued throughout the day; his transport and troops withdrawing down the coastal road were under constant attack from the Desert Air Force. Nevertheless, Rommel felt that Montgomery failed to exploit his opportunity: 'I had not dared hope that the British commander would give us such a chance.' And indeed from this point (though he had many anxious moments) Rommel was able to breathe more freely; for the *coup de grâce* never followed. Montgomery created an Alamein without contriving a Beda Fomm: a victory without a morrow.

Hitler rapidly relented: but as always his cancellation of a 'fight to the last man' order was too late—in theory. In fact Rommel had time to disengage his mobile troops in the north (though the Italians were caught in their thousands in the centre and south) because 8 Army proved incapable of cutting off his retreat.

Montgomery's brother-in-law, Hobart, was one of the pioneers of armoured warfare. He, Liddell Hart, Fuller, Martel and others had evolved during the 'twenties and 'thirties an ideology and a technique for what the Germans, following their forerunners, called the *Blitzkrieg*. Montgomery was not close to his brother-in-law, but their paths crossed from time to time; they talked for hours about war, and Hobart, a stern critic who had trained, before 1939,

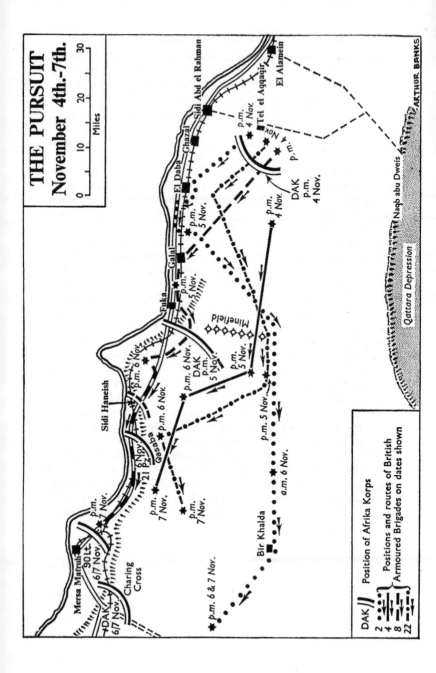

THE PURSUIT
November 4th.–7th.

0   5   10   20   30
Miles

Mersa Matruh
901 t.
6/7 Nov.
DAK 6/7 Nov.
Charing Cross
21 P 6 Nov.
Qasaba
p.m. 6 Nov.
Sidi Haneish
p.m. 6 Nov.
DAK p.m. 6 Nov.
p.m. 6 Nov.
p.m. 5 Nov.
Bir Khalda
p.m. 5 Nov.
a.m. 6 Nov.
p.m. 7 Nov.
p.m. 7 Nov.
p.m. 7 Nov.
p.m. 6 & 7 Nov.
p.m. 5 Nov.
Minefield
Fuka
Galal
El Daba
Ghazal
Sidi Abd el Rahman
Tel el Aqqaqir
El Alamein
p.m. 4 Nov.
p.m. 4 Nov.
DAK p.m. 4 Nov.
DAK p.m. 4 Nov.
p.m. 4 Nov.
p.m. 5 Nov.
Qattara Depression
Naqb abu Dweis

ARTHUR BANKS

DAK   Position of Afrika Korps
2   ⬤⬤⬤ Positions and routes of British
4 ⎫
8 ⎬ Armoured Brigades on dates shown
22 ⎭

the troops who were to become 7 Armoured, considered that Montgomery had more understanding of the nature of armoured warfare than most of the contemporary British generals. Yet here at Alamein Montgomery declared beforehand that he was creating a *corps de chasse* of armour which was to break through and pursue: the battle followed approximately the course he had predicted: a point was reached on 4 November when Rommel had to retreat, sacrificing his right flank and extricating his left as best he could in view of his shortage of fuel . . . and nothing significant happened! Rommel must be applauded for the skill with which he took advantage of an opportunity he could scarcely have believed possible. As the perspectives lengthen, Montgomery will be praised for his confident leadership, his calm and his flexibility: but he must be condemned for his failure to finish off effectively what he began so well.

It is clear that as the Axis line cracked, and a break-through became possible, 8 Army was not organised either administratively or morally to cope with the opportunity it had created. This was not the fault of the tanks. Briggs of 1 Armoured Division, for example, had proposed that a suitable force should be loaded in advance with the necessary fuel, food and ammunition to support it in a sudden advance. The New Zealanders were alert: Kippenberger remembers his orders for the 4th: 'we were to load up with eight days' water, rations, petrol for 500 miles, the gunners with 360 pounds per 25-pounder and 200 rounds per medium gun. This was great news.' The zeal and the foresight were there, at divisional level. What was missing was the foreknowledge, higher up, that when the break-through occurred the situation in the minefield gaps would be, as it was, chaotic: and that a most rigorous method of control would be essential if the armour was to pass through with speed. Also lacking was an appreciation that a punch through the Axis line would need steady logistic support if it was to succeed: the story of British tanks halted in their pursuit because they ran out of petrol is deplorable. Montgomery's excuse that the British armour was checked in its chase by rain and mud is not sufficient. He displayed at Alamein his ability to orchestrate the battle of position, but he offered no more evidence here than at Alam Halfa of his ability to master Rommel in a battle of manœuvre.

Still, all said and done, it was 'a famous victory'.

XII

Alamein to the Alps

'The armour was going headlong. Plainly there was a real gap.' This—Kippenberger's first impression of how 8 Army might advance from Alamein—was dramatic but unfounded: in fact the armour limped.

Its laggard progress was the result—as has been pointed out—of Montgomery's lack of foresight and the absence of meticulous plans for driving his army's *corps de chasse* through the Axis defences and deep into their hinterland before Rommel could withdraw.* If a commander may be compared with the conductor of a large-scale musical work, there appear to have been certain types of composition which were not Montgomery's *forte*. Further along the African coast, for example, at Wadi Akarit, the infantry of his 4 Indian Division by sheer endurance made possible an armoured penetration which never occurred: had it done so, it should have concluded the desert campaign. Another classic example is, of course, Arnhem. (It may be argued that his corps commanders let him down in the practical execution of his ideas: but they were his own men—hand-picked.) The fact is that before and after Alamein Montgomery planned what should have been decisive assaults in which, due to some lack of prevision or leadership, he was robbed of his potential reward. With his generals he was firm and even ruthless: he could browbeat and sack: and he certainly inspired his troops. But when the critical moment of exploitation arrived in Africa Rommel proved to be his superior at driving an army forward, at 'turning on the heat', and at leading from the front. Rommel grasped what Montgomery failed to understand: in the desert you could not conduct or invigorate a *mobile* operation (however

* This, it should be remarked, is a judgement delicately proffered by, among others, the *Official History*, which often implies gently what its authors clearly feel strongly.

well you might control a battle of position) from a caravan in which you went to bed each night leaving strict orders that you were not to be disturbed.

Before Alamein there was indeed a scheme whereby Major-General Gairdner (whose 8 Armoured Division had been dissipated) was to command a group-of-exploitation with air support which would be ready to dash to cut off Rommel's anticipated retreat. But this force was to be made up from bits and pieces, drawn from miscellaneous units: the truth is that at Alamein there was no properly considered plan for handling a break-through effectively . . . even Gairdner's non-existent force was cancelled, just as Briggs' proposal that an armoured division should be pre-loaded for the pursuit was rejected. As Kisch said when setting up his task forces for clearance of the minefields, a *drill* was required: but it was not evolved. The enthusiasm of Kippenberger and his New Zealanders was premature.

Rommel was thus left to extricate himself without the likelihood of being pulverised. His method was the hard but inevitable one of passing his main German units back down the firm coastal road while he let his Italian formations make their own way through the southern and inhospitable desert. 'The paratroopers and Italians in the south had to march.' Rommel recognised that for these units supply would be impossible; 'as a result these formations suffered severely from petrol and water shortage'. (Attempts by the British to round them up in the south developed an almost humanitarian aspect!)

His contempt for the Italian officer was always considerable and sometimes complete: but it must be observed that the Italian army contained many brave and self-sacrificing leaders who did their utmost on the battlefield, in spite of shoddy equipment, a logistical system which was a comedy, feeble support from their navy and a nervous control by *Comando Supremo*. One such was Caccia-Dominioni, who got his unit out of the shambles in the south at Alamein with courage and skill. Looking back, in his memoirs he wrote the epitaph of the hapless Italians. 'Names steeped in history', he says, 'passed out of existence alongside others, newer but no less glorious. The infantry of the *Pavia* had had a hundred years or more of life, though they really dated back to the French-named regiments of Savoy; the *Brescia* had originally been composed of volunteers of 1848; the *Bologna* of men recruited in Venetia and Romagna in 1859. Nothing was left of them. Nor of the youthful *Ariete* and *Littorio*. Nor of the new-born *Folgore*, reduced finally to the most painful of all sacrifices. They suffered a cruel misfortune and were powerless to stave off humiliation; it was like an ant-hill being overwhelmed by a flood.' After Alamein there was lament in the British Isles for the way that the 'flowers of the forest' had been taken in their prime: ancient Scottish battalions, the cream of the cavalry regiments, infantry units with a great tradition were decimated. In Germany the distress—obviously no less for next of kin—was in the main for casualties in newly formed units without a history: but some, at least, of the Italians shared with the British a poignant sense of the past.

Now the Commonwealth divisions at Alamein also presented the picture of an ant-hill overwhelmed by a flood . . . in this case from the skies. During the evening of 6 November the heavens opened. Montgomery, incorrectly, claims that 'only the rain on 6 and 7 November saved them' (the Axis divisions) 'from complete annihilation'. Rommel himself recognised the difficulties these conditions created for his enemy as well as for himself—'the result was a considerable slowing up of speed on both sides': a just comment. Montgomery's statement, however, is so self-defensive that it misrepresents the facts.

The New Zealand Division was right to feel elation as it passed through the minefields at Alamein, a mood reflected in the regimental histories of many of the units engaged; but this feeling was temporary. From the Alamein Line to Fuka was some 60 miles. 1 and 10 Armoured Divisions were ordered to make a quick loop from south to north within these limits and cut the coastal road at Daba, while 7 Armoured and 2 New Zealand Divisions were told to make a wider reach to Fuka by the conventional left hook. But the Desert Fox got away. It was not just rain which prevented 8 Army from forestalling him. Its advance was also delayed by skilful rearguard actions somehow contrived by the Afrika Korps; by what appeared to be minefields but turned out to be dummies laid earlier by 8 Army; and by an unpardonable failure in supply. This, for example, halted—admittedly in heavy going which might have been foreseen—the Sherman tanks of 2 Armoured Brigade, perfect instruments for a pursuit, because of lack of fuel. And the outflanking moves should have been bolder—with a larger scope.

The way Rommel extricated the core of his army from the complexities of the Alamein position was by any standard a considerable achievement, bearing in mind the distraction caused by Hitler's *pronunciamento* and the superiority in numbers and equipment of his opponent. This cannot be simply ascribed to the consequences of a downpour. It was technical dexterity and professional competence which enabled Rommel to withdraw the residue of his defeated divisions to and beyond Fuka before the main weight of Montgomery's army arrived. His success was aided by the fact that the R.A.F. was unable to take full advantage of the superb targets offered by his convoys retiring across the desert or down the one road available to them: R.A.F. doctrine had not as yet incorporated an effective method of low-level attack.

The rain, which was indeed severe and turned the desert into what is differently described as a bog, a morass and a quagmire, made its main effect *after* Rommel's army had extricated itself. This is not to say that confusion did not exist behind the German front: all retreats are chaotic, and some more chaotic than others. 'There was wild confusion on the coast road between Fuka and Mersa Matruh', Rommel noted of 5 November. 'Vehicle columns, their lorries full of stragglers, jammed up and choked the whole road . . .'; and again, on the 6th . . . 'conditions on the road were indescribable'. But though Rommel speaks of the R.A.F. reigning supreme—the *Luftwaffe* indeed did little to help him—in fact he managed to maintain his mobility and, as he sensed developing pressures from the south, was able to push back from Fuka to Mersa Matruh by taking avoiding action. On the 6th some of his men were actually approaching Sollum . . . a day during which he was visited by an emissary of Cavallero, General Gandin, who had obviously been despatched to obtain a situation report. 'This suited me very well.' Rommel, pulling no punches, told the Italian that as things were developing there was no hope of making a stand 'anywhere'—the British were free to run through Tripolitania. Such petrol as reached him would have to be employed for retreat, not for counter-attack. 'Gandin left my H.Q. visibly shaken.' This is the kind of confrontation which caused rather more to be made out of Rommel's attitude to his Italian allies than is warranted: certainly he thought little of them, militarily, but in such interviews—of which he suffered many— he was really the embattled general talking brusquely to the man from a comfortable base. It is not surprising, therefore, that between Gandin and Rommel there was a certain economy of communication!

During the evening the torrents of rain, as General Carver puts it, made 'captors and captured alike fellows in sodden misery'. Next morning Rommel's plan, put to De Stefanis, commander of the evaporating Italian 20 Corps, and Bayerlein* at Afrika Korps, was to avoid battle where possible, and to continue the retreat. He was agonisingly short of petrol: 5000 tons had reached Benghazi on 4 November, but 'what was the good of petrol in Benghazi?' He was also desperately short of tanks: of the 30 with which 21 Panzer had retired from Alamein, 4 only were now intact and his artillery had been similarly reduced. Ramcke, indeed, reported to him that morning from the deep south with 600 of his parachutists, a remarkable achievement. (His unit was so imbued with Nazism that Rommel, though he admired their fighting qualities, always distrusted them as a component of his army.) They had virtually no transport, however, and thus added to his administrative burden; nor did their truculence help.

Montgomery's own administrative problem was difficult to solve. Use of

---

* Once again in temporary command: Von Thoma, on reconnaissance as the Alamein Line collapsed, had been captured.

the coastal road was essential: but Rommel was clutching on to it. 8 Army's delays at and after Alamein were indeed an early warning of a lesson which would be driven further home as Rommel retreated along the African shore, and by what subsequently happened in Tunisia; in Italy; in north-west Europe; in Korea and in Vietnam. This is that even an army rich in *matériel* cannot succeed, unless means are found to keep these riches moving forward to the point where they can function . . . the battlefield. The 'B' echelons of his fighting divisions; the technical staff and equipment for bringing advance aerodromes into action; engineers and stores required to overcome the Germans' rearguard devices; the food, the fuel and the ammunition for a victorious spearhead could not be moved by Montgomery in a decisive way unless he controlled the road along the coast. This was imperative: and from Alamein to Mareth, where Rommel finally departed from the African front, it was what he dexterously denied to his adversary. Montgomery was always preoccupied by 'balance', yet in spite of what was by now a magnificently organised administrative base in Egypt, and in spite of skilful improvisations along his line of supply, he rarely enjoyed peace of mind about his logistic support during the long march to the west.

The Axis convoys slowly ground their way along the road to Halfaya and Sollum and dragged up the passes—'a vast column of vehicles, 30 to 40 miles long', as Rommel put it, which has often been graphically represented in photographs of the desert campaign: a long black crawling serpent of steel, looking so vulnerable that to this day it is hard to understand why it was not more punished by the R.A.F. or fatally decapitated by the British armour. Nevertheless, it was moving towards an inevitable fate; on the morning of 8 November Rommel informed Bayerlein that over 100 ships were approaching north-west Africa. *Torch* was in train, and Rommel immediately saw that 'this spelt the end of the army in Africa'. Mussolini sent out instructions that a line must be held at Sollum, but Rommel had no illusions. Short of tanks and men and fuel, he appreciated the certainty of further outflanking movements around the south of any line he might attempt to establish—a threat of which he was constantly reminded by reports of Allied probes along his right —and concluded that 'the vital thing now was to get every German and Italian soldier and as much material as possible away to the west to enable us to make stand somewhere further back, or *to ship them back to Europe*' . . . (my italics).

In these early days of retreat, as during the main Alamein battle, Rommel clearly began to change his concepts. Until now he had been mainly governed by the idea of the attack *à outrance*. As he retired towards Tunisia—and this was to cause much bitterness between him and the German and Italian commands in Africa and Europe—his conviction grew that the proper course was to evacuate completely from Africa: later, when he exercised his shadowy command north of the Alps, his recommendation was that the unreliable Italians should be abandoned and that the Germans should fall back on the strong Alpine bastion; and finally, in Normandy after D-Day, he again spelled out to Hitler the need for an immediate retreat—this time to the line of the Seine. It is difficult to think of an Allied commander in the Second World War who endured a similar experience.

For the Commonwealth, for the Americans and for the Russians the graph of success moved steadily upward after an initial descent into troughs of defeat. Rommel's career, on the other hand, began with triumphs: but during its final months it placed him in one situation after another where he himself could envisage nothing but disaster. From Alamein until his death, the strain must have been intolerable. But there can be no doubt in the mind of anyone who has studied his writings that he would have been deeply satisfied with the results of his refusal to abandon his principles. To mark the 25th anniversary of Alamein the *Sunday Times* printed a series of articles which included an interview with Dr. Hans-Adolf Jacobsen of the University of Bonn who, when Hitler killed Rommel, was serving in the *Wehrmacht*, as a youth of 19, in the Arctic Circle. Now a distinguished historian of his own times, he said in this interview: 'Ten years ago, when we were starting to build up the new idea of "civilians in uniform" inside the German Army, I was asked for a genealogical tree of suitable German generals who could be used as examples for the young German soldier of today. The question which of course arose immediately was which of the generals from Hitler's Third Reich could we include? I prepared a list, with historical reasons, and Rommel was at the top . . . among the highest military leaders of the Third Reich, Rommel is one of the very few who genuinely changed his spots . . . even allowing for the fact that Rommel was in a strong position because of the propaganda value to the Germans of his victories, he was one of the very few generals who had the strength to refuse to carry out one of Hitler's orders.' Rommel was in fact a man who undoubtedly would have wished to bequeath this image of integrity and moral strength, rather than one of conventional success in his chosen career: and it is gratifying to learn that this has happened.

In the retreat of the *Panzerarmee* the next two bounds were Mersa Brega–El Agheila (reached by 23 November) and the line Tarhuna–Homs covering Tripoli and its vital port (which was evacuated during the night of 22–23 January). Immediately after Alamein, on 8 and again on 10 November, Mussolini pressed on Rommel through Cavallero the need to hold on to a firm defensive position at El Agheila. On the 13th Cavallero and Bastico decided, independently of Rommel, that this must be the sticking point around and behind which their shattered divisions might re-form. On the 22nd Hitler intervened with one of his dogmatic 'hold-out-to-the-last' instructions; his army *must* stand at Agheila. But Rommel was unshaken in his appreciation of what was required. He saw that, even if it took time, the British would build up their strength in the forward areas remorselessly: and he realised that there was no hope of catching them again, as in the springs of 1941 and 1942, when they were most vulnerable—by a quick counter-attack before their spearhead units had been stiffened. It was he who was now short of reinforcement: 'what we found really astonishing was to see the amount of material that they' (the German and Italian High Commands) 'were suddenly able to ship to Tunisia, quantities out of all proportion to anything we had received in the past.' For 8 Army *Torch* was already paying dividends: the Afrika Korps was starved.

The thesis Rommel presented in his various arguments with Cavallero, Kesselring and Bastico was based on three main propositions. 1. The correct line on which the *Panzerarmee* should stand was the 'Gabes gap', where defences could be prepared to cover the short stretch between the sea and the impassable watery expanse of the Shott el Jerid. Here he saw an Alamein in Tunisia, with protected flanks and a distance between them not beyond the capacity of his diminished army to defend. As was shown by the hard-fought battle of Wadi Akarit (which opened on 6 April), had this position been properly developed in the time available it would have been a very hard nut to crack. 2. During the months Montgomery would need to ferry forward to Gabes sufficient troops and supplies, the *Panzerarmee* must be substantially reinforced, must then turn its face from east to west and unexpectedly attack Eisenhower's positions in Tunisia from the flank, and thereafter, having dealt them a crushing blow, must immediately re-organise, turn about once more, and hurl back Montgomery.

In the circumstances this—had he been allowed to put it into effect—was probably the best of the strategic options open to Rommel. But it is doubtful whether even this would have succeeded . . . as he well knew, for his third proposition was that 'in the long run neither Libya nor Tunisia could be held . . . the African war was being decided by the battle of the Atlantic'. And by the battle of the Mediterranean: for after the 'Stoneage' convoy, which successfully delivered four merchant vessels to Malta on 20 November, and the 'Portcullis' convoy which arrived safely with a tanker and five more cargo ships, the island was never again in serious danger. All Kesselring's forebodings were justified. Supplies now continued to flow in steadily, and as the stock-piles grew Malta's offensive capacity expanded. Before the end of the year more air squadrons had been introduced, and Force 'K' was back again with three cruisers and four destroyers. Increased submarine effort, minelaying, bombing, strafing, and surface naval action took a larger and larger toll: in October the Axis ships of over 500 tons sunk in the Mediterranean amounted to 17 (56,944 tons), but in December the comparable figures were 32 (90,730). Rommel, in effect, now presented the picture of the dying gladiator with a wound in his side through which his life-blood was draining away.

Yet in fact he was full of fight. Subordinated once more to Bastico, by a decision which on 22 November placed under Bastico's *Superlibia* the liaison group formed the previous August under Barbasetti di Prun (to act as a channel of communications between Rommel and *Comando Supremo*, to whom the Field-Marshal had a direct responsibility), *Delease (Delegazione del Comando Supremo in Africa Settentrionale)*, Rommel saw that he was making no progress by arguing with the Italians in Africa or by his signals to Germany. So to Germany, he now decided, he would go—taking advantage of the temporary lull in the pressure on his front. He went there—in the conditions of late 1942 a brave act—to tackle Hitler himself, and to try to make the Führer see both what ought to be done for his Army if it was to remain in Africa and also how much better it would be if the Axis could pull out.

This visit was disastrous. Rommel got to Rastenburg during the afternoon of 28 November and first talked to Keitel, Jodl and the ever-present Schmundt. 'The two former were extremely wary and reserved.' Soon he was ordered into Hitler's presence: 'there was a noticeable chill in the atmosphere from the outset.' He was treated like some Uriah the Hittite who had suddenly returned from the front to explain to the men in the rear a whole order of realities of which they had had no personal experience. Most of the staff present at his interview, he recorded (though rage may have coloured his recollections), 'had never heard a shot fired in anger'. Hitler worked himself up into one of his famous tantrums, but Rommel was not overawed. He described frankly his shortage of equipment ... to which the counter-charge was that his men had thrown their arms away! He explained the effect of the Allied superiority in armour and in the air, and was met by incomprehension. 'I stated that all other armies would suffer the same fate if the Americans succeeded in setting foot on the Continent.' Churchill grilled his field commanders when they returned to Whitehall, and in his communications to them gave ample evidence of his displeasure about their performance: but during their unhappy relations with London neither Wavell or Auchinleck had to deal with misunderstanding or insults at such a frenetic level.

For Rommel this was a most important stage in the diminution of his loyalty to Hitler. The seed was sown at Alamein. Now 'I began to realise that Adolf Hitler simply did not want to see the situation as it was, and that he reacted emotionally against what his intelligence must have told him was right.' Rommel, in effect, got small change from his visit. His views proved unacceptable: and Göring was sent back with him to Italy for further discussions. Rommel's distaste for Hitler's entourage was enhanced by a journey at close quarters with 'the antics of the Reichsmarschall in his special train'. In Rome, joined by Kesselring, they had a discussion with Mussolini during which Göring went so far as to accuse Rommel of having left the Italians in the lurch at Alamein: an accusation which even the Duce himself could not accept. The Rome conversations led to no definite conclusions about either logistics or strategy, and Rommel flew back to Africa with a heavy heart, convinced that he was now thrown back on his own resources—both of skill and supplies. Many times in the past he had fulminated about leading a Forgotten Army: now he knew it to be the truth.

For an estimate of Rommel's capacity as a military commander the tactical details of the British advance on Tripoli are unimportant; it was his appreciation of the larger realities which revealed his clarity of vision and—in his refusal to reject what he saw as the right course of action—his integrity and courage. In the story of the retreat there are certain constants: domination by the Allies in the air; a fertility of invention on the part of the Germans in obstructive engineering—mining and demolitions; a reiteration in Rommel's *Memoirs* of a plea for petrol, petrol, petrol; and a wearing succession of arguments about policy with the Italian commanders in Africa, with *Comando Supremo*, and with O.K.W., in which opinion veered and shifted like a weathercock. Even between the German H.Q.s in Africa there was no sense of solidarity. On 10 December 5 *Panzerarmee* was established in Tunisia under von Arnim, but, Rommel noted, 'unfortunately very little co-ordination existed between this new command and ourselves. We badly felt the need during this period of a single authority on African soil which could have welded together under a single command the two armies whose fates were so closely dependent on each other.' This was the system the British and Americans established a few months later. In spite of internal stresses and strains, it subsequently directed them into the heart of Germany and to victory.

During this phase there occurred two events which might have affected Rommel profoundly, had their possible consequences followed. The first was a summit conference at Rastenburg between 18 and 20 December at which there was a general review of the Axis position. Ciano represented an ailing Mussolini. Its conclusion, in respect of Africa, was that Rommel must gain time for the Tunisian front to be consolidated—which suited the Italians. Mussolini therefore signalled to Bastico a mock-Hitler message on the 19th: 'Resistance to the uttermost. I repeat resistance to the uttermost, with all the troops of the *Panzerarmee* on the Buerat line.' (Rommel asked himself how the Duce thought such battles were fought. 'I had really done all I could to arouse some understanding of the art of desert warfare in our higher commands and had particularly emphasised that to concern oneself with territory was mere prejudice.')

In strict military terms Rommel was of course correct; but when he spoke like this he betrayed himself. In modern war, where rapid communications are available, the political requirements of what Sir Henry Wilson in the First World War called 'the Frocks'—the politicians—form a factor which the soldier must take as much into account as his enemy. Wireless and now the satellites have given to civilian 'hawks' and 'doves' an unprecedented influence in the conduct of battles. Rommel was not like, say, Wolseley in the Ashanti campaign, operating in a situation where he and Whitehall were out of touch for weeks: Rommel had to face the fact that political pressures might bear immediately on his military decisions. He says in his *Memoirs* that non-motorised forces cannot create a centre of gravity quickly enough. Hitler, by a *Diktat* sent over the air, could do this more rapidly and effectively than all the tanks in the Afrika Korps.

During his pre-war career Rommel stood aside from politics: he never grasped, therefore, how the kind of orders transmitted to a commander in the field from Rastenburg or Whitehall or Washington could be coloured by more than military considerations. His era was that of radio rather than Telstar: but in effect he faced . . . as did Auchinleck during his badgering by Churchill . . . the same problem as that with which the American generals in Vietnam have had to live. When the home front can communicate with the battlefront in a matter of hours or even seconds, not only the status of the commander on the spot but also the very nature of the decisions he takes may be transformed. So it was in Africa.

Rommel was not alone in suffering the effect, but not understanding the meaning of this revolution in communication. An instruction from Churchill or Hitler might contain manifold nuances which only a sophisticated awareness of the political realities could interpret. Rommel was not a member of either the General Staff or the Nazi hierarchy which surrounded Hitler; Auchinleck came from the Indian Army and was a stranger to his Prime Minister; Montgomery was a law unto himself . . . perhaps the most astute and aware of the three, but not adept politically. None of them was of 'the establishment'; and none was able to decode with subtlety the motivations of the orders they received or to understand the domestic consequences of delays or retreats which, on purely military grounds, seemed to them inevitable. It is doubtful, for example, whether Montgomery to this day really comprehends the effect in Whitehall of hearing that he was pulling divisions out of the line of attack at Alamein for what to him seemed the sensible purpose of re-grouping. Rommel's own inability to understand the politico-military complex was especially a weakness during his withdrawal to the west. He never, for example, put himself fully into the mind of Italians who were losing an Empire. He was not *simpatico*.

But during discussions with Bastico about what to do at Buerat in the light of Mussolini's directive, this insensitivity on Rommel's part was restrained. Of course he was right to argue that to make a stand here was absurd . . . as Montgomery proved. The correct tactical decision was to pull out. But Bastico was Mussolini's mouthpiece, speaking for a dictator desperately attempting to retain some small corner of his disappearing dominions. For the Duce in his decline a delay on the battle front was a victory in Rome: this Rommel failed to see, and he pressed his Italian *confrères* hard. Still, they came to a tacit agreement. Bastico made his political point, and Rommel understood Bastico's ambivalent position, for he sensed that his own military appreciation was accepted in their hearts by the Italian military command in Africa. He therefore bowed to Mussolini's instruction, and did his best to prepare a stop-line at Buerat . . . with the secret reservation that he would retreat immediately it became untenable. Montgomery helped him by assaulting his carefully fortified position with a frontal attack which pinned his troops down, and an outflanking move by 7 Armoured and 2 New Zealand Divisions which offered him no alternative but withdrawal. The Italians' face was saved; the advance swept on past Tripoli; and Rommel was able to take a further step towards his true objective, Gabes.

The second event which might have had important consequences for Rommel was a storm. On 3 and 4 January a gale off Benghazi badly damaged both port installations and shipping in the harbour, while later in the month, between the 13th and the 16th, more rough weather disrupted the work of unloading. Here was a possibility of disaster for 8 Army. From Benghazi to Tripoli, still uncaptured, there was no port of substance, and for various technical reasons beach-landings would be unprofitable. East of Benghazi there stretched hundreds of miles and a single road back to the Egyptian base. The administrative plan on which Montgomery's not especially powerful spearhead rested was to obtain by the end of December about 2380 tons per day through Benghazi; a further 2200 were to be pushed up daily to Tobruk by rail, and most of these were to be ferried on to Benghazi by sea. The port was thus a nerve-centre in the administrative nexus. At the beginning of January everything fell apart.

On the 3rd the mole of Benghazi harbour, already weak, was cracked by the storm. Outside it and behind it supply ships and landing craft were damaged or sunk, berths were destroyed, and warehouses drowned. For two days all landings ceased. The rate then built up, interrupted by the second gale, but for the month of January the amount of supplies landed daily averaged 1800 tons as compared with the predicted 2380. This potential aid to Rommel had, however, been offset by foresight. 8 Army's staff had planned, contingently, to meet just such an Act of God: 10 Corps was immediately grounded, and its vehicles set up a shuttle-service from Tobruk to Benghazi (2,700,000 gallons of fuel were moved by road from one port to the other between 8 and 25 January). And yet, as the *Official History* points out, 'the problem was relentless. Once the army and air force moved they *had* to reach Tripoli without pause in a set time or withdraw for want of supplies.' In the event, Tripoli was reached and it was Rommel who withdrew. But it is an odd co-incidence that in Africa, as in the period after D-Day, Rommel nearly found salvation in a storm at sea.

There now began a period of grave uncertainty about his future which in one way and another persisted until his final return to Europe. He was, in effect, dismissed from his post. Bayerlein recalls that towards the end of January the Italians, and Kesselring, and O.K.W. were all scheming for Rommel's departure—on 20 January, indeed, he had received via Cavallero a reproach from Mussolini upbraiding him for his decision to withdraw from the Homs–Tarhuna line, although the Duce had instructed him to hold it for three more weeks. 'We gasped when we received this signal': and rightly. But Rommel's critics had their way, for at midday on 26 January *Comando Supremo* signalled that on account of his bad state of health he would be released from his command once the Mareth Line was reached, '*the actual date being left to me*' . . . (my italics).

This proved to be an escape clause. It enabled Rommel to maintain his position for the time being, to 'stick it out to the limit' (for he could not endure the thought of abandoning his faithful troops). He determined even to disregard his doctor's orders—in spite of his chagrin he was honest enough to admit to his wife on 28 January that he was unfit, suffering from severe headaches and overstrained nerves. He was also taking sleeping draughts. The Italians' face-saving formula may have contained this element of truth, but the ignominy of such a dismissal was more than Rommel could stomach, and he soldiered on, even though his appointed successor, General Giovanni Messe, arrived in Africa at the beginning of February. Messe had

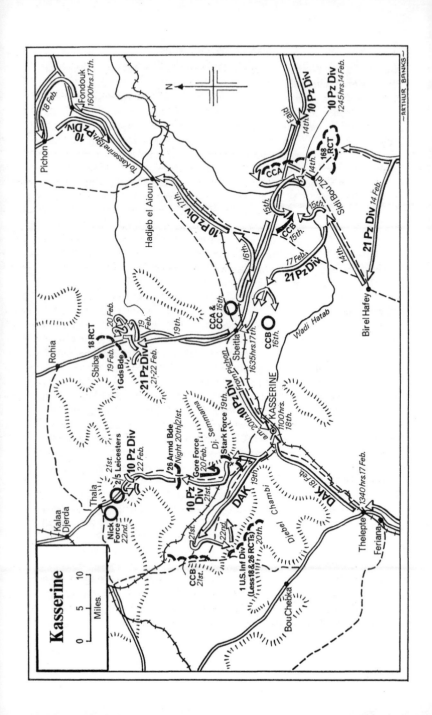

~ARTHUR BANKS~

Kasserine

Miles
0   5   10

N

Fondouk
1600 hrs.17th.

18 Feb.

10 Pz Div

10 Pz Div
1245hrs.14 Feb.

Pichon

To Kasserine 19th.

10 Pz Div

14th.

168
RCT

CCA

14th.

15th.

21 Pz Div

Sidi Bou Zid

21 Pz Div
14 Feb.

Hadjeb el Aioun

16th.

CCB

15th.

14th.

15th.

Bir el Hafey

17 Feb.

21 Pz Div

Rohia

18 RCT
20 Feb.

19
Feb.

21 Pz Div
21-22 Feb.

Sbiba
19 Feb.

1 Gds Bde

19th.

CCA &
CCC 16th.

Wadi Hatab

CCB
16th.

Sbeitla

1635hrs.17th.

Leicesters
21st.

10 Pz Div
22 Feb.

/26 Armd Bde
Night 20th/21st.

Gore Force
20 Feb.

Dj. Semmama

Stark Force 19th

10 Pz Div from Pichon

a.m. 20th

KASSERINE
1100 hrs.

18th.

Thala

10 Pz
Div
21st.

10 Pz Div
21st.

DAK
19th.

Djebel
Chambi

Kalaa
Djerda

Nick
Force
22nd

2/5

DAK
1340 hrs.17 Feb.

CCB
21st.

21st.

22nd

22nd

1 US. Inf Div
(Less 18 & 26 RCTs)
20th.

Wadi

Thelepte

Feriana

BouChebka

commanded the Italian Expeditionary Force in Russia and, as Rommel sardonically put it, 'like most people who came from Russia, he looked on things with considerable optimism'. But fortunately he disclosed no considerable desire to pick up the reins of command from Rommel—whose overlord, Bastico, a man he understood, had returned to Italy on 31 January. Cavallero had also been sacked in the shake-up . . . 'welcome news'.

His army was now getting into position along the Mareth Line. There was a moment of poise, during which new strategic possibilities could be reviewed. The old French frontier positions at Mareth, covering Tunisia against an Italian attack from the east—an 80-mile stretch between the Mediterranean and the Matmata hills—were strong enough, in view of the terrain and in spite of Rommel's contempt for French concrete, to make it certain that Montgomery would prepare a set-piece assault and take time in building up supplies; as Rommel savagely noted in his retrospective paper, *From Alamein to Mareth*, 'Montgomery had an absolute mania for always bringing up adequate reserves behind his back and risking as little as possible'. Montgomery has his answer—there is an air of sanity about a steady succession of victories which leads to an ultimate conquest. But his cautious methods, which by now were all too evident, enabled a quick-thinking commander like Rommel to exploit his opponent's Achilles' heel.

The option offered by this pause was the second of the propositions Rommel placed before his superiors earlier in the year—a two-fisted stroke, whereby the Allies in Tunisia could be fatally punched in the back and then, by a reverse turn, Montgomery could be given a final blow in the face. Arguments, messages and meetings in early February between the Axis commanders led to a typical compromise, in which Rommel's ideas were applied in theory, but nullified in practice because the Axis plan was not properly thought out in advance or effectively exploited—against what turned out, at first, to be a collapsing enemy. The actions collectively described as 'Kasserine' could have been a triumphant swan-song for Rommel. But inexperienced Americans and a few British troops—inexperienced also—were allowed by the Axis command to recoup after the initial shock from what Rommel intended to be the first of two decisive victories: they recovered at Kasserine, they reinforced, and in the end it was Rommel who retired, and who, in the other half of the two-pronged operation he had planned, Medenine, was conclusively defeated in a single day. Because he and 5 *Panzerarmee* did not speak the same language and were unable to compose a joint battle-plan, Rommel's swan-song in Africa was a double defeat, in what were essentially armoured engagements, for the most brilliant tank commander of all those who served along the Mediterranean shore.

With the Mareth Line as a pivot of manœuvre in his rear, Rommel was offered two main lines of attack by the geography of Tunisia. He could advance along the coastal strip, via Sfax and Sousse; but this could hardly have produced that brilliant, fatal stab into the Allies' entrails which he envisaged, and it would have exposed him to forces debouching through the passes in the mountains which marched from the north along what would have been his open left flank. In fact mountains and passes offered a better target. From Tunis (see map on p. 197) southwards to Gafsa there stretches the Eastern Dorsale, through which there are two viable passages: the Fondouk pass west of Sousse and the Faid west of Sfax. Another range, the Petite or Western Dorsale, runs in a rough parallel with the Eastern until it joins the Atlas Mountains: this too was penetrable by two passes, at Sbiba to the north and Kasserine to the south. Such was the geographical layout which Rommel chose to exploit; if he could burst through the passes he might once again hope to disrupt his enemy's rearward installations, as he had done in France and, for example, by his 'dash to the wire'. Beyond Kasserine lay Tebessa, where British supplies were gathering and which offered a rich harvest. A preliminary sally-port through the mountain chain (whose passes were so far held by the Allies) was achieved on 30 January when 21 Panzer (already transferred to von Arnim's command) hit the slight and ill-equipped French force holding Faid, brushed off a feeble attempt at relief by the Americans, and penetrated the pass. This was a useful overture.

But it would have been more useful had the Germans been able to see eye to eye. Rommel and von Arnim were aiming at different targets, from different points of view. On 9 February Kesselring came over to Africa to confer with them, in the hope of establishing a common policy. At this conference von Arnim spoke in support of caution. He was a member of the Prussian élite, a 'Russian front' general—he had commanded a corps in Russia—and he was conservative in temperament and in every sense Rommel's opposite. He doubted whether the two *Panzerarmeen* had enough men or *matériel* to force a way through to Tebessa, and preferred a limited operation, designed to manœuvre the French and Americans into withdrawing on to the Western Dorsale by an attack in the area of Pichon, north-west of the Fondouk pass. Division produced compromise—two virtually independent operations. Arnim in the north would launch *Frühlingswind*, with a centre-line through the Faid pass directed on Sidi Bou Zid, while Rommel's *Morgenluft* followed the line Gafsa–Feriana–Kasserine. After this meeting Kesselring had a private word with Rommel and told him that, should these moves make possible the 'big operation' against Tebessa, Rommel would become Generalissimo. In this event, Kesselring reckoned, he could carry

Comando Supremo with him. It was an inspiring message for a man who was at the end of his tether and was now about to embark on his final fling.

Von Arnim, however, does not seem to have grasped Rommel's intentions, or indeed his own responsibilities in regard to them. He assumed that exploitation would occur primarily in the north. He had a vague understanding that he should release some of 21 Panzer in the course of the battle, to support Rommel in the south, but he seems to have thought that Rommel's concern was to cover his rear at Mareth, rather than to make a damaging stroke towards Tebessa: though on 13 February Rommel, von Arnim and the latter's second-in-command, General Ziegler, did meet on the eve of the battle—Ziegler was directly, but incompetently, responsible for *Frühlingswind*.

'Kasserine' was a complicated action. It is complicated to follow because of the moves on the ground and even more so because of the nature of the ground itself. But in its opening phase the operations on Rommel's front developed with a relative simplicity: it was in von Arnim's area that the fighting was involved. Put shortly: von Arnim pushed forward from the Faid pass during the early hours of 14 February and Rommel ordered the Afrika Korps to attack Gafsa (evacuated already by the French and the Americans) on the 15th. By the 17th Rommel was in Feriana and had captured Thelepte, with its important airfield, some miles further to the north: von Arnim had by then taken Sidi Bou Zid and Sbeitla. Thus both *Frühlingswind* and *Morgenluft* were attaining their objectives, and the *Panzerarmeen* were nicely poised for a further thrust—poised, but still differing about their objectives. The Americans had certainly been disorganised in this first phase: 2866 prisoners, 169 tanks, and 63 guns were lost on the northern front alone.

But as Martin Blumenson, writing as an American, fairly observes in his study of Kasserine, 'if the loss of Sbeitla and Feriana had been the work of bumbling Allied commanders who were only amateurs, the next phase of operations would show how much better the Axis professionals and veterans could be at the business of bungling'. Rommel, with his *coup d'œil*, saw that there was now a golden opportunity to implement what he had always seen as the purpose of the attack, the capture of Tebessa. This could have unhinged the Allied line. But von Arnim was lukewarm. Rommel argued that an attack on Tebessa could only succeed if Arnim's tanks could be sent south in support; Arnim, determined to fight a private battle, held 21 Panzer back at Sbeitla and ordered 10 Panzer northwards to Fondouk. Thus the Axis army was dissipated among the mountains in a way reminiscent of some of 8 Army's more egregious dissipations of its strength in the desert. Disenchanted, Rommel ordered his Italian *Centauro* Division back to Gafsa and then on to the Mareth Line. He saw no future in the battle. On the 18th he wrote despondently to his wife: 'there will probably be a change of command here shortly. I need hardly tell you how hard this hits me. . . .'

His plan was based on previous experience of how the enemy would react, and was justified by the Allies' response. 'Commanders', he wrote, 'whose battles have so far all been fought in theory tend as a rule to react directly rather than indirectly to the enemy's moves. Beginners generally lack the nerve to take decisions based on military expediency alone, without regard for what is weighing most heavily on their minds.' This is good psychology: after a disaster one tends to concentrate on one's own front. In other words, the raw American and British troops who had just been shattered on his right would be so preoccupied with their predicament that they would not be able to react with sufficient speed to halt a sudden move round their own flank, directed on Tebessa.

Rommel perceived the truth. Eisenhower had instructed Alexander to take overall command of operations during the critical situation created by the Axis attack, and Alexander's appreciation was that Rommel would not strike for Tebessa but for Thala. It was at Thala, therefore, that General Anderson, the local commander, gathered his forces for a stand: and there is little doubt that if Rommel had been allowed to drive rapidly and ruthlessly on Tebessa he would have both caught his opponents on the wrong foot and also opened up further opportunities of exploitation, whereby the first strategic objectives of the 'two-pronged' idea would have been reached, and the Allied armies in Tunisia would have been hamstrung.

But war, as Thucydides observed, is a hard master. Rommel protested to *Comando Supremo* and Kesselring on the 18th about von Arnim's intransigence: 'we sat down in a fever of impatience to await the decision.' The unreasonableness of war was implicit in the answer: it was calculated to satisfy neither of the dissenting commanders, though it accepted Rommel's argument that the next thrust should be somewhere along his southern front. At 0130 the order arrived, giving as an objective not Tebessa, but El Kef. 'This was an appalling and unbelievable piece of shortsightedness, which did, in fact, cause the whole plan to go awry.'

The actual wording of the order was so ambiguous that Rommel might easily have warped it to suit his own purposes. 'With all available mobile troops of the G.I. Pz Army and 10 and 21 Pz Divisions under command, Field-Marshal Rommel, concentrating his forces and strongly protecting his west flank, is to advance from the general line Sbeitla–Tebessa–Maktar–Tadjerouine, with El Kef as his first objective. Weak forces will be adequate for protection of the line Tebessa–Tozeur.' *Comando Supremo*'s geography was odd. Rommel chose to interpret his directive literally, as meaning that he must strike at El Kef through Thala, and consider a move on Tebessa as merely a protection for his left flank. In the order the significant fact for Rommel was that it put the two panzer divisions under his direct control, while he retained responsibility for the Mareth Line. He took immediate advantage of this change of heart—believing always in the quick counter-attack—and warned *Comando Supremo* that an alteration in the command structure in Africa had now become imperative.

He gained his point. On the 19th 'Group Rommel' was established. The Mareth area became the direct responsibility of Messe and Rommel's old *Panzerarmee*, which was now rechristened 1 Italian Army: though Rommel still retained an overall control. He recovered 21 Panzer, acquired 10 Panzer, and retained the detachments of the Afrika Korps and the Italian *Centauro* Division which were already on his front. Since his 'order of release' on 26 January the up-turn of his fortunes was remarkable: but there was one flaw . . . von Arnim still stayed outside his command. (In spite of Rommel's occasional outbursts against Kesselring in his *Memoirs*, and in spite of their frequent disagreements in Africa, this rearrangement seems to have owed much to Kesselring's advocacy, and to his decision to back Rommel rather than von Arnim. Kesselring favoured the drive on Tebessa, and thought that, of the two diverging commanders, Rommel was the one who could produce the sudden hatchet blow which might shatter the Allies in the Tunisian mountains.) Action was now the word. At 0450 on the 19th Rommel told his Afrika Korps units to seize the Kasserine pass; thus beginning the critical struggle on which the whole operation ultimately turned, and after which it is properly named. The successful Allied defence of the route to El Kef may be compared with Rommel's defence of the minefield gaps at Gazala: in each case a failure of nerve would have been fatal. At Kasserine there was indeed first a failure (though Rommel had not been optimistic during the first hours of Gazala), but the Allies' line was not finally broken.

Rommel's orders directed 21 Panzer on Sbiba and recalled 10 Panzer to a concentration area around Sbeitla, for his intention was to use the latter as a reserve which might reinforce whichever of his attacks made headway. It is interesting to note how, as soon as Rommel took charge, he imposed on the disorderly Axis front a pattern which—granted his terms of reference—was logical and, as Montgomery would have said, 'balanced'. This instantaneous grasp of the facts, and the ability to propose the right answer almost instinctively, place commanders like Rommel in a category of their own. (Alexander also displayed these qualities. Rommel's orders on the 19th were paralleled by Alexander's quick assessment of the Allied front when it was put into his hands. He too summed up the situation swiftly; seeing that French, American and British units were in a hopeless *mêlée*, and that the first necessity was to disentangle them so that command and supply might function more efficiently.)

General Buelowius, now commanding the Assault Group of the Afrika Korps on Rommel's front, decided to rush immediately through the Kasserine pass with 33 Reconnaissance Unit—the 11 Hussars of the Afrika Korps. But the Germans had shown their hand. On the evening of the 18th their exploratory patrols had implied an attack: the defence was alert, and 33 Reconnaissance Unit made no headway. The Panzer Grenadiers came up in support, but when Rommel arrived at the Afrika Korps H.Q. and saw what was happening he realised the truth. Like Montgomery at Enfidaville, he had to accept that divisions expert in the desert could be tyros in the hills. Rommel criticised Menton's panzer grenadiers at Kasserine because 'he should have combined hill and valley tactics and should have taken possession of the hills on either side of the pass in order to eliminate the enemy artillery observers and get through to the enemy's rear'. This is the voice of a man who had fought on the Italian front in the First World War; the voice of experience. Many of the errors committed on both sides in the hills of Tunisia arose because neither British nor Germans appreciated the special problems involved—nor, certainly, did the Americans: Rommel lacked even a single division, like 4 Indian, which had specialised in mountain warfare and was commanded by a general who was prepared to press his expert point of view. In his Group he had no one like Tuker, so sure of the way to fight among mountains that he was prepared to resign (as Tuker was before Medjez el Bab) if the basic principles of hill fighting were being ignored.

By 1700 on the 20th Rommel had captured the Kasserine pass—but only by dint of personal pressure. 'Valuable time was being squandered. I was extremely angry and ordered the commanders to take themselves closer to the front where they could get a proper view of the situation.' This was his first experience of the fact that while Germans could sometimes be slothful, Americans were capable of reacting swiftly on the battlefield. For example, Fredendall, the general commanding 2 U.S. Corps, having realised that a German attack was imminent, 'requested that all the mines available in North Africa be supplied to him'. His conduct of the battle was so unsatisfactory that Eisenhower later posted him back across the Atlantic: but the mines mattered. There were hasty searches among the depots, and as a result 52 plane-loads delivered some 20,000 mines at the forward airfield of Youks-les-Bains, whence they were ferried by truck up to the pass and were being laid as late as 30 minutes before Rommel attacked. The American military image has suffered unfairly as a result of Kasserine. During the battle there was much incompetence, folly and fear: but all these deficiencies had been earlier displayed by 8 Army, and to the historian what is now significant is that, in spite of them, the line held.

The key to Rommel's cracking of the pass was his recall of 10 Panzer to Sbeitla, which provided him with a mobile reserve. But it was ominous that he had to use it. His decision to deploy it at Kasserine rather than in support at Sbiba—following a visit to 21 Panzer on the 19th, when it became clear to him that progress there was too slow—was a straw in the wind. The scratch defences at Sbiba were giving the veteran 21 Panzer a bloody nose. Rommel accepted his losses. He pulled back his troops at Sbiba seven miles into a defensive position, and told von Broich of 10 Panzer (on the move to Sbeitla) that he must be prepared, at dawn on the 20th, to break through Kasserine towards Thala. . . . Buelowius forming a flankguard in the direction of Tebessa. The second sinister fact was that at Kasserine the defences had proved sufficiently resilient to compel Rommel to commit his *masse de manœuvre*.

In the meantime, however, things were going well—even though von Arnim had withheld from 10 Panzer the heavy tank battalion with its Tigers. Rommel summoned *Centauro* from Feriana as a make-weight, and its units reinforced at Kasserine during the night of the 19–20th. He kept up an unremitting pressure on the pass throughout the 20th, and by late afternoon his Germans and Italians were through and driving north towards Thala, while his opponents were retiring in scattered disorder. His units on his left, feeling out towards Tebessa, had also made good progress. It was typical of Rommel that he stopped, as he advanced with his armour, to examine the American equipment abandoned by its crews—20 tanks and 30 half-tracks towing anti-tank guns were taken—and that he noted not only the luxurious scale of American supply but also the *standardisation* of vehicles and spares: he made a correct and perceptive comment when, as a result of his examination, he observed, 'British experience had been put to good use in American equipment'!

The same afternoon Kesselring called von Arnim to a conference at Tunis, and strongly criticised him for his failure to support Rommel. Arnim was evasive. Kesselring renewed his instructions to send the heavy tanks south—but nevertheless von Arnim held on to them. (A detailed study of the Kesselring–Rommel–von Arnim relationship would certainly reveal that the 'belly-aching' which Montgomery was determined to stop before and during Alamein, and which had been so prevalent in 8 Army at, for example, Gazala, was no monopoly of the Allies.) At Tunis Kesselring also told a representative of *Comando Supremo* that he proposed to recommend that

Rommel should assume command of all elements of 5 *Panzerarmee* on his front.

But it was all in vain. On the 21st, having spread his reconnaissance antennae into the hills which blocked an advance leftwards on Tebessa via Djebel Hamra, and also along the direct route to Le Kef via Thala, Rommel opted for the latter and instructed von Broich at 1130 to move on Thala while Buelowius masked his eastern flank. There now occurred a classic 'thin red line' action. The British 26 Armoured Brigade slowly withdrew in the face of 10 Panzer, moving from bound to bound, throughout the morning and afternoon. By 1745 they were only two miles short of a battalion of the Leicestershires behind whom lay nothing but a few field and anti-tank batteries. In the evening the British armour pulled back through the infantry, with German tanks on their heels: there was confused fighting during the darkness, and the infantry started to withdraw through the gun line.

For artillery the sight of infantry pulling back through their lines is always unnerving. But at Thala firm orders rejecting the idea of a retreat were issued, stragglers were collected, the guns held their ground, and somehow the line was still solid at dawn. By then a Blücher had arrived for the British at this Waterloo. In *The Struggle for Europe* Chester Wilmot observes that Americans have an affinity with machines: an affinity which explains, for example, how Patton's armour was able to race through France and how, during the German offensive in the Ardennes, he was able to switch his centre-line so rapidly from east to north, to enable him to relieve the Americans at Bastogne. At Thala something similar occurred. The artillery column of 9 U.S. Division—12 155-mm.s, 24 105s and 12 75s—which in four days had raced 800 miles from Morocco, drove into action that night straight off the line of march.

By contrast the supplies of Rommel's *Group* were now down to about one day's ammunition, six days' food and 120 miles of fuel per vehicle. At 1300 on the 22nd Rommel met Kesselring with Westphal and the *Luftwaffe* commander, Seidemann, and they decided to break off the attack. The gamble had failed. Kesselring asked Rommel if he was prepared to take over complete command of the two *Panzerarmeen*: but the offer came too late. Ill and dispirited, Rommel refused.

By the 23rd his troops were again south of the Kasserine pass and were being heavily attacked from the air. Later that day there came an order from *Comando Supremo*, nominating Rommel as commander of a new 'Army Group Africa', with authority over both Messe and von Arnim. El Kef and Tebessa were now forgotten, and 8 Army once again became Rommel's prime target. Ill and unhappy as he was, he could not refuse twice. So. . . .

24 February 1943

Dearest Lu,

I've moved up a step in command and have given up my army as a result. Bayerlein remains my Chief of Staff. Whether it's a permanent solution is doubtful. . . .

Even a temporary solution was in doubt. It has often been observed that Montgomery's main victories were preceded by a defensive success: Alam Halfa before Alamein; the offensive/defensive battle on the British left in Normandy which made possible the Americans' runaway break-through at St. Lo; and certainly a perfect defensive action at Medenine as a predecessor to Mareth and Wadi Akarit. At Medenine Rommel walked into a trap and was utterly defeated. He moved on 6 March, but de Guingand noted that 'by March 5th we were ready. . . . Rommel had missed his opportunity.' Why was this first operation of Army Group Afrika a failure?

The first reason was that the Group was still fissured by disagreement and argument over policy, and by unco-ordinated action. On 28 February von Arnim flew to Rome, on his own initiative, to press his private plans for a development in the north towards Medjez el Bab—countering Ambrosio's* proposals put forward the previous day for an attack in the south around Gabes. Messe, by contrast, felt he could not longer contain 8 Army, and yearned to fall back on Enfidaville and the central *massif*.

On 1 March Rommel reported to Kesselring his analysis of this split between his staff. He himself favoured Messe's scheme, which would shorten his front and offer his opponent an increasingly difficult terrain. But as ever *Comando Supremo* and Hitler were adamant (as was Kesselring)—no withdrawal except in emergency! And so Rommel (already contemptuous of von Arnim for the failure of his *Ochsenkopf* manœuvre, which on 26 February had been launched in the direction of Beja and, after hard fighting, had been stopped dead with many German tanks destroyed) accepted the situation and prepared to attack 8 Army at Medenine with the Afrika Korps and 10 and 21 Panzers. In the very planning of the attack argument with his subordinates continued. Badgered and weary, and responsible for the acts of a staff he was no longer able personally to select, Rommel in these days was a man without faith. His image is that of a dogged professional boxer going through the motions without conviction of success. The final plan—how inconceivable a year ago!—was left to Messe and Ziegler, now temporary commander of the Afrika Korps.

* Cavallero's replacement as Italian Chief-of-Staff: anti-German in influence, as opposed to the co-operating Cavallero—whatever a frustrated Rommel may have thought, Cavallero tried to make the Axis function.

10 Panzer was to descend from Hallouf on the New Zealanders and 7 Armoured between Metameur and Medenine. The Afrika Korps, driving down from Djebel Tebaga, was to attack on 10 Panzer's left. Their aim was to cut off and decimate the British front line between Medenine and Mareth.

But the second reason for Montgomery's victory was that he had been granted Napoleon's prime requirement—time. Had Kasserine not been attempted, had Rommel been made to concentrate his tanks and supplies (including all he lost at Kasserine), he might in latter February have been able to 'bounce' Montgomery's spearhead while it was weak; and it seems improbable that 1 Army could have thrust eastwards a sufficiently powerful force in Montgomery's aid. A week before Rommel attacked, de Guingand was told by his chief that as a result of having pushed ahead for his part to help to relieve pressure on 1 Army at Kasserine, he 'now found himself unbalanced'. But by 6 March all was in order. 30 Corps, holding the front, had been supplied through the efficient administrative network with some 350 field and medium guns, 460 anti-tank guns, 300 tanks and enough ammunition. The Desert Air Force was fully on the alert. There was an adequacy of infantry on the ground. And during the time allowed to him Montgomery had been able to emplace his guns—including the new 17-pounder anti-tank gun—in killing positions. I remember passing through the Medenine defences very shortly after the battle and reflecting that the enfilade siting of the anti-tank guns implied a self-confidence which earlier seemed a German prerogative. Medenine reversed, in fact, the process begun during *Battleaxe*: at *Snipe* during Alamein the British used their anti-tank artillery, as so often, with indomitable courage, but what now impressed was the sense of a cunning flowing from assurance. In the event the British held their fire; their infantry was scarcely engaged; the guns got off 30,000 rounds and destroyed some 50 Axis tanks. By mid-evening Rommel decided to call off the action—his last and most decisive defeat in Africa.

Hitler commented at one of his Führer Conferences: 'there you have the opposite ends of the scale. Rommel has become the greatest pessimist and Kesselring the complete optimist.' For Rommel this was now true: there was nothing left for him to do in Africa. New men were on the scene, new divisions, new ways of thinking: after Medenine he was like Gott before the Cairo Conference . . . a man from whom much was expected but who was too tired and too deflated. Rommel's view was simple: 'for the Army Group to remain longer in Africa was now plain suicide.'

Rommel departed from Tunisia for ever on 9 March and was succeeded by von Arnim. Various reasons have been advanced for his departure—Hitler seeing that the Italians found him intolerable; Hitler wishing to extract

Rommel before his useful image was damaged by a Tunisian Dunkirk. But the straightforward explanation in his *Papers* is the most credible: Rommel 'finally decided to fly once again to the Führer's H.Q. I felt it my duty to do all in my power to rouse a true understanding of the practical operational problems of Tunisia.' Once more he failed. Passing through Rome he talked with Ambrosio and Mussolini (whom, oddly enough, he understood: 'he was certainly no Roman, though he tried to act the part'), but found, in effect, that the political consequences of surrendering Tunisia outweighed, in Rome, the military arguments in favour of a withdrawal.

Rommel's record is one of growth not only in military skills but also in intellectual awareness and humane perceptions. Both as a commander and a person he steadily broadened his range. One of the check-points in this process is his subsequent comment on his interview with Mussolini in March. 'Now the Duce saw his dreams crumbling. It was a bitter hour for him, and he was quite incapable of shouldering the consequences. *Perhaps I should have spoken differently to him at the end*, but I was so heartily sick of this ever-lasting false optimism that I just could not do it.' Bearing in mind all Rommel had endured, this is a very charitable observation.

Having declined a journey from Rome in Göring's train, Rommel reached Hitler in Russia on 10 March. Hitler's answer was the same as Mussolini's—Africa must be held, and he must go on sick leave. Rommel pleaded to be allowed to return for a few weeks, but Hitler—wisely—refused. Rommel was decorated with the highest order of the Iron Cross (Oakleaves with Swords and Diamonds) and returned to Germany for treatment.

Hitler's attitude towards Rommel—though it zigzagged hectically—was more steadfast and more simple than has been suggested by those who have misunderstood their relationship. Hitler perceived that Rommel was a capable soldier on whose loyalty he could rely. There were no political implications: just a sense on Hitler's part that, give or take a victory or defeat, Rommel was one of the few men he could trust to keep on winning. During this phase of his relations with Hitler, however, Rommel increasingly came to understand what the Führer and his entourage were doing, and the way their minds were working. 'If the German people are incapable of winning the war then they can rot', Hitler said one day to Rommel. 'Sometimes', Rommel commented to his son, 'you feel that he's not quite normal.'

During the following months, from March to November 1943, Rommel's role was unrewarding. He observed with despair from a distance the inevitable collapse in Africa: 'not even a Napoleon could have done anything about it.' His son describes how he paced impotently up and down his study while Mareth and Wadi Akarit were being fought, condemning Hitler in front of 'a then enthusiastic member of the Hitler Jugend' . . . never a wise act in Nazi Germany! Hitler, however, relieved him to some degree by first attaching Rommel to his own staff as a 'military adviser'; then, in May, ordering O.K.W. to prepare Plan *Alarich*—an insurance against an Italian surrender— in which Rommel was earmarked to run an Army Group north of the Alps whose function would be to provide both a firm base for the German troops in Italy and also a service of reinforcement; next by despatching him on 23 July to Salonika to 'report in detail and direct to him on conditions in Greece'; and finally, following Mussolini's arrest on 26 July, by recalling him to Rastenburg to tell him that 'I am to prepare the entry into Italy . . . without being myself allowed, for the present, to cross the old 1938 frontier'. In other words, Hitler still retained sufficient confidence in Rommel to use him as a fire brigade officer, and Rommel's loyalty, diminishing steadily in respect of his Führer, was sufficiently strong towards the Reich for him to stay in business. But during his 'Italian period' the business was very different from the old days of the Afrika Korps: it was now Kesselring who conducted the battles, and Rommel who manned the rear.

Not surprisingly. As Major-General Jackson puts it in his valuable *The Battle for Italy*, 'the Rommel and Kesselring schools of thought on Italian policy vied with one another'. The broad distinction between the views of the two Field-Marshals was that Rommel's conviction about the Italians' inadequacy persisted, and the tenor of his advice to Hitler was that the Germans should face an undeniable fact and withdraw to the base-line of the Alps. Kesselring argued with more cogency his own case, that among the mountains of Italy effective lines of defence could be established even without Italian troops . . . and then proved in battle that this was true.

On 17 August Rommel's H.Q. actually moved over the Alps: by now his Army Group was feeding divisions southwards and preparing the position between Pisa and Rimini later known as the Gothic Line. But after the exhilaration of the desert these, like all his activities north or south of the Alps, seemed mundane. For Rommel it must have been a profound relief when his Führer decided in October to put the whole Italian zone under one C.-in-C. For a while Hitler thought of Rommel for the post; but, in the end, gave Kesselring the command and transferred Rommel to the unexpected task of inspecting the defences of the Atlantic Wall.

XIII

The Atlantic Wall

The Führer's inspector was a difficult person for C.-in-C. West to assimilate in his command. Understandably, von Rundstedt disliked the notion of a roving Field-Marshal examining areas partly within his field of responsibility and partly not: a Field-Marshal, also, who could report directly to Hitler. But the problem was soon resolved. 'On 31 December', the *Official History* states, 'the war diary of the Armed Forces High Command (O.K.W.) Operations Staff included an entry to the effect that, acting on the previous day's request by C.-in-C. West (that is by von Rundstedt) Rommel's command, now known as Army Group B, would be integrated in the western command machinery. It would cease to be directly under Hitler and in future Rommel would submit his proposals and receive his orders through von Rundstedt.'

This decision was a relief. It gave Rommel an operational command—he now had armies with which to fight—and von Rundstedt's face was saved. His territory was divided and his power decentralised, but he still remained C.-in-C. Rommel took over responsibility for the Netherlands, 15 Army (between Ostend and Le Havre), and 7 Army which covered the coasts of Normandy and Brittany, between Le Havre and the Loire. Later Army Group G was formed under General Blaskowitz to control the coast from the Loire southwards—the 'Bay of Biscay front', the Pyrenees, and the Mediterranean shore. On paper this structure looked sound.

But arrangements which form neat diagrams depend on the men who must make them work. The combination of Rommel and von Rundstedt, though it was sustained by mutual respect, was unhappy. Von Rundstedt was an aristocrat, and Rommel came from the middle class. Von Rundstedt was a trained staff officer, while Rommel's reputation derived from his success in

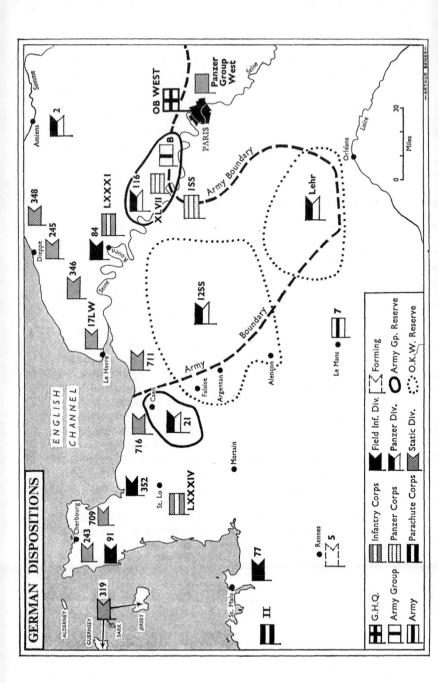

GERMAN DISPOSITIONS

ENGLISH CHANNEL

ALDERNEY
GUERNSEY
SARK
JERSEY

OB WEST

Panzer Group West

PARIS

Somme
Amiens

Dieppe

Le Havre

Cherbourg

St. Lo

Caen

Falaise
Argentan
Alençon

Mortain

Rennes

St. Malo

Le Mans

Orléans

Seine
Rouen
Seine
Loire

Army Boundary

Army Boundary

Army Group Boundary

2
348
245
346
17LW
711
716
352
709
243
91
319
77
II
5
7
12SS
21
Lehr
84
116
XLVII
17SS
LXXXI
LXXXIV

30
0
Miles

—ARTHUR BANKS—

G.H.Q.
Army Group
Army

Field Inf. Div.
Panzer Div.
Static Div.

Forming
Army Gp. Reserve
O.K.W. Reserve

Infantry Corps
Panzer Corps
Parachute Corps

the field and from Hitler's support—he was not a member of the closed shop of the German General Staff. And a Württemberger was always a Württemberger, whereas von Rundstedt, in Chester Wilmot's words, was 'the doyen of the Officer Corps, the only Field-Marshal who had never lost a battle'. Had they been able, in collaboration, to overcome these social handicaps, they would still have been separated by differences of temperament. The truth was that in the spring of 1944 von Rundstedt was finished.* He had triumphed in Poland in 1939, in France in 1940, and in the great drive through southern Russia in 1941. But he was now little more than a figurehead. Rommel, on the other hand, was still an alert and energetic professional soldier determined to achieve victory even when victory seemed unattainable.

Under von Rundstedt the Channel frontier had been only feebly strengthened; indeed, he told Rommel that the Atlantic Wall was a 'Propaganda Wall'. Rommel's own attitude is well summarised in his Letter of Instructions to Army Commanders, 22 April 1944. This was a restatement of orders previously issued in February. 'In the short time left before the great offensive starts, we must succeed in bringing all defences to such a standard that they will hold up against the strongest attacks. Never in history was there a defence of such an extent with such an obstacle as the sea. The enemy must be annihilated before he reaches our main battlefield. . . .'

Class and temperament separated by a gulf the two men on whom Germany's future in the West most depended. Age might also have provided a barrier. But the *Official History* is too facile in distinguishing between 'the old and sober strategist' and 'the young and ardent tactician'. None of the reasons which have been offered for the division between Rommel and von Rundstedt—neither class, nor age, nor status, nor temperament—was fundamental: though each made its contribution. Experience was the real reason for their disagreement—Rommel's experience. And von Rundstedt (who by now was drinking heavily) had been the supreme applicant of the 'staff solution'. During the early years of the war he had been particularly successful in following the text-book. But, as Chester Wilmot says, 'he lacked imagination and because his own approach was conventional and direct he presumed that his opponents would think similarly. In 1940 when he was planning the invasion of England, he had been compelled by the weakness of his air and naval support to prepare for a frontal assault across the narrowest part of the Channel. Three years later, applying his own plan in reverse, he assumed

* But this had an important consequence. Dismissed in July and reinstated in September as C.-in-C. West, von Rundstedt was one of the reasons why Allied intelligence could not believe that the Ardennes offensive was possible—until it happened. It seemed incredible that under von Rundstedt the German army in the West could attempt anything so ambitious.

that the Allies would inevitably make their main effort in the Pas de Calais.'

Rommel thought differently. He placed the possible invasion front somewhere between Dunkirk and Cherbourg. But the chief variance between the two commanders became evident when, early in 1944, Hitler sent a team to investigate the preparations along the Atlantic Wall. Jodl, the Wehrmacht's Chief of Staff, examined the front of 15 Army; General Baron Treutsch von Buttlar that of 7 Army; and Warlimont inspected the south. Their report revealed to Hitler that Rundstedt and his staff believed that a central armoured reserve should be maintained around Paris, because it was necessary to be able—having appreciated the line of thrust of an enemy landing—to launch a fully co-ordinated, even though it might not be an immediate, counterattack. 'Rommel', as Blumentritt says, 'on the grounds of his experiences in Africa and Italy maintained the view that it was a question of holding the *coast*, and to that end putting all the divisions, including the panzer divisions, into the coastal front or close behind it.' He then adds, 'Rundstedt's concept was strategic, Rommel's tactical'. Blumentritt is as unjust to Rommel as is the *Official History* when it observes that 'according to Colonel-General Jodl's diary notes for April the 13th, "Rommel says mobile operations with armoured formations are a thing of the past". This *surprising* opinion was apparently derived from Rommel's own experiences in North Africa.' (The italics are mine.)

One definition of strategy might be that it is the evolution of general plans whose particular execution, by tactical methods, is likely to be effective. Rommel's assessment was in this sense strategic. He was now a sagacious veteran. 'The day of the dashing cut-and-thrust tank attack of the early war years', he told Bayerlein on 17 May, 'is past and gone.' He had then examined the Atlantic Wall and its weaknesses, had estimated the capacity of the divisions guarding it, and in formulating his plan for its defence was pragmatic. What would actually *work*, when the inevitable day of invasion came? This was where experience counted. In all his triumphs von Rundstedt had never been faced with the problem of moving armour without air superiority, and his advocacy of a central reserve in the Paris region was much influenced by Geyr von Schweppenburg, the General in command of Panzer Group West, who also had no notion, from practical experience, of how failure to command the skies must inhibit the deployment of his armour.

Von Schweppenburg was fanatical, and the effect of a fanatic on another man already convinced that he is right can be disastrous. Even in the 1960s, Liddell Hart has told me, von Schweppenburg is still certain that Rommel was mistaken: on von Rundstedt in 1944 his persuasive power must have been formidable. (And yet when the R.A.F. bombed Geyr's H.Q. on 10 June, after which his Chief of Staff and 17 of his other dead officers were buried in one of the craters, and Geyr was dismissed from his post and sent back to Paris to recover from his wounds, he wrote to Rommel: 'Dear Field-Marshal, on relinquishing my command may I be permitted to add a few words to my official leave-taking? The recent battles in a theatre of war more exacting than any I had hitherto experienced have, in addition to providing me with my posting to Army Group B and uniting me in purpose with yourself, wrought an inner change in me. Your soldierly qualities and experience have transformed the temper of my obedience into something different and finer than the effort of will it had hitherto been. . . .') This speaks much for the validity of Rommel's argument in the tense discussions which preceded D-Day, and is also, incidentally, a handsome confession of error by a General whose military career was disrupted by the air force in whose power he had refused to believe.

During the spring of 1944 Rommel was looking back to Alam Halfa. He remembered how, after that distant battle, he had decided that 'anyone who has to fight, even with the most modern weapons, against an enemy in complete control of the air, fights like a savage against modern European troops'. All his later experience in the desert, all that he had learned about the final collapse in Tunisia and the conduct of the Italian campaign, and his present awareness of what was happening in the air daily and nightly over Germany and France supported these conclusions. The 'Russian generals' had never known pattern bombing. 'Our friends from the East', Rommel said to Bayerlein, 'cannot imagine what they're in for. It's not a matter of fanatical hordes to be driven forward in masses against our line . . . here we are facing an enemy who applies all his native intelligence to the use of his many technical resources.' His premonitions were justified on D-Day. Out of the whole force of bombers, fighters, reconnaissance and transport planes available for the German Third Air Fleet on 6 June only 200 were capable of flight. In the great Order of Battle of the Allied air forces on the same day two figures stand out: on the British front, during the bombing of the beaches before the assault went in, 1056 heavy bombers and Mosquitoes were used, while on the American front the comparable number for the U.S.A.A.F. is approximately 1600 planes. Rommel was right, in his conversation with Bayerlein, to remark that 'we, of course, thanks to the Allied air forces, will have nothing there in time'.

Rommel reckoned that the first 24 hours of an Allied landing would be critical. Without control of the air it would be impossible to move armour rapidly from the rear to deal with an assault on the beaches, and therefore the tanks the Germans could provide in the West would have to be placed near to every potential landing-point. (On 21 May he wrote to his wife: 'The enemy successes in Italy are very unfortunate. Strength on the ground was not unfavourable to us. It's simply that their superiority in the air and in ammunition is overwhelming, the same as it was in Africa.')

The interdiction programme of the Allied air force and the interference of resistance groups certainly foiled a major counter-attack by German panzers. Yet the possibility of an instant reaction such as Rommel envisaged is illustrated by the abortive attempt of a battle-group from Feuchtinger's 21 Armoured Division to cut through to the coast on D-Day, and separate the airborne spearhead in the east from the landings on the beaches. Rommel was right in believing that this kind of counter-attack would cause confusion and, possibly, disaster: he also correctly perceived that it could not be launched from a distance. (The two commanders in Normandy who had experienced the full effect of air power and realised that troops on the ground must revise their tactics, Rommel and Montgomery, were of the same mind in their appreciations. On 13 June Montgomery wrote, in a personal letter to Alan Brooke: 'The answer to invasion across the sea is a strong counter-attack on the afternoon of D-Day when the invading force has not proper communications and has lost certain cohesion. That was Rommel's chance. It was not taken, and we were given time to recover—thank goodness!') Feuchtinger's was the only dangerous drive of the kind Rommel had imagined which penetrated the Allied bridge-head in any strength on D-Day: when it finally broke in, it had already been so weakened that its stroke was powerless. Yet a situation can be conceived in which similar and stronger battle-groups of armour and infantry, working in consort in the inimitable German way, might have pressed instantaneously upon the beaches where the British and the Americans were struggling ashore. The terrain would not, indeed, have allowed this kind of assault on the first few miles of some of the bridge-heads. Still, Phase Two of a landing, when exhausted troops are trying to establish themselves in the ground behind the beaches, is their most vulnerable moment. During this chaotic period the possible consequences of the armoured intervention Rommel had in mind are incalculable. In spite of the predominance of the Allies in the air, it might have been decisive.

Feuchtinger's plan for an immediate penetration was delayed irreparably by orders from 7 Army, instructing him to move down the west bank of the Orne, whereas his own sensible objective was the positions which 6 Airborne was establishing on the Orne's eastern bank. By the time this confusion was disentangled, and as a result of attacks on his armour from the air, his plan was null before it was properly launched. Yet there is a precedent which, like

Feuchtinger's lonely raid, suggests that Rommel was right. Against the un-stable Anzio beach-head the Germans sent in a counter-attack of four infantry divisions on a 4000-yard front, backed by two armoured divisions; 452 guns were in support. This local *Blitzkrieg* split the Allied front at Anzio, and came near to creating disaster.

All the same, von Rundstedt deserves sympathy. He was hidebound, unimaginative, old. But as C.-in-C. West he had to face the fact that though landings in some sectors of his large perimeter were inevitable, he was not supplied with intelligence firm enough to predict these areas with precision. It was therefore reasonable (particularly in view of the British deception measures which suggested that an invasion of the Pas de Calais was probable*) to think that his army in the west was too small, and that a concentrated reserve which could be moved swiftly against an actual area of invasion would be more valuable than frail and dissipated forces spread in anticipation around the front line of the coast. His strategic appreciation was sensible enough—in theory. But such appreciations are useless if they cannot be implemented in fact, and what happened, on D-Day and after, proved that Rommel's realism was more relevant than the 'staff solution' of Rundstedt. Neither, however, was allowed to put his personal plan into action, for Hitler intervened.

Speidel has remarked that 'the organisation and chain of command of the major commands in the West was somewhere between confusion and chaos'. Hitler's response to the disagreement between his two Captains provides a significant example, since it effectively sabotaged control of Germany's armoured forces behind their front. The Führer ruled that Rommel could have direct command of 2, 21 and 116 Panzer Divisions, but that the rest of the armour, 1 and 22 S.S. Panzer and Panzer Lehr, would from 26 April form an O.K.W. reserve under Hitler's personal supervision. The effect of this ruling was to eliminate von Rundstedt. But it was also obvious before D-Day, as became abundantly clear afterwards, that such an arrangement was bound to create confusion. Tanks on the ground, like fighters in the air, are in special need of swift and sensitive direction to enable them to do what they are capable of doing. Hitler, pursuing by remote control his policy of 'divide and rule', severed the command of his armour in Normandy and ensured its destruction. During the crucial days of 6 and 7 June his long-distance handling of his tank reserve was slow, ill-informed and disastrous.

Amid all these debates and distractions Rommel carried out relentlessly his chief assignment—the improvement of the fortification of the Atlantic

* By various methods they conveyed the convincing impression that an invading force of 12 divisions would gradually be enlarged to one of 50. None of these existed.

Wall. At first he was appalled by what he was told and what he saw for himself. Blumentritt has described how Rommel was given a strategic *tour d'horizon* by von Rundstedt and then 'information about the troops themselves, their equipment, arms and the construction of the fortifications, etc., was given to Rommel in detail. In talking to Rommel, Rundstedt sarcastically alluded to the Atlantic Wall as a "Propaganda Wall". Finally Rommel was informed that an effective strategic reserve, particularly of panzer and good infantry divisions, was lacking. Positions to the rear were not available; there was merely a line marked on the map, which ran approximately: Somme–Marne–Saône–Swiss frontier. But it was only theory! Discussions with Rommel ended with Rundstedt's comment: "things look black." Rommel was visibly affected. . . .'

But he was not daunted. In the period before his *Gummibefehl* (the elastic responsibilities Hitler provided in making him the Führer's inspector) was terminated by the placing of Army Group B in an operational command, Rommel was a tireless traveller. Between the middle of December and the middle of February he assessed the coasts of Holland and then moved westwards, via the Somme region, to the Atlantic and the Mediterranean. He set in motion various technical schemes for the stiffening of the Wall which acquired such a momentum during the next six months that the Allies were lucky to be able to invade in June. Had D-Day been two months later, Rommel's drive and invention might have provided that immediate bar to the invading divisions which, during the vital first two days, could have brought them to a full stop in the sea and on the beaches, and allowed the ramshackle German command in the West to produce its own clear and definite line of policy; to consult with and obtain intelligible instructions from the distant Führer; and to organise a counter-offensive powerful enough to obliterate a beach-head whose follow-up divisions and logistic support had still not arrived. Here is one example. In the first half of 1944 inland minelaying around the coasts was tripled: between five and six million mines were planted. But Rommel was thinking in terms of 50 million, and the pace of planting was continually quickening. Every week counted.

Blumentritt's biography of von Rundstedt is a most valuable piece of evidence about Rommel's activities during this phase. The Chief of Staff of C.-in-C. West must necessarily have had doubts about Rommel. He did indeed, and he has uttered them. But he is fair and explicit about the tactical policies of the man whose strategic ideas he and his Chief deplored. He analyses them as follows:

'At that time there were three problems which haunted him day and night:

'1. Minefields. He could not get enough mines and demanded millions to lay in extensive fields. As he could not obtain them in sufficient numbers he set French factories to work. His vivid imagination was always furnishing him with new ideas. Thus he wanted these new minefields to be concealed under brambles, and the most cunning ideas suggested themselves to him whereby sham minefields were to be laid by way of deception.

'2. "Rommel's asparagus" was the humorous name given by the troops to those great forests of stakes which he erected. Their object was to obstruct enemy landings from the air in threatened areas. Thus the idea came to him to stud such zones with tree-trunks about ten to fifteen feet high in the hope that aircraft would then not be able to land. Countless numbers of trees were solemnly planted artificially by driving them into the ground. He determined to requisition the male population for this. He let it be known that he would provide meals and wages if volunteers report for this work. They did so and thus presented the remarkable picture of German troops and French volunteers working together with great zeal to lay out "Rommel's asparagus-beds".

'3. His special interest lay in obstacles on the foreshore. With them he wanted to obstruct the landing of enemy boats on the beaches, so that at the ebb-tide he had whole rows of stout stakes driven in like a stockade. This was laborious work, for it often happened that a storm would tear the whole lot down again and the uprooted stakes would all be swept on to the land. But these simple obstacles did not satisfy the ingenious marshal. The idea struck him to provide each stake with a mine at the top as a kind of hat.'

The 'kind of hat' was no joke on D-Day.

Hitler's appointment of Rommel to make his Western Wall a reality was another example of his intuition. Here was an ideal challenge for the man who in his youth had been unable to buy a motor-cycle without immediately taking it to pieces and re-assembling it*; who in the dash through France in 1940 (though now a General commanding an Armoured Division) was always ready to stop to give advice about the building of a bridge; and who, in Africa, always forgot military protocol and joined enthusiastically in the solution of problems like the lifting of a minefield, the siting of his anti-tank guns, the leading of a supply column through the enemy or the navigation of his 'Mammoth'. In Normandy all the practical Swabian in Rommel's character was once more released.

---

* The affinity of Rommel and T. E. Lawrence in their understanding of the essentials of desert warfare has often been noted: but they also shared an instinctive need to understand practical techniques. Lawrence in his different desert sought constantly to master the know-how of weapons, vehicles and explosives. Like Rommel, he was an addict of the motor-cycle.

His impact on the divisions there—divisions disillusioned by a long wait for an invasion, or exhausted in Russia—was galvanising. It was no less than that of Montgomery on the divisions in Britain—divisions which had either been training for years in the expectation of a Second Front, or brought back for refreshment after decimation in Africa and Italy. Rommel's naval adviser in Normandy, Admiral Ruge, puts this well. He says that Rommel 'fundamentally altered the underlying idea, thus changing the atmosphere of despondency and vague hope to one of hard work and clear plans. He was untiring in his efforts to instil his ideas into his men and they took them up eagerly because they appreciated his personality, his experience, and his common sense.' This capacity to elevate the morale of an army, which Montgomery particularly displayed in Africa and Slim in India and Burma, is one of Rommel's many qualities that place him among the Great Commanders of the Second World War. If military command is more of an art than a science, as I think it is, then this is a field in which artistry can be best disclosed: Rommel disclosed it at its best.

Blumentritt's summary does not adequately cover the whole range of Rommel's improvisation and his directions to the divisions scattered around the Atlantic coast. Rommel demanded, for example, that for seven miles inland from the sea the ground should be obstructed by his 'asparagus', and that where this was impossible the lowland gaps between the higher ground should be flooded. He wanted mines to be broadcast on the land just as he wanted them to be distributed over the beaches. And he pressed for a massive improvement in the wiring and thickening of the concrete protection of the coastal batteries and strong-points: rightly, for he was looking ahead to the likelihood of saturation bombing and local attacks by commandos. 'Throughout the spring of 1944', says Chester Wilmot, 'the Atlantic Wall grew in strength as Rommel stumped the coast examining the defences and haranguing the garrisons.' His furious application of his foresight made the invasion more difficult.

The scale, the variety and the ingenuity of Rommel's preparations not only delayed the evolution of the Allies' plans but also caused them to be, in some respects, radically altered. Increased and intimate surveillance of the Normandy beaches and their hinterland became necessary: by photography from the air, by night-landing parties, by midget submarines. The 'asparagus', growing where airborne divisions might land, was threatening enough; but ramifying obstacles on the beaches now offered a particularly sinister menace. As they advanced further and further from high-water-mark into the sea they presented the invaders with a progressively unacceptable set of alternatives. Either the first waves of the assault divisions would have to disembark at high tide—in which case many of their landing craft would be holed and therefore useless for the next waves: or they would have to land at low tide, in which case the infantry would be faced with a struggle through a 'beaten zone' of bare beach swept by German fire—a new Gallipoli.

The Allies found an answer. Montgomery ordered that the first touchdown should occur approximately at half-tide, and the specially developed armour of 79 Division and the DD (Duplex-Drive) tanks, which could float and propel themselves, were given the highest priority in the landing tables so that they could shoot the infantry ashore. (Rommel expected and warned his troops of this development. On D-Day, nevertheless, the sight of tanks emerging like sea-monsters from the ocean caused a psychological shock in some units of his army.) But the need to assess manifold intelligence reports about the growing complexity of the Wall's defences, and the subsequent argument among the planners about how to overcome these unexpected snags, hampered Eisenhower and Montgomery unquestionably during the last few months and weeks when their plans were being completed.

Montgomery, however, had shrewdly assessed the intentions of his old adversary. On 15 May he revealed his scheme for the invasion of Europe at his H.Q. in St. Paul's School, London, before an audience which included his King, his Prime Minister, his Chiefs of Staff, representatives of the Allied forces, and his immediate commander, Eisenhower. (It is, incidentally, a token of the difference between the climates in which Rommel and Montgomery existed that such an address, presenting the strategic and tactical thinking about a forthcoming operation on which the whole future of the country depended, could not conceivably have been given in Germany in 1944 before a comparable audience.) Montgomery then said: 'Last February Rommel took command from Holland to the Loire. It is now clear that his intention is to deny any penetration: OVERLORD is to be defeated on the beaches. . . . Rommel is an energetic and determined commander; he has made a world of difference since he took over. He is best at the spoiling attack; his *forte* is disruption; he is too impulsive for a set-piece battle. He will do his level best to "Dunkirk" us.'

But though Rommel could exercise his initiative on the beaches, he was hobbled in his command of the armies lying behind his front line, and even on the beaches his command was not absolute. The big guns in the coastal batteries, for example, were mainly sited and controlled by the Navy, and their disposition was frequently criticised by Rommel and his subordinates. The anti-aircraft defences, as well as his fighter cover, were the preserve of the *Luftwaffe*. Such was Hitler's system. C.-in-C. West and Rommel had no authority over the Third Air Fleet in France or over Admiral Krancke, the naval commander responsible for the waters around the Atlantic Wall.*

In effect, therefore, Rommel had to prepare for the defence of the *Reich*'s western frontier without firm control of the men on the ground, the planes in the air, or the few ships available at sea. There were deep fissures of disagreement in the Allied headquarters both before and after D-Day: Leigh-Mallory doubting the chances of the airborne drop on the right flank of the beach-head; Tedder virulently criticising Montgomery's strategy in Normandy; Bradley and Patton, and the Americans in general, always ready to pounce on the presumption of a British mistake. Nevertheless, in spite of its many weaknesses, the integration of the three British Services and their U.S. equivalents was incomparably more effective than the Nazi system of divided authority and the internecine rivalries with which Rommel was beset. At no time before or after D-Day was Rommel able to dispose of troops under his command as he would have wished. His service as C.-in-C. Army Group B must therefore be held aside in any final assessment of his generalship.

The fluctuations of the Russian front, for example—and Hitler's incalculable reactions to them—affected his army in ways which made it impossible for him to plan a stable and efficient system of defence. By the middle of March the Russians were on the Polish frontier. The West, nevertheless, was still being reinforced, and by the end of March von Rundstedt controlled 57 divisions. In the *21st Army Intelligence Review* of 2 April the Chief Intelligence Officer, Brigadier Williams, wrote: 'For the moment it would seem that the enemy is courting further and deepening disaster in the East to retain a good chance in the West; a strange gamble militarily, made intelligible politically by the prospect of a compromise peace if the Western decision bore fruit: in short, more and more Stalingrads in the hope of one Dunkirk.' Hitler (who, strongly influenced by von Rundstedt, had made Dunkirk possible by refusing to commit his armoured divisions to a final assault) could not now face the prospect of yet another Stalingrad. The inevitable happened: Rommel had to accept a switch of 9 and 10 S.S. Panzer, *Panzer Lehr*, and 349 Infantry Divisions to the eastern front. Then, of course, there came the spring thaw, and the mud which prevented armoured action. So *Panzer Lehr*, and four other armoured divisions which had been shattered in Russia, crept back to the armies in the West.

---

* Admiral Ruge recalled in *Decisive Battles of World War II* that Navy Group West had a plan for *Blitzsperren* (lightning barrages), a system of minefields to be laid by all available vessels as soon as the attack was recognised as being imminent. But on D-Day they were mostly laid in the wrong place . . . 'not a single one in the attack area where they were needed most, for the enemy forces arrived there before the minelayers were ready. Therefore, a very important part of Rommel's plan for the defence was not executed.'

Rommel was essentially a practical and matter-of-fact commander, and for him these sudden shifts were disconcerting. He was, indeed, experiencing no more than had happened to his earlier opponents—Wavell, Auchinleck—when sudden and unpredictable demands from other theatres of war required the immediate reduction of their strength. But a repetition of history was no help to him in Normandy.

Yet history repeated itself again on D-Day. It is a strange coincidence that at the beginning of the three major battles of his military career—*Crusader*, Alamein and Normandy—Rommel was absent. (On the eve of *Crusader*, it will be remembered, he was on his way back from a conference in Italy; and on the eve of Alamein he was again in Europe, a convalescent.) On 4 June the chief meteorologist of the 3 Air Fleet prophesied that there could be no invasion within the next fortnight: on the 5th, therefore, Rommel set out from Paris to visit his family and then, on the 6th, to go to Berchtesgaden to persuade Hitler that 12 S.S. Panzer Division should be moved into the St. Lo–Carentan area. His diary for 3 June reads: 'The most urgent need was to speak to the Führer personally on the Obersalzberg, convey to him the extent of the manpower and material inferiority we would suffer in the event of a landing, and request the dispatch of two further panzer divisions, an A.A. Corps, and a Nebelwerfer brigade to Normandy. . . .' But he was recalled by the news of the invasion, and did not see Hitler, so the 12 S.S. was not moved: a mischance which must have saved many American lives. Rommel was not the only absentee. Of the five principal German commanders in the West three, in fact, were not at their headquarters when the invasion began. Dollman, C.-in-C. 7 Army, was supervising an anti-invasion exercise at Rennes, while Sepp Dietrich, commander of 1 S.S. Panzer Corps, was far away in Brussels: the third was Rommel.

At 0645 on the morning of the invasion Speidel telephoned Rommel at his home in Heerlingen, and thereafter ordered 21 Panzer to counter-attack immediately. A full counter-attack, as has been seen, never developed. Indeed from the start of the invasion until his wounding next month Rommel was never able to grip and control the battle: its unfolding was taken out of his hands before it began. Most of 21 Panzer had been established, on Rommel's instructions, in and around the city of Caen, but though its presence stopped the penetration and exploitation which Montgomery had anticipated it failed to prevent the bridge-head. This and other factors were fatal for the Germans.

During the first critical hours the *Luftwaffe*, for example, was a broken reed. Only 319 sorties were flown during the whole of 6 June, and in the long appreciation which Rommel wrote on 10 June he estimated that the Allied air forces had by then achieved total cover of the battle area up to a point some 60 miles behind the front. 'During the day, practically our entire traffic—on roads, tracks, and open country—is pinned down by powerful fighter-bomber and bomber formations.' He also noted the effect of the Allies' naval artillery and the vast preponderance of their material strength. (Another of his African forecasts was proving to be true. As he wrote despairingly to his wife on 13 June, 'the long-husbanded strength of two world powers is now coming into action'.) And he was further depressed by his opponents' use of their airborne troops. All this he had prophesied to von Rundstedt.

A detailed account of the Normandy campaign is not relevant in a broad appreciation of Rommel's career. Within four days after the landings it became clear to him (as he had always assumed) that once the Allies made firm lodgements ashore his situation was hopeless and victory in the West was impossible. Restricted by Hitler in the deployment of his tanks, uncovered in the skies, short of men and arms, he never had in Normandy the opportunity for creative generalship *on the battlefield*. There his role was the ignominious one of desperately plugging holes. His main achievement in these weeks was to perceive the realities instantly, and to attempt, at what in 1944 meant the risk of his life, to bring them home to Hitler. He failed. But he saw what should be done, he advocated it, and no commander during the Nazi régime spoke more courageously (in Martin Luther's tradition) on behalf of what he knew to be the truth.

For some time he was as much in the dark as von Rundstedt about the *Schwerpunkt* of the invasion. He still thought that landings (and perhaps the main landings) might follow further north: even in Belgium. But he also saw that the defence of the port of Cherbourg was vital. Pressure in the Cotentin must contain the Americans before they could extricate themselves from the blocked beaches and the floods on their front. But Bradley, beneath his air umbrella, broke out before the Germans could reinforce. He was aided by Hitler's order on the 16th that (contrary to Rommel's intention) there should be no planned withdrawal from Cherbourg but simply the usual and wasteful policy of standing fast. Thus on Rommel's right, as along the rest of his line, his troops were destroyed piecemeal.

Well before the 16th, however, von Rundstedt and Rommel had agreed, without demur, on the impossibility of holding Normandy. On the 11th they met to review the battle and then reported independently to O.K.W.—in the same vein. Some of Rommel's pessimistic conclusions have already been mentioned; he also added: 'the enemy forces in the bridge-head are growing at a considerably faster rate than reserves are flowing to our troops still holding out at many points along the coast. . . . I request that the Führer be informed.' This was a nightmare repetition of his experience during the retreat along the African shore, when to Rommel the only answer appeared to be to withdraw from Africa if his men were to be saved from destruction. The immediate answer now was to withdraw behind the line of the Seine. Hitler's reaction was to order the transfer of 11 S.S. Panzer Corps from Russia (two divisions: of which *one* arrived by *July*) and to promise infantry from Germany and Scandinavia. For the two Field-Marshals, attempting hourly to patch their collapsing front, this was useless. Nor did it help when on 17 June Hitler came forward to confer with them at Margival, near Soissons, where, according to General Speidel, he was 'worn and sleepless, playing nervously with his spectacles and an array of coloured pencils which he held between his fingers. He was the only one who sat, hunched upon a stool, while the Field-Marshals stood.'

Rommel then put forward a desperate but characteristic stratagem: to hold the British front with infantry divisions in the Orne area, while massing German armour on the flanks, and, by a calculated withdrawal of the infantry, to entice the British forward into an armoured trap . . . 'fighting the battle outside the range of the enemy's naval artillery'. But Hitler was more interested in talking about the potentialities of the V-1 rocket than in deluding the British into believing that they were being offered another Battle of the Marne. One of these rockets (off course for Britain) exploded near Soissons; so the Führer returned, for ever, to Germany.

Nothing had been decided at Margival, except—if this was a *military* decision—that Hitler reiterated his principle that his armies in Normandy 'hold fast tenaciously to every square yard of soil'. (It was at this conference that Rommel protested, typically, against the recent atrocity by S.S. *Das Reich*. At Oradour-sur-Glane this division, as a reprisal, had massacred the inhabitants. Rommel dared to ask to be allowed to punish *Das Reich*. Those who think of him as one of 'Hitler's Generals' might well weigh the courage and the humanity which such a protest involved in June 1944. Astonishingly —in view of his other protests—Rommel survived: Hitler just told him that this was none of his business.)

Rommel had therefore to rely on what he had got without much hope about what he might get. And what he had got was not enough: not enough infantry, in particular. Without more infantry divisions he could not pull his armour out of the line, reform, and concentrate to attack both the Americans in the west and the solid British line in the east. After Hitler's departure he was still uncertain (and cannot be blamed for an uncertainty prevalent in the German Higher Command) about the possibility of a second landing on the

coasts held by 15 Army: 'A large-scale landing', he reported to von Rundstedt on the 19th, 'is to be expected on the Channel front on both sides of
Cap Gris Nez or between the Somme and Le Havre.' So the process continued
of feeding reinforcements parcel by parcel into the battle, as they arrived, and
of running down his armour by using it in relatively small groups to plug
gaps as they occurred. Sepp Dietrich had already reported, 'I am being bled
white and am getting nowhere.' All this was not and could not be a creative
act of generalship: it was what Haig had to do after 21 March 1918—the
gesture of a plumber dealing with a flood.

Another kind of flood brought for Dietrich, Rommel and Rundstedt a
temporary easement, on which Omar Bradley's comment was, 'this damned
weather is going to be the death of me'. The Allies' luck had held on D-Day:
but it broke on the 19th, when the most vicious June gale for 40 years hit the
coasts of Normandy. On the beaches the effect was ruinous. Landing-craft
were hurled ashore, completed and unfinished portions of the Mulberry
harbours were damaged or destroyed, and the supply line across the Channel
was broken. Apart from shipping sunk, it was estimated that 800 vessels had
been stranded, while 140,000 tons of stores and 20,000 vehicles were seriously
delayed in transit. The Allied air offensive was also temporarily stifled. But
whereas, in Africa, Rommel had been able to exploit immediately he sensed
that his enemy was unexpectedly embarrassed or weakened, in Normandy
this was beyond his power.

Hitler on 20 June ordered him to attack as soon as armoured reinforcements reached him: but what Hitler saw as a fact on paper was, as usual, a
'paper tiger' for Rommel. 9 and 10 S.S. Panzer Divisions, which had started
back from Poland on 12 June, were still struggling westwards over shattered
communications and were not due to assemble around Alençon until the
25th. So it was not Rommel, but Montgomery, who attacked that day—
between the Odon and the Orne. The troops with which Rommel had hoped
to break through in a drive to Bayeux were, once again, used up unit by unit
as stop-gaps: Dollmann of 7 Army died of what is thought to be a heart
attack: and by 29 June Rommel and von Rundstedt were again conferring
with their Führer, at Berchtesgaden, about the continuing crisis.

This was Rommel's last throw. It seems that he decided that if, at this
conference, Hitler once again failed to see reason, Rommel would collaborate
more constructively with those who were plotting Hitler's removal. Precisely
how he might have acted must always remain obscure, because of his wounding
on 17 July. But the meeting was undoubtedly the last step in his abandonment
of his allegiance to his Führer.

Hitler behaved intolerably at Berchtesgaden. He accepted the undeniable fact that his enemy was superior in the air, at sea and on the land. But from the dream world which he now inhabited he produced visions of 'confining him to his bridge-head, by building up a front to block him off, and then fighting a war of attrition to wear him down and force him back'. He spoke of 7 Army being supplied by 'several strong anti-aircraft highways, protected by a large number of flak emplacements and covered by fighter patrols'. (There were few guns available, and fewer planes.) He ordered mines to be laid in the Bay of the Seine 'with the tenacity of a bulldog': the *Blitzsperren*, the crucial mine-laying operation, having of course failed to occur on D-Day.

Rommel then, according to Bayerlein, asked Hitler how he expected the war to be won. His mood is well reflected by Admiral Ruge: 'He had sworn his oath to a man whom he recognised more and more as a usurper and a criminal, he knew the Allied demand for unconditional surrender, and he felt responsible to the Allied people and to Europe. As a rule, high commanders are isolated in war. In this situation where no satisfactory solution could be seen, each had to solve these moral problems by himself, according to his conscience and his knowledge.' Von Rundstedt's mood is reflected in his telephone conversation with Keitel after his return from Berchtesgaden. 'What shall we do?' asked Keitel. 'What shall we do?' Von Rundstedt replied, 'make peace, you fools, what else can you do?'

Both the Field-Marshals expected to be relieved of their commands as a result of this summit conference: but it was only von Rundstedt who was dropped. Keitel told Hitler of his exchange of views with Rundstedt, Hitler sent the latter a mollifying letter, and von Kluge came west to replace him: a man with a mixed mind; wavering in his loyalty to Hitler, dubious about the way the West had been managed, and uncertain about the Nazi régime. 'He arrived at Rommel's H.Q.', says Bayerlein, 'full of that exaggerated optimism which was shown by most Eastern front commanders on the day they first entered the western theatre, and administered a severe censure to Rommel.'

H.Q., *5 July 1944*

To C.-in-C. West

HERR GENERALFELDMARSCHALL VON KLUGE

I send you enclosed my comments on military events in Normandy to date. The rebuke which you levelled at me at the beginning of your visit, in the presence of my Chief of Staff and Ia, to the effect that I, too, 'will now have to get accustomed to carrying out orders', has deeply wounded me. I request you to notify me what grounds you have for making such an accusation.

(*Signed*) ROMMEL
Generalfeldmarschall

To this letter Rommel attached a copy of the strategic arguments he had advocated since D-Day; it ended: 'only unified, close-knit command of all services, after the pattern of Montgomery and Eisenhower, will vouchsafe final victory.' This was the correct diagnosis: and it is to von Kluge's credit that though he was one of the German High Command who, unlike Rommel, had been seduced by Hitler's system of bribery (in his case a 'gratuity' of the equivalent of £20,000) and though he had arrived in the West in a spirit of optimism, he rapidly became a realist and accepted Rommel's appreciation of the true state of affairs.

Rommel sensed what was coming. He anticipated Montgomery's attack on his right flank, 'strong in armour'. (It might well be maintained that of the two Rommel usually benefited from his instinct about the use of armour.) Montgomery, at Alam Halfa and Medenine, certainly defeated Rommel by his ability to create a defence against tanks: but Rommel, like all successful commanders in mobile warfare, had a flair which Montgomery lacked—a flair which now warned him that a major armoured attack was about to be launched against his defences east of the Orne. He therefore built up a five-layered system of defence which, when the time came, brought to a halt Operation *Goodwood* (the attempt by 11, 7 and the Guards Armoured Divisions, heavily supported by the R.A.F., to smash through his eastern flank). Montgomery's theory that 'the air must hold the ring' was not justified in this battle, where bombardment from the air increased the difficulty of the troops on the ground in their endeavour to break out of the ring.

It was from the air, however, that Rommel received his *coup de grâce*. Before *Goodwood* began he was out of action because near to a village called, appropriately, Ste. Foy de Montgommery his car, on its way back from the Battle H.Q. of Panzer Group West, was observed and attacked by one of the omnipresent British aircraft. In the crash that followed Rommel was severely wounded: and at that moment his military career came to an end.

XIV

Murder of a Field-Marshal

The plot against Hitler which reached its climax on 20 July 1944 eliminated by its failure many of the men whose moral qualities would have been invaluable in post-war Germany: among them was Rommel. His death on 14 October, from poison offered to him by Hitler's emissaries, was a direct consequence of the events of that day. But the reasons for his death began to accumulate long before the summer of 1944. The story of his end is reminiscent of some episode in Gibbon's *Decline and Fall of the Roman Empire.* Phase One—the dedicated commander of the Praetorians (Rommel at the head of Hitler's personal guard during the invasion of Poland); Phase Two—the victorious general on the frontiers (Rommel in Africa); Phase Three—the general's disillusion about the imperial court; and Phase Four—the gradual growth of suspicion in the neurotic emperor's mind and the quick merciless stroke finishing his favourite. The analogy is not fanciful. Such was life under Hitler: such was Rommel's experience: and such is the way that a Gibbon writing in the 1960s would interpret what happened.

Rommel's understanding of Hitler's nihilistic disregard for the true interests of Germany and the German people began, as has been pointed out in Chapter XI, at Alamein. This was the moment of truth when a non-political* commander became aware that war in the twentieth century is not simply a matter of winning battles: that total war requires, among other things, a proper attitude towards the society you are defending. At Alamein Rommel started to realise that Hitler's attitude towards the German nation was irresponsible. His experiences in Italy, and indeed all his relations between

---

* The sharp-eyed Dollman noted of Kesselring that at the time of the Anzio landing 'he was one of the few senior officers who possessed political flair, a respect in which he differed widely from the other two Field-Marshals then on Italian soil, Rommel and Richthofen'.

Alamein and Normandy with Hitler and his entourage, deepened this feeling of doubt and distrust.

In all I have read about Rommel, nevertheless, I have found nothing to disturb my view that his steadily developing antipathy to Hitler was mainly based on a conviction that Germany's *military* ruin was being caused by Hitler's policies. Those involved in the 20 July plot with which he was to be implicated had many other ideas (social, political or theological) which never entered his head. Rommel had one aim: to win the war for Germany. He had been serving on the frontiers; he had little first-hand knowledge of what Hitler had done to Germany nor—it is fair to say—any vision of what society a Germany released from Hitler might become. He simply grew more and more aware of the material damage that Germany's enemies might inflict on her as a result of Hitler. In fact he finally abandoned his military allegiance because Hitler seemed to him to be failing as *Der Alte Fritz*, the Frederick the Great of the 1940s, the successful Führer of a Germany at war.

Rommel's outlook was entirely honourable. While many of his colleagues and peers in the German Army surrendered their honour by collusion with the iniquities of Nazism, Rommel was never defiled. He and Guderian, in particular, are outstanding examples of men who by keeping detached from the moral decay of Hitlerism were able to concentrate on 'the military necessity'—the soldier's task of fighting without other preoccupations on behalf of a country to which they were devoted and to which their lives and services had been dedicated. There have indeed been Great Commanders who were also political animals: but there have been others who functioned as no more than professionals. Rommel essentially belongs to the second category. It is therefore remarkable that he should have been shifted into the first because of a disinterested passion for his country and in spite of the personal risks involved.

Rommel's connection with the 20 July plot sprang from two sources—his developing ideas about Hitler, and his own image in the eyes of the German people. The latter was, in the end, perhaps more fatal than the former.

During the winter of 1943–44 there was no German general who more than Rommel represented to the German people the character of the *chevalier sans peur et sans reproche*. He had won dramatic victories: he had won them, too, on a foreign field which summoned up for the ordinary German none of the awful connotations of the Russian front—the vast casualty lists, the mystery and the misery. Rommel had done nothing like this to their menfolk. He was not even identified with the surrender in Tunisia. For the burgher in Hamburg or Düsseldorf or Stuttgart the Field-Marshal was the nearest thing they knew, in this unknightly war, to the knightly tradition. (It is worth observing that the racial memory of the German people still contained a concept of Teutonic knights defending and advancing their frontiers against the enemy; and Goebbels' propaganda had presented Rommel to them in shining armour.) Moreover, for a people still committed to Hitler he seemed the soldier who fitted acceptably into the Hitler/Nazi complex without any taint of disagreeable rumour—rumour about the beastliness of his private or public life. Rommel was, in fact, the Good German General at a time when there were not—in German or Allied eyes— many such available to convince either camp.

This acceptability of Rommel had been noted by the plotters. Their fundamental problem—apart from the practical one of killing Hitler—was that if the plot succeeded an alternative government, however temporary, must be immediately announced. Who should be its head? Some of the conspirators (especially General Beck and Goerdeler, the Mayor of Leipzig) decided in their tentative way that Rommel was the man.

The Nazi promotion of Rommel thus proved self-defeating. Görlitz points out in his book on the German General Staff that *thanks to National Socialist propaganda* Rommel, since the days of his African victories, was the most popular of German commanders. And he seemed a possible saviour to those working outside Germany. Max Ritter von Pohl, for example, a general of the German Air Force in Rome in June 1944, wrote about a conversation with Dollman that 'we both considered that this task' (the elimination of Hitler) 'could only be carried out jointly by the armed forces, under the leadership of Rommel or some other big name. . . .' In this way, whether he liked it or not, Rommel was inescapably caught in the network of the conspiracy. But it was not uncongenial to him. During a meeting at his house near Ulm in February 1944 with a representative of the plotters, a meeting whose conclusions have been variously described in various documents, Rommel seems to have said something like, 'I believe it my duty to come to the rescue of Germany'. In the spring of 1944 the question was, how could that rescue be achieved?

Those most deeply involved in the conspiracy were quite clear about their objective. They believed that Germany's rescue depended on Hitler's assassination. During the second half of 1943 this had been planned six times, but the circumstances had always proved unfavourable. Rommel was never allowed to know their final purpose: he was drawn into the plot by consultation but not by approval of its real aims. In a closed circle he was certainly prepared to make statements like 'Hitler's orders are nonsense; the man must be mad', or 'every day is costing lives unnecessarily; it is essential to make peace at once'. But in all his thinking about Hitler and what was happening to Germany he never—publicly or privately—went beyond the notion that Hitler should be arrested by the army and brought to trial. He was obsessed with the idea that if only the Germans could have the truth about Hitler revealed to them they would understand and reject him. In this he was very naïve.*

The overtures which were to draw him into the plot began effectively with the meeting at his house near Ulm in February 1944. The contact between Rommel and the plotters was Dr. Karl Strölin, a leading civic dignitary in Stüttgart who had served with Rommel on the Italian front in 1918, had maintained a friendship with him, had started to soften him up via Frau Rommel in the autumn of 1943, and now came to the point. Strölin risked a great deal in visiting Rommel. He was on the Nazi list of suspects. His telephone was being tapped. He endangered both Rommel and himself by his interview: but he talked.

'Rommel,' says Wheeler-Bennett, 'who had little or no understanding of politics, but much shrewd Swabian *Bauernschlauheit* (peasant cunning), listened attentively. He no longer entertained any personal illusion about victory. To his military understanding and his ordinary common sense the war was lost beyond redeeming.' Strölin was not at the heart of the matter; he had not been told about the plotters' final aims; but he was able to say to Rommel that 'you are the only one who can prevent civil war in Germany. You must lend your name to the movement.' And he was able to go back to Goerdeler and tell him that Rommel had responded. This—as it happened—was Rommel's death-warrant.

Goerdeler now thought that Rommel was prepared to become 'a modern Hindenburg'. It was a fatal conclusion: not only for Rommel, but also because it raised false hopes among the plotters. As Chester Wilmot put it, 'Rommel's adherence to the conspiracy, late and guarded though it was, encouraged Beck and Goerdeler to believe that when Hitler had been removed they would be able to treat direct with the Western Allies on a military level'. This was never possible: had von Stauffenberg's bomb been successful the plot must still have failed, for it was based on a fiction. It is now clear that the Allies would never have been prepared to negotiate with a group at the head

* And yet his misconception is pardonable. Wheeler-Bennett, *The Nemesis of Power*, p. 607 refers. 'Not only those of his fellow officers who shared his gloom as to the outcome of the war frequented his headquarters, but also disgruntled Nazi hierarchs, such as the *Gauleiter* and *Reichsstatthalter* of Hamburg, Karl Kaufmann, and frightened collaborators of the régime, such as Julius Dorpmüller, the Reich Minister of Transport, begging him to deliver Germany from her desperate straits. Nor were the voices of men and women in the street silent. The postbag at La Roche Guyon was augmented daily by many letters from humble and unknown writers bearing testimony to their trust in the Field-Marshal as their potential saviour.' It is ironic to think that at the time of Munich Chamberlain had the same experience.

of the German state, even a group led by Rommel, on the kind of terms which the conspirators envisaged.

But coincidence continued to press Rommel closer to the plot. His inspectorate of the Western Wall, during the last months of 1943, further diminished his belief in Germany's capacity to resist an invasion of the European fortress. Then Gause, his faithful Chief of Staff who had shared his African ventures, was compelled to retire because of his African wounds. In his place Rommel asked for and got Speidel, an old comrade-in-arms and a fellow Württemberger. Speidel (though Rommel did not know this at the time) was part of the inner web of the conspiracy. He used his 'special relationship' to work on his old commander during those spring months when the Field-Marshal, by a curious paradox, was struggling night and day to improve the *Reich*'s defences around the western coasts of Europe, while his doubts about the government of the *Reich* were growing. This supports the view that Rommel's rejection of Hitler was primarily a rejection of his military capacity. His revulsion from the *Führer* never entailed a revulsion from the *Reich*. He continued to guard its frontiers conscientiously, in Europe as in Africa, at the same time as he was surrendering, in his heart, his allegiance to its leader.

Speidel was not the only link with Rommel. The Military Governors of Belgium and France, von Falkenhausen and von Stülpnagel, were old acquaintances from the days at the Dresden School of Infantry where von Falkenhausen, as Commandant, had had the other two under him as instructors. With Wagner, the Quartermaster General, they kept up the pressure on Rommel. Stülpnagel was close to the inner ring: moreover, he was a friend of Speidel. 'Together', says Desmond Young, 'he and Speidel worked out the heads of an armistice agreement with Generals Eisenhower and Montgomery. If Hitler had not already been removed, it was to be made independently of him. It provided for the evacuation of the occupied territories in the west. In the east a shortened front would be maintained.'

On 27 May an important meeting was arranged in Speidel's flat at Freudenstadt between himself (representing Rommel), Strölin and von Neurath (the former German Foreign Minister). Strölin took with him a document summarising the state of play. 'I had it copied in longhand by one of my employees. He was very frightened and burned the blotting paper afterwards.' (Rommel, the professional soldier, had now placed his life in the hands of amateurs.) Between them they evolved a draft agreement for an armistice. Rommel was, according to it, prepared to take over command of the army, unwilling to let Hitler be assassinated, and not eager to replace him as Führer. The document proposed, in fact, that after a radio announcement had declared the termination of the Nazi régime control of the state would be taken over by Beck, Goerdeler and the socialist Wilhelm Leuschner. The army was to arrest Hitler, who would then be tried in a court of justice. 'Such', says Wheeler-Bennett, 'is the first part of the Rommel Saga of the Resistance, and it is full of problems for the historian.'

The problems arise from the very nature of the twilight world in which the conspirators moved. It is by no means clear how far Rommel realised that he was being vicariously committed. On the other hand it is certain that he was ignorant of the von Stauffenberg plan, and also certain that von Stülpnagel was the only senior officer in the West wholly dedicated to the irrevocable attempt at an assassination.

This brief review of the preliminaries to 20 July reveals how Rommel, whatever the extent of his commitment to the conspiracy, had matured since the time when the only problems he had to deal with were the taking of Tobruk or a spoiling attack at Kasserine. He had now entered the politico-military dimension; the area within which Marlborough lived before 1688. He was beginning to develop a capacity to think as a statesman as well as a soldier. It is tantalising, therefore, to ask whether he would have continued, had he lived, to expand the moral and intellectual awareness of his country's needs which was his chief concern during the winter and spring of 1944.

Some of his private thoughts at this time are reflected in an account by General Blumentritt, in his book on von Rundstedt, of a three-day journey on which he accompanied Rommel in an inspection of the Atlantic Wall. It occurred in February 1944 and reveals, among more serious matters, that after the war Rommel's greatest desire was to lay out large fruit and vegetable gardens at his home, as he had admired them in Holland. But it was not glass and greenhouses, nor even the Atlantic Wall, that were now Rommel's pre-occupation: just as he 'thought big' about the strategic possibilities in the Middle East, so now he was 'thinking big', or at least feeling his way towards so thinking, about Germany. Between Alamein and Normandy he was transformed from a man who might have made a successful *condottiere* into something more substantial. It would be absurd to pretend that this mutation converted him into a statesman of stature: but it certainly changed him from a simple soldier into a man prepared to renege on his sacred oath to prevent his country's ruin.

The stage was now set for the penultimate act of Rommel's tragedy: an act full of irony. The period is that immediately before and immediately after D-Day. During these weeks Rommel bravely sent his memoranda to Hitler expressing, without qualification, pessimistic views about the German Army in Normandy. Once the Allied bridge-heads had been established he knew, and he told Hitler, that the only action which would make military sense would be to withdraw beyond the line of the Seine. Few of the *Reich*'s commanders had ever dared to address Hitler like this: of those few not many had survived. Rommel also was to die. The clarity with which he presented military truth clouded the *Führer*'s mind, and led inevitably to a finale.

Yet while Rommel pushed his professionalism and patriotism to a point which could only be suicidal, and while he was steadily drawn deeper into the plot, it seems doubtful whether the combination of conspirators would have survived a success.

In the nexus of the conspiracy many incompatibles were brought together. Goebbels' promotion of Rommel had been so efficient that most Germans thought he was irreproachable; but the diehards in the conspiracy took a very different view. Their attitude is well described by Wheeler-Bennett. 'Though he may have been the darling of the German people as a whole, Rommel was anathema to the majority of the veterans of Resistance, who saw in him the very epitome of military opportunism and irresponsible casuistry which had nourished and supported National Socialism up to the moment of its downfall. It is greatly to be doubted, for example, whether von Stauffenberg and his followers among the plotters, or those surviving friends of Dietrich Bonhoeffer, such as Otto and Hans John, would have continued in Resistance in such a contingency. To have placed Rommel at the head of the new régime, or even in command of its armed forces, would have been to disintegrate almost irreparably the whole moral fabric of the conspiracy, and it is almost inconceivable that it was ever seriously considered except by the little ring of Württembergers, who would, perhaps, have been not averse to establishing a Swabian ascendancy in the new *Reich* and the new Army.' This is both perceptive and too subtle. The plotters were indeed acting from various motives. Some were impelled by a refined religious conviction: some sought social reform: some were vague but good. It is understandable that to many of them Rommel seemed dubious. But the committed Swabians who tried to draw their Field-Marshal into the conspiracy did so, in the main, because they had weighed him up and felt they could trust him. Wheeler-Bennett is wrong in suggesting that theirs was simply a political manœuvre. Indeed, one of the imponderables about the plot is what might have been the consequence if von Stauffenberg had been able to take the measure of Rommel. Meetings between them were attempted, but never successfully arranged. Yet the *Bauernschlauheit* of Württemberg, the peasant cunning, had not misjudged Rommel: and von Stauffenberg conceivably might have been able, appreciating this, to marry his aristocratic fervour and Rommel's earthy common sense. Here would have been a formidable combination.

Speculation about what might or might not have occurred is, however, ᴜrought to a stop by the facts. There is no doubt about what happened in the final act of the tragedy. It began with the failure of von Stauffenberg to plant the bomb successfully at Hitler's H.Q. on 20 July, after which the plotters' network of communications broke down. For Rommel's future the crucial figure was von Stülpnagel in Paris.

The latter had committed himself irrevocably by the orders he issued on the assumption that Hitler was dead. But Hitler survived. At 9 a.m. on the morning of the 21st von Stülpnagel was summoned to Berlin, and the significance of the summons was unmistakable.

He decided to drive to Berlin by way of Verdun, where in the earlier war he had been a battalion commander. As he passed through the area of the battle-field he tried, suitably, to shoot himself—but even in his attempted suicide he was inefficient. So he was taken to the Military Hospital at Verdun, and thus fell into the hands of the Gestapo. He was now blind: and on 30 August he was hanged after a trial before a People's Court. Von Stülpnagel was a man incapable of firmly grasping the nettle, and even in his death he was inept. It was during his delirium after his failure to kill himself at Verdun or, possibly, under torture by the Gestapo, that he uttered the word 'Rommel'. This was a sentence of death. Hitler's mood after his own 'miraculous survival' was merciless and inappeasable. Among a multitude of others the Field-Marshal was doomed.

Most of those connected or suspected of being connected with the plot were immediately slaughtered. Rommel was given a moratorium. After he recovered from his wound he was allowed to return to his house at Herrlingen, and there—though even in this there was something sinister—he was left alone. On 6 September Speidel came to warn him that Keitel and Jodl were calling him a defeatist: soon afterwards Speidel himself was arrested and taken to the Gestapo prison in Berlin. Yet Rommel, in theory, still commanded Army Group 'B'; Speidel in theory was still on his staff. Rommel wrote to Hitler protesting about Speidel's arrest and—there was menace in the silence—received no answer.

On 7 October Keitel summoned Rommel to Berlin 'for an important interview'. But Rommel was suspicious, and refused to go, pleading that his doctors would not let him travel. On 11 October Admiral Ruge stayed the night with him and Rommel then said, 'I shall not go to Berlin: I would never get there alive.'

On 14 October, however, Berlin came to him. Generals Burgdorf and Maisel of the Army Personnel Branch arrived at his house at noon. After talking to them Rommel went to his wife and told her, 'I have come to say good-bye. In a quarter of an hour I shall be dead. . . .'

The generals had offered Rommel a choice. He could drive back with them to Berlin and face a trial before a People's Court, knowing that he would be condemned to death and be branded as a traitor (in which case his wife would receive no pension): or he could drive away with them, and quietly swallow the pill they had brought for him, with the assurance that the *Reich* would take care of his family and that he would be honoured by a state funeral. If he accepted the second alternative it would be covered by a convenient explanation: he had 'died as a result of his wounds in Normandy'. Rommel naturally chose death by the poison which, the generals said, 'would only take three seconds to act'.

The promised and ghastly ritual was then carried out. Messages of sympathy arrived from Hitler, from Goebbels, from Ribbentrop. When von Rundstedt entered the hall at the elaborate state ceremony in Ulm—the hall where Rommel's bier had been decorated with his Marshal's baton and officer's sword—he did so to the funeral march from the *Götterdämmerung*, and then delivered a eulogy. Alas for von Rundstedt! He too had been tricked; when he spoke his *éloge* about his old comrade-in-arms he had no reason to believe that Rommel's death was due to anything other than his wounds.*

In this chapter I have inevitably drawn on Desmond Young's biography of Rommel. It ends:

'Early in March 1945, when his world was visibly falling about Hitler's ears, Frau Rommel received a letter dated 7 March. It was from *Der Generalbaurat für die Gestaltung der Deutschen Kriegerhofe* or, as I should say, the War Graves Commission.'

' "The Führer has given me an order", it ran, "to erect a monument to the late Field-Marshal Rommel, and I have asked a number of sculptors to submit designs. At this moment it would not be possible to erect this monument or to transport it. One can only make a model. . . . I think that the Field-Marshal should be represented by a lion. One artist has depicted a dying lion, another a lion weeping, the third a lion about to spring. . . . I prefer the last myself but if you prefer a dying lion, that, too, could be arranged."

' "The slab can be made immediately, as I have special permission from Reichminister Speer. Generally monuments cannot now be made in stone. But in this special case it can be made and quickly shipped. . . . "

'To this letter Frau Rommel sent no reply.'

---

* Five thousand, more or less, were executed and thousands more were committed to concentration camps as a result of Hitler's paranoiac reaction to the plot. In Rommel's funeral oration, which von Rundstedt read as a duty, he had to say that 'his heart belonged to the Führer'. This, now, was nonsense.

XV

'An ordinary
German general'?

In his biography of Wavell John Connell records that throughout the African campaign Rommel carried with him and carefully annotated the German translation of Wavell's Lees-Knowles Lectures on the theme of *Generals and Generalship*, which he delivered at Cambridge in 1939. 'Many years later', Connell says, 'Frau Rommel presented the battered and historic little volume to Lady Wavell.'

At Cambridge Wavell had an audience of between 20 and 30 under-graduates. But subsequently the *Times* published his lectures first as turnover articles and then as a pamphlet; Penguin Books re-issued them; and they have been translated into a number of languages. They were, in fact, an extraordinarily prescient analysis of the qualities which a military leader would require in the war which Wavell predicted: they forecast Rommel. 'The commander with the imagination—the genius, in fact—to use the new forces may have his name written among the "great captains". But he will not win that title lightly or easily; consider for a moment the qualifications he will require. On the ground he will have to handle forces moving at a speed and ranging at a distance far exceeding that of the most mobile cavalry of the past; a study of naval strategy and tactics as well as those of cavalry will be essential to him.' Rommel himself thought of his battles in the desert in terms of an action at sea. This correlation of armoured operations and naval engagements was a dramatic and colourful way of presenting the desert conflict during the war. It does not now stand up to the cool analysis of peacetime and hindsight. But this was how Rommel and his opponents interpreted their role. In attempting the necessary task of estimating why a study of Rommel should take its place in a series on the Great Commanders nothing, therefore, could be more appropriate than to use as 'heads of discourse' some of the basic points which Wavell made in these seminal lectures.

The prime requirement, he thought, was 'the quality of robustness, the ability to stand the shock of war'. By this he did not mean the simple gift of hardihood—the kind of hardihood exhibited by Lord Uxbridge and Wellington at Waterloo, when after the former's right knee had been shattered by grape-shot he observed, 'By God, Sir, I've lost my leg', and Wellington (in the popular version of the story) removing his telescope from his eye replied, 'By God, Sir, you have', and then replaced his spy-glass. Nor was it mere physical endurance: though this is certainly one element in the Great Commander's constitution—and one which Rommel possessed. In 1933 he was appointed to command of a Jaeger battalion expert with the ski. Its officers immediately gave Rommel a test on the snow slopes. There was no lift. They trudged to the top, and descended; honour was satisfied. But Rommel had his officers up and down the ski-run twice more before he let them wearily fall out. This was his spirit in both wars—to be physically more robust than the troops he led, and always to show them an example.

By robustness Wavell meant something more subtle . . . 'delicate mechanism is of little use in war; and this applies to the mind of the commander as well as his body'. In other words, one of the qualities which separate the Great Commander from those effective at a lower level—the Lieut.-Colonel, for instance, who genuinely earns a D.S.O. because of the consistent success of his well-ordered battalion—is his mental and emotional capacity to accept very large responsibilities and, in consequence, to absorb very large shocks over very long periods of time. Such a man must be able to face with resilience the strains and stresses which even victory involves: the disappointment of defeat when victory was expected: and (even more testing) the assimilation of defeat when defeat had been seen to be inevitable. On the British side, Alexander and Slim were notable for this gift.

Rommel was exposed to these three tests, and overcame all of them: between Alamein and Tunisia he was continually tried by perhaps the most exacting of the trio. As O'Connor was driving up to Beda Fomm, after his troops had achieved their astonishing victory, Dorman-Smith, who was travelling with him, asked him what it felt like to be a successful general. O'Connor replied, 'I would never consider a commander completely successful until he had restored the situation after a serious defeat and a long retreat'. This is the standard of resilience Wavell demanded—the standard by which, for example, the performance of Foch and Haig after the German attack on 21 March 1918 is to be judged—and if it is applied to Rommel he emerges as exemplary. He was capable of creating a Kasserine after losing an Alamein.

Wavell devoted the third of his lectures to *The Soldier and the Statesman*, discussing in it a special form of robustness with which the best of the Great Commanders have been endowed, of which he himself would prove to be deficient when his own time of testing arrived, and which Rommel displayed superbly. This is the possession of both a moral strength sufficient to enable a general in the field to stand up to the pressures, often unreasonable, of his political masters at home, and also the verbal capacity to articulate his protests. Wavell was the Wully Robertson of the Second World War. He had moral strength, but he lacked the gift of speech. Rommel had both. He was never afraid to fly back from Africa, or to go to Berchtesgaden from Normandy, to express in uncompromising terms his condemnation of the Führer's policies. It requires an imaginative exercise to understand the moral courage which such actions demanded during the collapse of the Third Reich. Yet Rommel used the rough edge of his sergeant-major's tongue when speaking or writing to Hitler in a more audacious way than most of his generals did in speaking or writing to Churchill.

Wavell would also have respected the robustness, both physical and mental, which Rommel displayed during the months and the moments which preceded his death. When his car was hit by cannon-shells from a fighter plane on 17 July 1944, and crashed into a tree-stump and overturned, Rommel's injuries were grave. He was taken to a French hospital with his driver, Daniel. 'The doctor', according to Captain Helmuth Lang (who was travelling with Rommel), 'said that there was little hope of saving his life. Later he was taken, still unconscious, with Daniel to an air-force hospital at Bernay, about 25 miles away. The doctors there diagnosed severe injuries to the skull—a fracture at the base, two fractures on the temple and the cheek-bone destroyed, a wound in the left eye, wounds from glass, and concussion.' But his great physical power enabled him to survive—to face, in due course, the climax of his life, when two generals from Berlin called at his house to tell him that he must die. In those last minutes his fortitude was at its finest.

The next of Wavell's criteria was that of 'character . . . a genuine interest in, and a real knowledge of humanity, a raw material of his trade'. To this I would add an expert knowledge of the tools of his trade. In both these respects Rommel was pre-eminent among the commanders of the Second World War. General Hobart, who raised 11 Armoured Division and, more significantly, 79 Armoured Division, whose diversified tanks played so important a part on D-Day, was one among the very few British generals who might have addressed Rommel as a peer. (The Americans, because of their lack of experience during 1914–18 and their withdrawal from military affairs between the wars, produced no senior officer who, like Hobart or Rommel, could speak as a veteran with that intimate knowledge of technical detail which only years of practice can generate.)

It is therefore relevant to note the shortage of Allied commanders who could match Rommel's professional experience and expertise. Men like Patton or Horrocks, who won distinction because of their leadership of armour, did not compare with him in precise knowledge of the tools of their trade. Throughout the First World War his outstanding achievements were due not only to his courage and initiative, but also to his technical understanding. In France, in 1940, he was always ready, in spite of his rank, to lend a hand at building a bridge or clearing an obstruction. In Africa the examples of personal intervention which derived from his sense of the technical possibilities are infinite. Whether he was carrying out private reconnaissance in a light aircraft, or advising on the clearing of a minefield, or navigating his own command truck when everyone else was lost, or leading his 88s to the right point at Sidi Rezegh, he had a special gift for being the man on the spot with the know-how. In Normandy his inventive skill vastly strengthened the weak Atlantic Wall. And always his grasp of how things should be properly done enhanced his sway over his armies, for both in battle and in peace his forthright criticism of officer and man stemmed from a professional awareness which those criticised had to respect as superior to their own. This was the reason for the trust which, even in defeat, Rommel always secured from his troops.

There is scarcely any need for comment about his sense of 'humanity', the 'raw material of his trade'. He was manifestly a soldiers' general. Austere himself, he demanded austerity from his staff, and the self-abnegation he exercised throughout his career was taken for granted by his *entourage*. They, too, had to live hard: Rommel was merciless. The men he led saw this, day by day, and out of their observation grew respect. Von Mellenthin says that 'between Rommel and his troops was that mutual understanding which cannot be explained and analysed, but which is the gift of the gods. The Afrika Korps followed Rommel wherever he led, however hard he drove them . . . the men knew that Rommel was the last man to spare Rommel.' This is not the adulation of a sycophant, but a statement of fact from an eye-witness.

Wavell remarked in his lectures that 'without placing himself at the head of his troops in battle a modern commander can still exercise a very real influence over the morale of his men'. Montgomery did this. After Dunkirk he was never personally involved in action, but he always imposed his image effectively. Rommel, on the other hand, could not keep away from the front line: he was continually and perhaps obsessively taking the place of Napoleon on the bridge at Lodi. (Balfour, on hearing Winston Churchill say about his service on the Western front that it gave 'opportunity for calm meditation', observed that he was 'like the Duke of Marlborough—most master of himself amid the din of battle'. This would be a good epitaph for Rommel.) But when he did this it came naturally: a reflex. The dash and courage which drove him to the front was guided by some deep instinct which habitually positioned him in the right place at the right time.

Yet the genuine feeling of Rommel's men about him was rather one of trust than of deep affection. He never, like Wellington's corps commander, acquired a nickname as revealing as 'Daddy' Hill. Allenby became 'the Bull': Slim 'Uncle Bill'. The Confederates in the Valley knew what they meant when they talked about 'Stonewall' Jackson. But though Rommel could teach, and harry, and lead, his domination of his 'raw material' never attained that rare and mysterious affinity between commander and commanded which has the warmth of a successful marriage. When men talk of Rommel, they talk of 'Rommel'. When they talk of Montgomery they talk of 'Monty'. And 'Ike' was always 'Ike'.

Wavell and Rommel held much the same view about the correct relation between soldier and general. Wavell's was pragmatic: a soldier will follow the leader who, he believes, will produce results. Rommel summarised his own thoughts in a paper on *Modern Military Leadership*: 'The commander must try, above all, to establish personal and comradely contact with his men, but without giving away an inch of his authority.' But, he added, 'when an attack is ordered, the men must never be allowed to get the feeling that their casualties have been calculated in advance according to the laws of probability' (a lesson from the Western front in 1914–18) 'for that is the end of all enthusiasm. The soldier must continually receive fresh justification for his confidence, otherwise it is soon lost. He must go into battle easy in mind with no doubts about the command under which he is fighting.' Wavell and Rommel in fact advocated a strictness which, they both knew, must be qualified in practice by a concern for the common man. Westphal remembered that Rommel's attitude to the war was that 'the important thing was to win it with as few casualties as possible. A saying of which he made frequent use was, "Germany will need men after the war also".' And this concern embraced his enemy. It was Rommel who burned the Commando Order issued by Hitler on 28 October 1942, which laid down that all enemy soldiers encountered behind the German line were to be killed at once, regardless of whether they landed from sea or air.

One of the most controversial questions about Rommel is raised by Wavell's point about a general putting himself at the head of his troops. Critics of his capability state, not without reason, that the place of a modern commander is in his command post, and that whereas in the simpler structure of eighteenth-century warfare a Marlborough or a Wolfe could properly direct a battle from the front, in the 1940s the elaboration of the network of command was such that their successors should sit back tranquilly in the rear. Rommel disproved this thesis. Among the papers Sir Basil Liddell Hart has made available to me from the multitudinous collection in his files is one entitled *Positioning of Commanders*. In this he calculated how 'the British commanders' influence in the battle suffered from their far-back position—in contrast to the way that the Germans, and Rommel above all, were usually well forward, and often took direct control of operations at key moments in the battle'. In *Battleaxe* Beresford-Peirse conducted the action from an H.Q. 60 miles behind the lines, and the H.Q. of 7 Armoured Division was 30 miles in the rear. Cunningham during *Crusader* worked from Fort Maddalena, 80 miles from Sidi Rezegh. At Gazala Ritchie's H.Q. was near Gambut—60 miles behind the front. Though figures can be used to prove anything, and though I would not wish to push the implications of these too far (since the position of headquarters and the movements of the commander himself are not necessarily connected—as Rommel's staff well knew!), nevertheless Rommel's instinctive desire to command from the front brought many benefits. His subordinates suffered: as Kesselring observed at Gazala, Rommel's method of control from the sharp end of the spearhead meant agony for his H.Q. But an objective reading of the battles along the African shore in which Rommel was involved will surely justify his appearances as the 'Feldherr of the front line'. In the spring of 1941, during *Crusader*, at Gazala, in the assault on Tobruk, his electric presence was an extra weapon.

The British commanders, trying to run the desert war from the rear (and this does not reflect on their undoubted courage), were usually late in making decisions and fumbled the management of their forces. So, while Wavell was not wrong in observing that in modern war a commander may successfully function from behind the battle, he was perceptive in following Liddell Hart's prophecies and adding, in his 1939 lectures, that 'in mechanised warfare we may again see the general leading his troops almost in the front of the fighting, or possibly reconnoitring and commanding from the air'. This was Rommel's method. He worked on the principle that 'no admiral ever won a battle from a shore base'. In the final assault on the position of 150 Brigade in the *Cauldron*, Rommel went in with the foremost platoon. He defied the text-books and inspired the Afrika Korps. By being up in front he was able to use his *Fingerspitzengefühl*, that natural ability to read the battle-field which all Great Commanders have possessed. The evocative and summary German word is constantly and rightly used by his colleagues whenever they talk about Rommel.

Wavell also hinted at a quality of the Great Commander on which he might have further enlarged—the ability to survive. He noted that, during Marl-borough's attack on the Schellenberg position, among the 1500 British casualties were four major-generals and 28 brigadiers or lieutenant-colonels. He then implied—but did not elaborate the thought—that the Great Com-manders are men who have managed to keep alive in battle long enough for them to make their mark. In this respect Rommel, before 17 July 1944, was fortunate. His immediate subordinates continually disappeared because of death or wounds,* but, in spite of many miraculous 'near misses' from bomb, mine, shell or bullet, Rommel seemed to lead a charmed life. Yet how important is the luck of survival! Stonewall Jackson certainly made a name and a reputation, but his death at Chancellorsville, when his gifts were still not fully developed, was a tragic loss for both the Confederates and the military historian. And who can tell what original paths Wingate might have followed had his plane not crashed into a Burmese hill-side?

Implicit in Wavell's lectures was the notion that the modern commander, even more than his predecessors (because of the speed of armoured warfare), must be a man with flexibility of mind. He must have a quicksilver capacity to change his ideas about tactics or strategy, and must constantly originate or cause his staff to originate new methods of employing the equipment available to him. T. E. Lawrence remarked that 'the greatest commander is he whose intuitions most nearly happen'. Rommel was a man who intuitively grasped new possibilities in both tactics and techniques; if he was not a great originator—though he was certainly not lacking in invention—he was quick at adopting and adapting the insights of others. Moreover he was supreme at converting a mistake into a masterpiece: an agile exponent of Marshal Saxe's dictum that 'there is more address in making bad dispositions than is commonly imagined, provided that they are intentional, and so formed as to admit of being instantaneously converted into good ones: nothing can more confound an enemy, who has been anticipating victory, than a stratagem of this kind'. Saxe would have commended the *Cauldron* manoeuvre. As a junior officer among the mountains of Italy and as a general in the sands of Africa Rommel constantly devised the essential element of victory—surprise. 'Rommel's asparagus' was not the only crop from the fertile field of his imagination. His creative energy in Normandy was a natural consequence of

* See p. 89.

his originality in Africa and in France during an earlier war. In what has been called 'the terrible etiquette of the battlefield' he was never a conformist.

This copiousness of invention is all the more surprising if it be remembered that in Africa Rommel, compared with his counter-parts—Wavell, Auchinleck and Montgomery—was held on the leash by his German and Italian masters while Churchill was constantly urging his generals into the attack. Here is another example of his robustness of temperament. He might easily have lost his aggressive instinct by developing a *je m'en foutiste* attitude: but it was never impaired. For Churchill the Mediterranean was vital: for Hitler, a side-show. Rommel's buoyancy does credit both to his appreciation of the strategic facts and to his mental stamina.

He was a quick thinker, and always a thruster. Whatever view may be taken of his 'dash to the wire', it is instructive to reflect about what might have happened if Rommel and not Horrocks had been in charge of the attempt to break through to the airborne bridgehead at Arnhem: merely to make the suggestion is to underline Rommel's mastery of the *Blitzkrieg*. He brought to a World War slowed down by the memory of its predecessor something of the dash and *insouciance* of the cavalry in the American Civil War. It might be said of him that in the 'forties he was the personification of the twentieth-century Captain about whom the British theorists, in their speculations about the future of war, had dreamed in the 'thirties.* 'He became,' says Liddell Hart in his introduction to the *Rommel Papers*, 'next to Guderian, the leading exponent of the new idea.' The effect on his opponents† can best be illustrated by the well-known and perhaps unparalleled instruction issued by Auchinleck—an ill-advised directive, because, as T. E. Lawrence once remarked, 'all our efforts to make our men hate the enemy just made them hate war'.

To: All Commanders and Chiefs of Staff
From: Headquarters, B.T.E. and M.E.F.

There exists a danger that our friend Rommel is becoming a kind of magician or bogey-man to our troops, who are talking far too much about him. He is by no means a superman, although he is undoubtedly very energetic and able. Even if he were a superman, it would still be highly undesirable that our men should credit him with supernatural powers.

* Rommel's essence, I suppose, is contained in his letter to his wife of 3 April 1941, which tells her about his first African offensive. 'I took the risk against all orders and instructions because this opportunity seemed favourable.' This was the practical exponent the theorists sought.

† Hitler's view about Rommel's predominance, expressed in his conversation of 7 July 1942 recorded in *Hitler's Table Talk*, is relevant here. Hitler ascribed Rommel's world-wide reputation to Churchill's speeches in the House of Commons in which for tactical reasons the Field-Marshal was presented as a military genius. 'The mere name', said Hitler, 'suddenly begins to acquire the value of several divisions.'

I wish you to dispel by all possible means the idea that Rommel represents something more than an ordinary German General. The important thing now is to see to it that we do not always talk of Rommel when we mean the enemy in Libya. We must refer to 'the Germans' or 'the Axis powers' or 'the enemy' and not always keep harping on Rommel.

Please ensure that this order is put into immediate effect, and impress upon all Commanders that, from a psychological point of view, it is a matter of the highest importance.

(*Signed*) C. J. Auchinleck,
General,
Commander-in-Chief, M.E.F.*

A capacity of the Great Commander which Wavell emphasised, and which Rommel's critics have suggested he lacked, is the ability to organise his supplies. 'There are 10 military students', Wavell pointed out, 'who can tell you how Blenheim was won for one who has any knowledge at all of the administrative preparations that made the march to Blenheim possible.' The truth is that in this matter a final, objective conclusion is impossible, because military studies are as bedevilled by subjective attitudes as literary criticism or the history of art. There will always be a division between those who like Montgomery prefer a 'balanced' attack, with administrative resources tidily arranged before the assault goes in (though even Montgomery took an administrative risk at Arnhem), and those who like Rommel are prepared to accept the minimum as a necessity. In war what counts is the result. Of course Rommel took risks—risks in regard to his supplies which many other commanders would not have been prepared to accept, and which, in his early days in Africa, were questionable. But he learned. His operations were increasingly preceded by an intense effort to secure the necessary stocks—and in North Africa, it must be remembered, he was never master of his rear: the inefficient Italians were mainly in control.

This was in part due to Rommel's own mistakes. His error of judgement about Malta made a victory at Alamein impossible, administratively; and he probably made a further error in racing from Tobruk to the Alamein area. But in most cases the risks Rommel took were justified, and he was usually aware that tactical success could be defeated by administrative weakness. Alam Halfa is perhaps an exception—he should have seen on the first morning of the battle that his potential supplies could not possibly furnish a further advance. But in general it is difficult to maintain that Rommel behaved more foolishly than those other commanders who, from time to time

---

* Critics of Montgomery as a 'showman'—there are many, and they are often justified—might remember that after Alam Halfa such an instruction would have been unnecessary and indeed unthinkable.

in military history, have found themselves far out on a flank of the line with much expected of them but little provided for its execution. The issue is the answer. When O'Connor pushed forward a small force, with worn-out transport, over rough terrain, to trap the Italians at Beda Fomm he took administrative risks as grave as any that Rommel accepted. But had O'Connor failed . . . ? And in 1942–43 it must be remembered that Lindsell and Brian Robertson built up for Montgomery an infrastructure of exceptional efficiency. The fourth volume of the *Official History* of the Mediterranean and the Middle East campaigns makes this point with an impressive repetition, while Tedder's memoirs, *With Prejudice*, show how the R.A.F. achieved similar and perhaps incomparable standards. But in the desert which his Chief of Staff once described as a Quartermaster's nightmare Rommel could never be confident that his spearhead would be firmly supported by its shaft. He was not, however, one of the careful compilers of victory, like Monash, or Allenby, or Haig. Rommel's type of instinctive, split-second command must always involve tactical and administrative hazards. In the war of sea-on-land (which was how he envisaged the desert campaigns), he was more of a Beatty than a Jellicoe.

Yet by comparison with the Russian front, the operations in Burma, and the unfolding of Allied power in north-west Europe, this was not more than a little war. Rommel in Africa was never in command of more than a few divisions. (At Alamein he had roughly 50,000 Germans and about the same number of Italians. At Kursk in Russia Modl commanded three panzer corps and two infantry corps, while Hoth on his right commanded the most enormous tank assembly ever granted to a German—apart from three infantry corps he had at his disposition nine of the best panzer divisions in the German Army: famous names like the *Totenkopf*, the *S.S. Leibstandarte*, the *S.S. Das Reich*, the *Gross Deutschland*.) Rommel never knew such riches. Both the Allies and the Axis, in fact—the Allies far more than the Axis—strained themselves to maintain in the Mediterranean a situation in which, like knights in tourney, their few men in armour fought symbolically, in a closed arena, with the whole world as spectator. So the tank actions during *Crusader* or at Alamein cannot be compared with an engagement like that at Kursk where the armoured forces of two nations met *en masse*, and where, because of the size of the armies involved, victory in the battle probably meant victory in the war.

This is important—for relativity is a factor which must be borne in mind in any final assessment of a Great Commander: in two ways. First, his performance must be considered in relation to what is known about the scale of military operations possible during his lifetime. Belisarius, Genghis Khan,

Marlborough and Zhukov must obviously be appreciated, from this point of view, by different standards. There is a relative magnitude of command in every century, and even every decade. Did the commander under review, it must be asked, have the opportunity to control the largest possible number of forces available to himself and his contemporaries; and, granted that he had such an opportunity, how did he make use of it?

Rommel presents an enigma. Command is the test of the commander: yet Rommel never had the chance of manipulating in action (for Normandy was no trial) those huge groups of divisions and armies with which other men—in Russia and north-west Europe—were able to demonstrate their skill. One can only make a projection from the known to the probable. At every step in his career, from junior officer to battalion commander, and then onwards to general and army commander, Rommel was quick to appreciate and apply the professional requirements of his rank. There is no reason to suppose that, had he been faced with the problem of directing larger forces, he would not have found the answer—technically. The doubt lies in whether his temperament, essentially that of a leader in the field, might have been unable to endure the loneliness which could not be evaded by a Haig or a Falkenhayn, imprisoned in their châteaux when the barrages lifted; and whether his inability to blend allies into a unity (shown so strikingly in his attitude towards the Italians, and indeed towards many of his German colleagues) might have proved ruinous if he had been put in charge of great groupings of armies.

The other 'relativity factor' is also one of scale. How far is it justifiable to compare the performance of a commander in a minor theatre of war with that of one working on a vast battlefront? In his study of T. E. Lawrence, Liddell Hart wrote: 'Few of the Great Captains can offer more than three or four battles for examination. Lawrence can only offer one. But that is a gem. His own mockery of his achievement cannot hide the fact that at Tafila he displayed a tactical artistry, based on consummate calculation, in the purest classical tradition. It was Cannae, or still more, Ilipa, adapted to modern weapons.' This sort of juxtaposition has always seemed to me to be like a comparison between the minute perfection of a lyric and the sustained orchestration of *Paradise Lost*: the dimensions of size and space and time make the two types of achievement incomparable. Rommel certainly revealed attitudes of mind similar to those of his famous predecessors: but there are dangers in setting his battles beside theirs in the hope of reaching a comparative estimate.

It therefore seems better to base an assessment of Rommel as a military commander on what is unquestionable. His merits as a strategist can be argued indefinitely; but as one of the last of the great cavalry captains his place cannot be denied. On whatever corner of Valhalla Jeb Stuart and Attila, Prince Rupert and Patton may assemble, Erwin Rommel will be of their company: and the final words of Colonel Henderson's famous appraisal of Stonewall Jackson seem appropriate as a conclusion. 'What is life without honour? Degradation is worse than death. We must think of the living and of those who are to come after us. . . .' The man who in two savage wars led his troops to victory among the Italian Alps, across the plains of France, and over the African desert, preserved his honour to the end; and his opponents, whatever their varying views of his vicissitudes, have never failed to hold him in honour.

APPENDIX ONE

Rommel's Military Record

(reproduced from his *Wehrpass*, the official register
of his attachments and commands)

19.7.10–3.10.15	Inf. Reg. 124
1.3.14–31.7.14	Z.Feld Art.Reg. 19
4.10.15–10.1.18	Württemberg. Geb. Batt.
11.1.18–20.12.18	Gen. Kdo. 64
29.7.18–19.8.18	Z. 4/Landw. Fulda Reg. 6 d. Bayr. L. Division
20.8.18–8.9.18	Z. 1 Landst. Fussart. Batt. xx A.K.
21.12.18–24.6.19	Inf. Reg. 124
25.6.19–31.12.20	R.W.Sch. Reg. 25 (Schwab. Gemund)
1.1.21–30.9.29	Inf. Reg. 13 (Stuttgart)
1.10.29–30.9.33	Inf. Schule Dresden
1.10.33–14.1.35	III/Inf. Reg. 17 (Jaeger Goslar)
15.1.35–21.1.35	R.W.Ministerium
25.1.35–14.10.35	II/Batt. J.R.Go.
15.10.35–9.11.38	Kriegsschule Potsdam
10.11.38–	Kommandatur der Kriegsschule W.Neustadt
23.8.39–14.2.40	Führerhauptq. Unterstab.
15.2.40–14.2.41	Stab. 7 Panzer Div.
15.2.41–14.8.41	Befehlshaber der Deutschen Truppen in Libyen
15.8.41–21.1.42	Kommando der Panzergruppe Afrika
22.1.42–24.10.42	Oberkommando d. Pz. Armee Afrika
25.10.42–22.2.43	Oberkommando d. Deutsch. Ital. Panzerarmee
23.2.43–13.5.43	Oberkommando d. Heeresgruppe Afrika
14.5.43–14.7.43	Arbeitstab Gen. Feldmarschall Rommel
15.7.43–3.9.44	Oberkommando d. Heeresgruppe B.
4.9.44–14.10.44	Führer Res OKH (V)

This *Wehrpass*, it may be noted, contains no specific reference to Rommel's service
on Hitler's bodyguards.

APPENDIX TWO

Codes and Intelligence

Since I wrote this book my attention has been drawn to *The Codebreakers*, by David Kahn, published in the United States in 1966 and subsequently published in Great Britain by Weidenfeld and Nicolson—a study of the history of codes and cyphers.

This is a world clouded by secrecy. A world where cross-checking on your sources and evidence is difficult and where corroboration is impossible because lips are sealed. But Mr. Kahn has produced a good deal of detailed evidence which in any study of Rommel must be taken into account. He describes the way that the Axis armies in Africa broke the Allied codes, and one must assume that he is correct because, in this twilight world, and in my experience, nobody is prepared to comment. Let us suppose that he is correct: let us pursue the argument in terms of the pre-war German philosophical system which presented itself as *als ob*, 'as if'.

Kahn states that an Italian called Gherardi provided in 1941 means for breaking into an American Embassy safe, as a result of which the Italians cracked what the Americans called their BLACK CODE—a most important cypher system, which they were using in the Mediterranean area. He quotes an entry in Ciano's *Diary* for 30 September 1941: 'The military intelligence service has come into the possession of the American secret code . . .' He also reminds one that Ciano on 12 February 1942 noted: 'I handed Mackensen the text of a telegram from the American Military attaché at Moscow, addressed to Washington. It complains about failure to deliver arms promised by the United States, and says that if the U.S.S.R. is not aided immediately and properly she will have to consider capitulating.'

For Rommel on the African front the importance of this codebreaking seems to have been considerable. From 1940 the Americans had in Cairo a military attaché, Colonel Fellers, who sent back to the Intelligence Section of the Pentagon a regular series of messages in which he appreciated the state of British equipment and even described their forward plans—messages which were readily interpreted by the Axis. Before Gazala, for example, Rommel received a number of intercepts. He had also, as is well known, another efficient method of surveillance . . . the *Fernemeldeaufklärung* Company commanded by Captain Seebohm, which listened in to 8 Army's radio traffic, at all levels, and learned a great deal because at this time 8 Army was notably weak in wireless discipline. Finally, British codes had also been cracked.

But in 1942 three things happened, in a more or less simultaneous fashion according to Kahn, which directly affected Rommel. First: in July Seebohm was killed, and most of his interception unit either died or was captured, at Gazala. In July, also, Fellers was recalled to Washington because of American doubts about the security of their communications. He was recalled with honour and was awarded the Distinguished Service Medal for work which 'contributed to the tactical and technical development of our Armed Forces'. And, finally, as a result of Seebohm's death and his papers falling into British hands, 8 Army 'profited from their capture of the *Fernemeldeaufklärung* files to institute an improved call-sign procedure, tauten cryptographic discipline forward of divisional headquarters, introduce radiotelephonic codes, impose rigid wireless silence on reserve formations, pad out real messages with dummy traffic, and create an entire fake signals network in the southern sector. The new *Fernemeldeaufklärung* staff had neither the talent nor the experience to penetrate these disguises and sift the true from the false.'

Since this is a field in which few will speak categorically . . . few British officers in particular . . . one must work on assumptions and the kind of private inquiry which does not allow the disclosure of sources. Assuming Mr. Kahn to be correct, the coincidence of timing is most significant: all these important sources of information for Rommel seem to have dried up in mid-1942. Now at Alam Halfa (see Chapter X) he was clearly short of information and he was not even in Africa when the battle of Alamein started. How far are these matters interconnected? If Rommel lost his wireless-intercept service at about the time when the unquiet American was recalled from Cairo and the British reorganised their vulnerable system of communications, then Montgomery had a double stroke of luck. He faced with an abundance of supplies an impoverished Rommel and also, with a powerfully reinforced intelligence network, an opponent whose own secret resources of information had been simultaneously destroyed.

What is not clear, of course (and in this respect the *Rommel Papers* provide little guidance), is the extent to which such intelligence as he did receive affected his planning. Experience tends to suggest that this may have been less than might be supposed. One of the most important intelligence facts of the war, the knowledge that the Germans were about to invade Russia, was communicated to Stalin by his own ambassador in London, Maisky, but it was disregarded. Commanders, like statesmen, have a way, as they put it in Scotland, of 'ganging their ain gait'.

Bibliography

The literature which spans Rommel's experience during and between two World Wars is of course enormous. I have listed here those books which I have found especially helpful.

Agar-Hamilton, J. A. L., and Turner, L. C. F. *Crisis in the Desert, May–July 1942*, O.U.P, 1952

Alexander, Field-Marshal the Earl. *The Alexander Memoirs, 1940–1945*, Cassell, 1962

Barnett, Corelli. *The Desert Generals*, Kimber, 1960

Belfield, E., and Essame, H. *The Battle for Normandy*, Batsford, 1965

Blumenson, Martin. *Kasserine Pass*, Houghton Mifflin, 1967

Blumentritt, Maj.-Gen. Günther. *Von Rundstedt*, Odhams Press, 1952

Bradley, General Omar N. *A Soldier's Story*, Eyre and Spottiswoode, 1951

Bryant, Sir Arthur. *The Turn of the Tide*, Vols. I and II, Collins, 1957 and 1959

Bullock, Alan. *Hitler*, Odhams Press, 1952

Caccia-Dominioni, Paolo. *Alamein, 1933–1962*, Allen and Unwin, 1966

Carell, Paul. *Hitler's War on Russia*, Harrap, 1964

Carver, Lieut.-Gen. Michael. *Tobruk*, Batsford, 1964

Carver, Lieut.-Gen. Michael. *El Alamein*, Batsford, 1962

Chaplin, Lieut.-Col. *The Queen's Own Royal West Kent Regiment*, Michael Joseph, 1954

Churchill, Winston. *The Second World War, passim*, Cassell

Ciano, Count. *Diary, 1939–1943*, Heinemann, 1946

Clark, Alan. *Barbarossa*, Hutchinson, 1965

Clarke, Brig. Dudley. *The Eleventh at War*, Michael Joseph, 1952

Clifton, Brig. George. *The Happy Hunted*, Cassell, 1952

Connell, John. *Auchinleck*, Cassell, 1959

Connell, John. *Wavell*, Collins, 1964

Cunningham, Admiral Lord. *A Sailor's Odyssey*, Hutchinson, 1951

Davin, D. M. *Crete*: Official History of New Zealand in the Second World War, 1939–1945, O.U.P, 1953

Deakin, F. W. *The Brutal Friendship*, Weidenfeld and Nicolson, 1962

de Guingand, Maj.-Gen. Sir Francis. *Operation Victory* and *Generals at War*, Hodder and Stoughton

Divine, David. *The Blunted Sword*, Hutchinson, 1964

Dollman, Eugen. *The Interpreter*, Hutchinson, 1967

Douglas of Kirtleside, Marshal of the R.A.F. Lord. *Years of Command*, Collins, 1966

Eisenhower, Gen. *Crusade in Europe*, Heinemann, 1949

Falls, Capt. Cyril. *Caporetto, 1917*, Weidenfeld and Nicolson, 1966

Fergusson, Brig. Bernard. *The Black Watch and the King's Enemies*, Collins, 1950

Frischauer, Willi. *Himmler*, Odhams Press, 1953

Fuller, Maj.-Gen. *The Decisive Battles of the World, Vol. 3*, Eyre and Spottiswoode, 1956

Gale, Gen. Sir Richard. *With the 6th Airborne Division in Normandy*, Sampson Low, 1948

Gale, Gen. Sir Richard. *Call to Arms*, Hutchinson, 1968

Gisevius, Hans Berndt. *To The Bitter End*, Cape, 1948

Glubb, Brig. J. B. *The Story of the Arab Legion*, Hodder and Stoughton, 1948

Görlitz, Walter. *The German General Staff*, Hollis and Carter, 1953

Guderian, Gen. Heinz. *Panzer Leader*, Michael Joseph, 1952

Hibbert, Christopher. *Benito Mussolini*, Longmans, 1963

Hitler, Adolf. *Hitler's Table Talk*, Weidenfeld and Nicolson, 1953

Hood, Stuart. *Pebbles From My Skull*, Hutchinson, 1963

Horrocks, Lieut.-Gen. Sir Brian. *A Full Life*, Collins, 1960

Jacobsen, H. A., and Rohwer, J. *Decisive Battles of World War II*, André Deutsch, 1965

Jackson, Maj.-Gen. W. G. F. *The Battle For Italy*, Batsford, 1967

Joly, Cyril. *Take These Men*, Constable, 1955

Kahn, David. *The Codebreakers*, Weidenfeld and Nicolson, 1966

Kennedy, Maj.-Gen. Sir John. *The Business of War*, Hutchinson, 1957

Kennedy Shaw, W. B. *Long Range Desert Group*, Collins, 1945

Kesselring, Field-Marshal. *Memoirs*, Kimber, 1963

Kippenberger, Maj.-Gen. *Infantry Brigadier*, O.U.P, 1949

Liddell Hart, Capt. Sir Basil. Many books, but in particular *T. E. Lawrence*, Cape, 1934; *The Tanks*, 2 vols., Cassell, 1959; *Memoirs*, 2 vols., Cassell, 1965

Lindsay, Lieut.-Col. Martin. *So Few Got Through*, Collins, 1946

Macintyre, Donald. *The Battle for the Mediterranean*, Batsford, 1964

Macksey, Maj. Kenneth. *The Shadow of Vimy Ridge*, Kimber, 1965

Macksey, Maj. Kenneth. *Armoured Crusader*, Hutchinson, 1967

Majdalany, Fred. *The Battle of El Alamein*, Weidenfeld and Nicolson, 1965

Martel, Lieut.-Gen. Sir Giffard. *An Outspoken Soldier*, Sifton Praed, 1949

Mellenthin, Maj.-Gen. von. *Panzer Battles, 1939–1945*, Cassell, 1955

Montgomery, Field-Marshal the Viscount of Alamein. *Memoirs*, Collins, 1958

Montgomery, Field-Marshal the Viscount of Alamein. *Alamein and the Desert War*, Sphere Books and the Sunday Times, 1967 (Contributor)

Moorehead, Alan. *Mediterranean Front; A Year of Battle; The End in Africa; Eclipse;* and *Montgomery*, Hamish Hamilton

Namier, Sir Lewis. *In the Nazi Era*, Macmillan, 1952

Official Histories. I refer *passim* to the relevant volumes in the Military Series of the *United Kingdom History of the Second World War*. (H.M.S.O.) Professor Postan's account of the development of weapons and M. R. D. Foot's history of *S.O.E. in France* have been instructive, as have, especially, Capt. Roskill's volumes on the war at sea.

Peniakoff, Lieut.-Col. Vladimir. *Private Army*, Cape, 1950
Phillips, Brig. C. E. Lucas. *Alamein*, Heinemann, 1962
Prittie, Terence. *Germans Against Hitler*, Hutchinson, 1964
Rommel, Erwin. *The Rommel Papers* (ed. B. H. Liddell Hart), Collins, 1953
Ryan, Cornelius. *The Longest Day*, Gollancz, 1960
Schmidt, Heinz Werner. *With Rommel in the Desert*, Harrap, 1951
Sherwood, Robert E. *The White House Papers of Harry Hopkins*, Eyre and Spottis-woode, Vol. I, 1948; Vol. II, 1949
Smyth, Brig. the Right Hon. Sir John. *Bolo Whistler*, Muller, 1967
Stewart, McD. G. *The Struggle for Crete*, O.U.P, 1966
Sweet-Escott, Bickham. *Baker Street Irregular*, Methuen, 1965
Tedder, Marshal of the R.A.F. Lord. *With Prejudice*, Cassell, 1966
Tuker, Lieut.-Gen. Sir Francis. *Approach to Battle*, Cassell, 1963
Verney, Maj.-Gen. *The Desert Rats*, Hutchinson, 1954
Wavell, Field-Marshal the Earl. *Generals and Generalship*, The Times Publishing Company, 1941
Westphal, Gen. Siegfried. *The German Army in the West*, Cassell, 1951
Wheeler-Bennett, Sir John. *The Nemesis of Power*, Macmillan, 1953
Willison, Brig. A. C. *The Relief of Tobruk*, The Leagrave Press Ltd.
Wilmot, Chester. *The Struggle for Europe*, Collins, 1952
Young, Brig. Desmond. *Rommel*, Collins, 1950

I have also found instructive a number of the articles in Purnell's *Illustrated History of the Second World War*. Admirably edited by Barrie, P. H., this weekly series has provided a number of insights which I am happy to acknowledge.

Index

INDEX

259

INDEX

INDEX

'S' mines *167*
Smuts, Field-Marshal Jan *142*
Snipe strongpoint *177, 178, 208*
Sollum *32, 43, 55, 126, 189, 190*; Mussolini orders that a line be held there *190*
Soluch *105*
Sonnenblume, Operation *28*
Sousse *200*
South African Air Force *56*
South African Army, *see* Commonwealth forces
Speidel, General *223, 225, 233, 236*
Spitfire fighter-planes *134, 140*
Sponeck, General Graf von *164*
ss *7, 9, 225*
Stalin *149*
Stauffenberg, Count von *232, 234*
Stephan, Lieut.-Col. *64*
Stoneage convoy *192*
Streich, General *33*
Strölin, Dr Karl *232, 233*
Stuart, Jeb *73, 77*
Student, General *108*
Stuka dive-bombers *39, 102, 120, 159*
Stülpnagel, General von *233*; executed *236*
Stumme, General *10, 89*; takes command of *Panzerarmee 163–166*; killed *174, 175*
Sudetenland *9*
Suez Canal *39, 50, 131, 134*
Sümmermann, Maj.-Gen. *66, 89*; killed *92*
Sunday Times 191
Supergymnast, Operation *97*
Syria *42, 43, 50*

Tactical weaknesses, British *151*
Taib el Essem *84*
Tanks
  British: *32, 45, 86, 99*; Crusader *46, 62*; DD (amphibious) *221*; 'flail' *168*; Grant *112, 114, 149, 158*; Honey *149*; Matilda *21, 46, 59, 62*; Sherman *149, 188*; Stuart *59, 62, 98*; Valentine *59, 62, 141, 159*; compared with German *99*
  German: *62, 86, 158*; dummy *32, 138*
  Italian: *62*
Tarhuna *191*
Tebessa *200–202, 206*
Tedder, Air-Marshal *52, 72, 222*; *With Prejudice 171, 247*
Tel Aqaqir *181*
Tel el Eisa Ridge *139, 140, 141*
Tengeder *36*
Tergestea, ss, sunk *177*
Thala *202, 203, 206*
Thelepte *201*
Thoma, General von *89, 158*; takes command of Afrika Korps *164, 187, 189*
Thompson's Post *173, 179*
Tiger convoy *41*
The Tiger Kills (qu.) *89*
Tmimi *93*
Tobruk
  prepares for siege *39*; Rommel's attempt fails *40, 44, 49, 51*; invested *55, 60*; 70 Division

sallies out *67, 73, 77*; 13 Corps HQ enters *84*; counter-attacks from *85, 107, 120*; siege and surrender *121*, Chapter IX; garrison and armament *127*; air raids on *128, 196*
Tomahawk fighter-plane *149, 157*
Torch, Operation *133, 142, 143, 190, 192*
Trigh Capuzzo *64, 71, 88, 112*
Tripoli *194*
Tripolitania *189*
Trommelfeuer 139
Tuker, General Sir F. *56, 96*; evacuates Benghazi *106, 204*
Tunisia *26, 190*; 5 *Panzerarmee* formed in *194*; Rommel leaves *208, 209*
Turkey *27, 50*
Turner, Colonel *178*

United States: enters the War *96, 97, 148*; Army Air Force *161*; Tenth Air Force bombers diverted to Middle East *149*; landing in North Africa, planning for *97*; Second Corps *204*; 9 Division *206*; troops in Normandy *224*

V-1 Rocket *225*
Vaerst, General von *89, 152*; takes over command of Afrika Korps *157, 159*
Valiant, HMS, damaged *97*
Via Balbia *88, 102, 123, 129*
Voss, Lieutenant (qu.) *81*

Wadi Akarit *186*; battle of *192*
Wagner, General *233*
Warlimont, General *214*
Water supplies *61*
Wavell, General *27, 32, 33*; vacillates over Neame *35, 38*; his many preoccupations *42*; launches June offensive *45, 46*; relieved of command *48, 128*; Lees-Knowles Lectures *238, 240, 241, 244, 246*
Wellington bombers *157*
Welshman, HM Mine-layer *84*
Western front (First World War) *7, 139*
Westphal, Lieut.-Col. *73*; ability and courage *80, 81, 89, 99, 114, 164, 206*
Wheeler-Bennett, Sir John, *The Nemesis of Power* (qu.) *232, 234, 235*
White scout-car *149*
Willkie, Wendell *161*
Williams, Brigadier *139, 179, 222*
Willison, Brigadier *132*
Wilmot, Chester *The Struggle for Europe 206, 213, 220, 232*
Wilson, General Sir Henry *32, 195*
Woodcock Strongpoint *177, 178*

Young, Desmond, *Rommel* (qu.) *2, 4, 58, 233, 237*
Yugoslavia *27*; invaded *38*

Zaafran *87*
Zamboni, General *35*
Ziegler, General *201, 207*